SECRETS OF RUSSIAN COOKING

Moscow Raduga Publishers 2003

ББК 36.99
С 28

Translated from the Russian by O. Chorakaev

С 28 Secrets of Russian Cooking. – М.: Raduga Publishers, 2003. – 144 p.

Much has changed in our life over the recent years, yet much has remained the same, such as Russian cooking, rich and hospitable, which customarily preserves the age-old traditions of our national cuisine.

We offer you the recipes of various dishes, both meat and vegetarian ones, which are meant for festive occasions as well as for everyday life.

The book has twelve sections dealing with the most interesting and simple recipes of salads, soups, hot second courses, drinks, beverages, and pastry. We hope they will help make your fare more diversified.

Bon appétit!

The book's artwork includes reproductions of the works of the following artists: A. Sashin, B. Kustodiyev, I. Khrutsky, Z. Serebryakova, I. Mashkov, N. Yevgrafov, I. Grabar, and N. Ivanov

Редакторы Е. Травникова, Н. Вергелис
Оформление Е. Кузнецова
Художественный редактор Т. Иващенко

Налоговая льгота — общероссийский классификатор продукции ОК-005-93,
том 2; 953000 — книги, брошюры.

Подписано в печать 27.08.2003. Формат 84х108/16.
Бумага мелованая. Гарнитура Newton. Печать офсетная.
Условн. печ. л. 15,12. Уч.-изд. л. 12,90. Тираж 3000 экз. Заказ № 1617. Изд. № 9813.
Лицензия ЛР № 020846 от 23 декабря 1998 г.
ОАО Издательство «Радуга»,
121839, Москва, пер. Сивцев Вражек, 43.
105005, Москва, Аптекарский пер., 4, стр. 1.

Отпечатано с готовых диапозитивов издательства.
ОАО «Тверской полиграфический комбинат»
170024, г. Тверь, проспект Ленина,5.

ISBN 5-05-005810-4   © Raduga Publishers, 2003

CONTENTS

APPETIZERS AND SALADS *9*

    Vegetable and Mushroom Appetizers, Salads and Russian Vinaigrette Salads *11*

    Meat Hors D'oeuvres and Salads *16*

    Fish Hors D'oeuvres *21*

SOUPS *25*

    Meat Soups *27*

    Fish Soups *31*

    Vegetable, Mushroom, and Milk Soups *35*

HOT MEAT DISHES *43*

    Dishes with Beef *45*

    Dishes with Pork *52*

    Dishes with Various Kinds of Meat *54*

    Dishes with Mutton *55*

    Dishes with Poultry *56*

    Dishes with Game and the Meat of Wild Animals *60*

HOT FISH DISHES *63*

HOT VEGETABLE AND MUSHROOM DISHES *77*

CEREALS, ROUND LOAVES, *KRUPENIKS,* AND PUDDINGS *87*

DISHES FROM EGGS, COTTAGE CHEESE, AND MILK *95*

KISSEL AND BEVERAGES *101*

MEAT DUMPLINGS, *KLOTSKAS,* AND NOODLES *109*

PASTRY *117*

    Pancakes and Pancake-like Pies *119*

    Pies, Rolls, and Spice-cakes *121*

DIFFERENT KINDS OF KVASS AND *SBITEN* *129*

SAUCES, DRESSINGS, AND GRAVIES *135*

You are about to read a book of recipes of Russian national cuisine. Many of them came down to us from long ago, others first became known in the 18th—19th centuries.

In old Rus, grain-that is rye, barley, oats, millet, and wheat - was always the main food product. Since days of old the Russians have been known as land-tillers, that is why bread remains their major national food. As early as the 10th and 11th centuries, Russians made rye bread from fermented dough. The secret of «sour» rye bread was in the special ways of leavening. Some ways of leavening such bread have been preserved till this day.

Pies have always been a part of the holiday fare. The pies are customarily filled with different kinds of meat, groats, fish, and berries.

As for the groats, millet was most often used since it was the main agricultural product. They also made various kinds of *kashas* (cereals), round loaves, baked puddings, and *krupeniks*.

Russians have always eaten vegetables. In old times it was the turnip, swede, cabbage, radish, and cucumbers. Since the 18th century the potato began to play an ever more important part as one of the most loved ingredients of the Russian board.

As Russia's international ties expanded, other vegetables, such as the pumpkin, and marrow, began to be introduced in the country. In the 16th century, Russians began to grow lettuce. As for tomatoes, they were brought to Russia only in the 19th century.

Russians have bred cattle and hunted since olden times, hence the great variety of meat dishes and game in their national cuisine.

Interestingly, until the 11th century they mostly ate horse meat; beef and especially veal were less popular.

The abundance of berries, mushrooms, and honey in Russian cuisine is accounted for by the country's vast expanses, especially in the north.

Fish dishes are worth mentioning too. The country's rivers, lakes, and seas have been a source of fish, which is a tasty and wholesome food. Russian cuisine is famous for its various fish dishes, especially the hors d'oeuvres.

The Russian stove was not only a source of warmth, that is of life itself, but also an excellent hearth for cooking. Many Russian national dishes, such as *schi* (cabbage soup) which is stewed in a stove in clay-pots, or stewed meat, came into being due to the Russian stove. And what delicious *kashas* were cooked in this wonder-stove! They baked meat and stewed and roasted ducks, chicken, and geese in the Russian stove. Suckling pigs were baked whole. Over the centuries, the kitchen utensils used with this stove have remained the same: cast-iron kettles, clay-pots, oven prongs, shovels, and frying-pan holders.

As the centuries passed, borrowings from western countries appeared in Russia. During the reign of Peter the Great, ovens became widely used in Russia, as well as sauce-pans, frying-pans, and skimmers. Early in the 19th century, Russian cooks began to make different French sauces in addition to purely national condiments, such as mustard and horse-radish.

All this has enriched Russian cuisine which is tasty, nourishing, and wholesome.

APPETIZERS AND SALADS

Most often Russian appetizers are rather spicy and look good enough to whet the appetite. They are served with various seasonings and condiments, such as horse-radish, kvass, garlic and piquant tomato sauces lending the dishes special pungency.

Vegetable and Mushroom Appetizers, Salads and Russian Vinaigrette Salads

GRATED RADISH WITH SOUR CREAM

10 oz (300 gm) sour cream, 6 tbsp. grated radish; dill and parsley

Grate the radishes, add the sour cream and some salt. Mix and then sprinkle minced dill and a parsley. Serve immediately.

RADISHES WITH VEGETABLE OIL

10 oz (300 gm) radishes, 1 tbsp. vegetable oil, 1 or 2 onions, 1 tsp. vinegar; salt to taste

Grate a peeled radish fine, pour a vegetable oil and vinegar dressing over it and salt it. Instead of oil you can dress it with sour cream or chopped onions fried in vegetable oil, or, better yet, in duck or goose fat. Top it all with greens.

RADISHES WITH GREEN ONIONS

15 oz (400 gm) radishes, 3/4 cup sour cream, salt, green onions

Grate peeled and washed radishes, salt and mash them with a wooden masher until juice comes out. Then put them in a salad bowl, add sour cream, mix and sprinkle minced green onions over them.

RADISHES WITH PICKLED CUCUMBERS

15 oz (400 gm) radishes, 4 pickled cucumbers, 2 onions, 4 tbsp. vegetable oil, salt, parsley or dill

Peel and grate the radishes, add some salt and mix. Cut the cucumbers into thin strips. Mince the onions. Add both to the radishes and mix. Pour the sour cream or vegetable oil over it, sprinkle finely chopped parsley or dill over it.

CARROT AND GREEN PEAS SALAD

2 big carrots, 1 cup canned green peas, 3 tbsp. mayonnaise, dill, salt

Grate the carrots, add the canned green peas and dill, then salt to taste, add mayonnaise.

CARROT AND GARLIC SALAD

3 or 4 carrots, 4 cloves garlic, 4 tbsp. mayonnaise, 2 tsp. sugar; salt to taste

Grate raw carrot, add the sugar, finely cut garlic, and salt. Add mayonnaise and mix well before serving.

CARROT AND APPLE SALAD

4 carrots, 2 apples, 3 tbsp. sour cream; sugar to taste

Grate the carrots fine, cut the apples into thin slices and mix with the carrots. Add the sour cream and sugar.

RADISHES WITH SOUR CREAM

Radishes, sour cream, dill

Chop the radishes into fine cross-cut slices (red radishes are more eye-appealing), salt, add sour cream, and

mix well. Sprinkle some minced dill over them and serve.

RADISH SALAD
The first variant

1 bunch of radishes, 1 egg, 1/4 cup sour cream, pepper, sugar, vinegar; salt to taste

Cut radishes into fine slices and add sour cream, salt, pepper, sugar, and vinegar. Mix. Top with slices of a hard-boiled egg and leaf lettuce, and sprinkle minced dill over it.

RADISH SALAD
The second variant

1 bunch of radishes, 1 cucumber, 3 tomatoes, 2.5 oz (75 gm) spring onions, 2 oz (50 gm) green lettuce, 1 or 2 eggs, and half a glass of mayonnaise

Cut radish, cucumbers, and tomatoes in fine slices, add small fragments of a hard-boiled egg, finely cut onion, and green lettuce. Dress it with mayonnaise.

RADISH SALAD
The Third variant

10 radishes, 2 fresh cucumbers, 5 tbsp. vegetable-oil dressing, 1 onion, dill

Cut the radishes and cucumbers into thin strips, add minced dill. Pour a sauce to which shredded onion has been added over it. Mix it all in a salad-bowl and top the salad with the minced radishes and dill rings.

GREEN-ONION SALAD

1.5 lb (600 gm) green onions, 7 oz (200 gm) sour cream, 1 hard-boiled egg, some parsley, and salt

Chop green onions, add salt and sour cream. Mix. Top with grated egg-yolk, slices of egg-white, and parsley.

WATER-CRESS, RUSSIAN STYLE

7 oz (200 gm) water-cress, 6 tbsp. vegetable oil, 3 tbsp. vinegar, 1 tsp. mustard, herbs; pepper and salt to taste

Put the leaves of water-cress in a salad-bowl, pour the vegetable oil and vinegar over it. Add some salt, pepper, chopped herbs, and mustard. Mix and serve.

DANDELION LEAVES SALAD

7 oz (200 gm) dandelion leaves, 4 tbsp. sour cream, horse-radish to taste

To lessen their bitter taste, leave the young dandelion leaves in salted water for thirty minutes. Then chop them with a stainless-steel knife and add the sour cream and grated horse-radish. You can add some chopped egg or grated cheese to it.

SORREL AND NETTLE SALAD

10 oz (300 gm) sorrel stalks, 10 oz (300 gm) young nettle, 3 tbsp. sunflower-seed oil, 1/2 cup nuts, half a garlic, citric acid; salt, and granulated sugar to taste

Pour salted boiling water over the sorrel stalks and boil them till they are tender. Pour some boiling water on the nettle and heat to the boiling point. Strain the water off in a colander and cool the nettle. Mix it with the boiled and cooled stalks of sorrel and add the sauce.

The sauce

Mash nuts and garlic into paste, add some boiling water to make a kind of gruel. Cool and stir oil into it, a little at a time. Salt it and add diluted citric acid and granulated sugar to taste.

SPRINGTIME SALAD

5 potatoes, 3 new cucumbers, 1 bunch radishes, 4 oz (100 gm) leaf lettuce, 1 egg, 4 oz (100 gm) green onions, 1/2 cup sour cream, 1 tbsp. sour cream, 1 tbsp. 3% vinegar; salt to taste

Peel the potatoes, then boil and cool them. Chop them with raw vegetables. Add sour cream, vegetables, vinegar, and salt, and put it all into a salad-bowl or a plate. Pour on more sour cream and adorn with vegetables and hard-boiled eggs.

POTATO AND PICKLED CUCUMBER SALAD

15 oz (400 gm) potatoes, 3 pickled cucumbers, 1 fresh cucumber, 2 tomatoes, 1 big onion, 1 egg, 3/4 cup sunflower-seed oil, 1 tbsp. finely cut parsley and dill; salt and pepper to taste

Shred an onion. Peel pickled cucumbers and slice them into small bricks. Boil the peeled potatoes till done. Pour out the water, dry the potatoes and, without letting them cool off, mix them together with shredded onion, pour all the oil into it and mash it into an even mass. Add finely sliced cucumbers and pepper, place it all on a board, roll it into a thick cylinder, place it on an oval plate. Sprinkle finely chopped egg and herbs on it. Slice the tomatoes in slices and stick them into the potato roll, the cut section down. Adorn the sides of the roll the same way. Place fresh cucumbers on a plate in the shape of rings, like scales. You can serve the salad with mayonnaise with finely cut tomatoes.

BEETROOT AND CUCUMBERS SALAD

15 oz (400 gm) beetroots, 1 or 2 fresh cucumbers, 1 fresh-salted cucumber, 1 tbsp finely chopped green onios, 5 tbsp. mayonnaise, 1 tsp. sugar

Cut boiled beetroots and fresh and fresh-salted cucumbers in bricks, add the green onions, sprinkle sugar over it and season it with mayonnaise.

POTATO AND BEETROOT SALAD

5 or 6 potatoes, 3 beetroots, 1 tbsp. boiled haricots (kidney-beens), 1 pod sweet pepper, 2 tbsp. vegetable oil, vinegar, parsley or dill

Boil and peel the potatoes. Bake the beetroots in the oven and peel them. Cut them into small cubes, add the haricots and finely chopped sweet peppers, salt and season them with vegetable oil and vinegar, top with shredded herbs.

FRESH CUCUMBERS WITH HONEY

15 medium-size cucumbers and honey

Peel the cucumbers, chop them in cross-cut strips, pour 7 oz (200 gm) of honey over them, and mix. Serve the honey separately.

BEETROOT AND APPLE SALAD

15 oz (400 gm) beetroots, 3 tbsp. mayonnaise, 2 tsp. sugar, 2 apples; salt to taste

Bake the washed beetroots in the oven or boil them in slightly salted boiling water, peel and cool them in cold water, chop fine or grate them, add the grated apples and sugar; top them with mayonnaise.

BEETROOT AND HORSE-RADISH SALAD

15 oz (400 gm) beetroots and 2.5 oz (70 gm) horse-radishes

For the sauce: *3 tbsp. 3% vinegar, 1 tbsp. vegetable oil, 1 tsp. sugar, 1/2 lemon (dried lemon peels), 0.04 oz (1 gm) spices, 1/2 cup water*

To make the sauce put the spices, lemon, sugar, and vegetable oil on a one-litre jar, pour boiling water over it and add some vinegar.

Boil the beetroots, cut them into small slices or shred them. Put them in a bowl in layers sprinkling grated horse-radish on each layer. Make a marinaded sauce. Pour the sauce over the beetroots in the bowl and let them stay that way for several hours till the beetroots are saturated with the prepared dressing. Serve with the sauce. Before serving add some sugar and dress it with the vegetable oil.

TOMATOES AND HORSE-RADISH

8 tomatoes, 3 tbsp. grated horse-radishes, 3 tbsp. vegetable oil, 1/2 cup sour milk, 1 tbsp. parsley; salt and pepper to taste

Wash the tomatoes and cut them into flat rings, lay them out on a flat plate the cut surface up, pour the sauce over them.

The sauce

Grate some horse-radishes, grind some salt and pepper, add some sour milk and whip it properly. You can add 1 tea-spoon of granulated sugar to the sauce.

TOMATOES AND GREEN PEAS

8 tomatoes, 2 tbsp. fresh green peas, 3 tbsp. mayonnaise; salt to taste

Pour boiling water over the tomatoes,

Vegetable and Mushroom Appetizers, Salads and Russian Vinaigrette Salads

remove the skin, cut them in cubes. Wash the peas thoroughly, dry them on a washcloth, mix with the tomato cubes and top it all with mayonnaise.

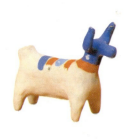

TOMATOES, GARLIC, AND ONIONS

5 tomatoes, 1 onion, 1/2 garlic, 5 tbsp. sunflower-seed oil; ground black pepper and salt to taste

Cut the tomatoes and onions in small cubes. Grind the garlic with salt. Mix, add some pepper, pour vegetable oil over the mixture, cool it for one hour. Before serving mix the salad thoroughly.

GREEN BELL-PEPPERS AND TOMATOES

8 green bell-peppers, 4 tomatoes, 1 cucumber, 1 onion, 1 tbsp. finely chopped parsley, 4 tbsp. sunflower-seed oil; salt to taste

Cut the peppers, tomatoes, and the cucumber in thin rings. Mix them with parsley and salt, put them in a salad-bowl, add some sunflower-seed oil, top with rings of sliced onions.

RICE AND TOMATOES SALAD

3/4 cup rice, 3 eggs, 3 tomatoes, 1 fresh cucumber, 3 tbsp. vinegar, and 4 tbsp. sunflower-seed oil: salt and ground pepper to taste

Boil and wash the rice thoroughly. Cut the tomatoes, cucumber, and hard-boiled eggs in small bricks. Mix and put them in a salad-bowl, dress the dish with a mixture of vinegar (or diluted citric acid) and sunflower-seed oil; salt and pepper to taste.

SAUERKRAUT AND APPLES

2 lb (1 kg) sauerkraut, 2—3 apples, 1 onion, 1 carrot, green onions, 3—4 tbsp. vegetable oil, sugar, and salt

If the sauerkraut is too sour, wash it with cold water, add course-grated carrot and apples, and rings of 1 onion. Salt and mix them. Dress with the vegetable oil or sour cream; sugar to taste. Lay the salad in a salad-bowl in the shape of a mound and top it with thinly chopped green onions.

ZAGORSKY SALAD (ZAGORSK-CITY STYLE)

7 oz (200 gm) fresh cabbage, 1 onion, 2 or 3 tbsp. green peas, 1/2 hard-boiled egg, 1 tsp. 3% vinegar, 0.1 oz (3 gm) granulated sugar, and 0.1 oz (3 gm) herbs

Wash a cabbage head several times in cold water. Remove the upper leaves. Cut the cabbage and onion in thin slices and salt them. Rub the cabbage well until the juice comes out and let it stay that way for a while. Add the chopped onion and green peas. Chop the egg fine and pour granulated sugar over the cabbage and onion and dress them with vinegar. Lay out the mixture in a salad-bowl. Add half the amount of the sour cream to it. Lay out the salad in the shape of a mound, pour the rest of the sour cream over it and top it all with the herbs.

MIXED SALAD

1 cup fresh shredded cabbage, 3 green bell-peppers, 4 tomatoes, 1 carrot, 6 cloves garlic, 1 tbsp. finely cut parsley, 2 tbsp. chopped green onions, 5 tbsp. sunflower-seed oil; salt to taste

Cut the peppers lengthwise into thin strips, grate the carrot and tomatoes coarsely, and grind the garlic with salt. Mix the vegetables, add some salt and put them in a salad-bowl. Pour the sunflower-seed oil over the mixed mass.

RUSSIAN VINAIGRETTE SALAD

2 potatoes, 1 beetroot, 2 carrots, 1—2 pickled cucumbers, 4—5 tbsp. shredded sauerkraut, 2 tbsp. 3% vinegar, 1 medium-size onion, 4 tbsp. vegetable oil, 4 tbsp. mayonnaise (as substitution for vegetable oil and vinegar)

Boil the potatoes, beetroot, carrots, and pickled cucumbers and cut them in thin slices. Cut one onion or the corresponding amount of green onions the same way and press the sauerkraut until the juice comes out. Put them all together, dress with the vegetable oil, vinegar, salt, pepper, and mustard. Mix. You can dress the salad with mayonnaise and add eggs, pickled or marinaded mushrooms, red herring, fish, and meat.

THE POKROVSKY VINAIGRETTE

2 apples, 6 prunes, 2 potatoes, 1 beetroot, 1 cup sauerkraut, several cloves garlic, mayonnaise, boiled field mushrooms or pickled mushrooms, $1/2$ egg; salt and herbs to taste

Wash the apples, remove the skins, stones, and the cores. Boil the prunes, the beetroot (unpeeled), and the potatoes. Make sure the potatoes are not overboiled. Peel and mash the garlic cloves. Cut them in thin strips and mix them with the sauerkraut and garlic. Salt to taste and dress the dish with mayonnaise. Mix well. Put the ready vinaigrette in a salad-bowl in the shape of a mound and adorn it with the prunes, mushrooms, boiled egg, and herbs.

CARROT PASTE

1 lb (500 gm) onions, 2 lb (1 kg) carrots, 1 cup tomato paste thinned with water, 1 cup sunflower oil, 5 bay leaves, 3 cloves garlic; salt and pepper to taste

Mix tomato paste with water till it becomes as thin as Russian sour cream and put it in a pan with finely chopped onions. Pour some sunflower oil into it, add the bay leaves, salt and cook over low heat with the lid on the pan. When the mass starts to boil, lower the heat and continue cooking it till the onions turn into a very soft mass covered in red tomato-coloured oil.

While the onion is cooking, peel the carrots, wash and grate them coarsely and fry them in a frying-pan in a small amount of sunflower-seed oil. Add a little water to help the carrots get tender without burners. When the onions and carrots are done, mix them thoroughly and put them in a heated oven. Add several bay leaves, the garlic crushed with salt, and pepper it all.

The paste can be kept in a glass jar for several months.

VEGETABLE-MARROW PASTE

5 medium-size vegetable marrows, 2 onions, 1 lb (500 gm) tomatoes, 1 cup vegetable oil, 2 oz (50 gm) 6% or apple vinegar; salt, ground cayenne, and sugar to taste

Lay the vegetable marrows out on a dripping-pan, put them in an oven and keep them there till they are softened. Remove the skin and pound the pulp with a masher. Fry the finely chopped onions in vegetable oil till semi-done, add the cut tomatoes, spices, and sugar.

Put it all in a cast-iron pan, add the remaining vegetable oil, and mix thoroughly. Salt to taste, add some vinegar, and mix it all again. Cook the mixture with the lid on the pan till the paste is thoroughly cooked and has an eye-pleasing yellowish-golden tint. Serve the paste cold, sprinkling finely chopped dill on it.

GARLIC PASTE

1 garlic, 1 cup shelled walnuts, 1 slice whole wheat bread, 1 tbsp. finely chopped parsley and 1 tbsp. finely chopped dill; lemon juice and salt to taste

Mash the garlic, pepper, and walnuts into a homogenious mass. Add the herbs, vegetable oil and a slice of soaked white bread. Put through a meat-grinder. Gradually add the lemon juice or diluted citric acid.

BEET PASTE

1 lb (500 gm) beetroots, 2 tbsp. vegetable oil or butter, $1/2$ cup sugar, dill, parsley, and green onions; salt and citric acid to taste

Put the boiled and peeled beetroots through a meat-grinder, add the vegetable oil, sugar, salt, and diluted citric acid. Mix it all and heat in a pan, stirring (10—15 minutes). It can be served hot or cold.

MUSHROOM PASTE

10 oz (300 gm) fresh mushrooms, $3/4$ cup mushroom broth, 5 cloves garlic, 2 tbsp. finely chopped green onions, vegetable oil for browning; salt, vinegar, and pepper to taste

Boil the mushrooms, mince or put them through a meat-grinder. Then mix the slightly browned onion with the mushrooms, add some of the mushroom liquid, and cook over gentle heat till most of the liquid boils away. Add spices and vinegar. Serve cold.

Vegetable and Mushroom Appetizers, Salads and Russian Vinaigrette Salads

FRESH MUSHROOM SALAD

1 lb (500 gm) mushrooms, 2 tbsp. vegetable oil, 1 tbsp. finely chopped parsley; vinegar, salt and ground pepper to taste

Pour slightly salted boiling water over the peeled and properly washed mushrooms. Boil till soft, cut into thin slices, and top them with oil and vinegar dressing. Add some salt and pepper to taste. Top it all with a considerable amount of parsley.

JELLIED BOLETUSSES

10 oz (350 gm) fresh boletusses, 2 tbsp. gelatine

The sauce: 1 egg-yolk, 1 tbsp. mustard, 2 oz (50 gm) vegetable oil; salt and sugar to taste

Boil the fresh boletusses in 2 pints (1 litre) of salted water and chop them fine. Pour the gelatine into half a glass of boiled cold water and leave it for an hour. Pour the gelatine into the mushroom broth, keep it over low heat until the gelatine is completely dissolved, but do not bring it to a boil. Pour the broth over the mushrooms and put them in the refrigerator until chilled.

The sauce

Beat the egg-yolk well, add some mustard and oil; salt, sugar, and vinegar to taste. Serve with hot new potatoes, cucumbers, and tomatoes.

FRESH MUSHROOM AND VEGETABLE MARROW SALAD

10 oz (300 gm) cooked fresh mushrooms, 5 eggs, 5 oz (150 gm) vegetable marrows, 2 cups vegetable oil, 1 tbsp. vinegar, about 1 tsp. ground pepper; salt to taste

Peel the vegetable marrows and remove the seeds, cut them into cubes $1/3$ in (1 cm) long, put them in a colander, lower it into salted boiling water for 2 or 3 minutes. Chill them. Cut the mushrooms and hard-cooked eggs into large strips and mix them with the dried cool vegetable marrows. Add an oil and vinegar dressing.

DRIED MUSHROOM SALAD

4 oz (100 gm) dried mushrooms, 1 garlic, 5 tbsp. sunflower oil; vinegar and salt to taste. 3 tomatoes for decoration

Mash the garlic with a pinch of salt. Cook the mushrooms till soft and cut them into thin strips. Mix the oil thoroughly with the garlic. Add some lemon juice or vinegar and pour over the mushrooms. Mix thoroughly and transfer to a salad-bowl. Adorn the dish with finely cut tomatoes.

Meat Hors D'oeuvres and Salads

SUCKLING PORK-ROLL (COLLARED SUCKLING PIG)

2 lb (1 kg) suckling pig, 1 lb (500 gm) pork, 2 oz (50 gm) of salted pork fat, 5 eggs, 1 carrot, 1 piece parsley, 2 onions, salt, pepper, and 1 bay leaf

Singe the suckling pig, then gut, wash properly, and cut it lengthwise on the chest. Remove the skin and bones from the meat. Cut the pork into pieces, put the pieces and removed meat through a meat-grinder. Cut the salted fat into small cubes, salt and pepper them, add them to the finely chopped meat and mix it all thoroughly. Put half of the ground meat on the skin of the pig and top it all with the quartered hard-cooked eggs. Top it with the rest of the ground pork. Fold the pork in a roll and put it on a piece of wet cloth, tie it up with twine, put it in a pan of hot water, add some salt, pepper, bay leaf, finely chopped carrot, parsley, and onion and simmer until done. Put the ready roll under a press and cool it.

SMALL HAM ROLLS WITH HORSE-RADISH AND WHIPPED CREAM

15 oz (400 gm) ham, 1 glass cream, 2 oz (50 gm) horse-radish, 7 oz (200 gm) grated apples, 2 oz (50 gm) grated carrot, 1 oz (30 gm) sugar, a little lemon juice, and an egg

Whip the chilled cream, add some sugar, lemon juice, grated horse-radish, apples, carrots, and a fried egg. Lay the stuffing on

Appetizers and Salads

thin slices of the ham, fold carefully in rolls and lay it all out on the dish. Top the small rolls with whipped cream to which the grated horse-radish has been added.

PIG'S HEAD, COUNTRY STYLE

1 pig's head, 4 carrots, 4 onions, 3 garlics, 3 pieces parsley, a bay leaf, peppercorns, ground cayenne; salt to taste

Cut the pig's head into three large parts and wash them thoroughly in warm running water. Put the pieces in a large pan or cauldron, pour hot water over them, bring to a boil over high heat, then lower the heat and simmer for 5 hours, from time to time skimming the froth and fat. Put in the onions, carrots, parsley, and salt when it has one hour left to cook and the peppercorns and bay leaf right before it is done.

Take out the pieces of pig's head, cool them a little, remove the bones carefully trying to keep the pieces whole. Lay out the prepared pieces on a board putting them together. Lay the small pieces of the pork left over after cutting the head, and chopped garlic in the middle. Top with the ground cayenne and bake in the oven for 30 minutes. Press down and keep that way in a cold place for twenty-four hours. Before serving cut it into slices. Serve with horse-radish sauce.

ROASTED PORK, À LA RYAZAN

2 lb (1 kg) pork, 4 eggs, 3 carrots, 2 oz (50 gm) salted pork fat, 2 tbsp. 3% vinegar, 1 tsp. sugar; salt, pepper (better cayenne), and sauce to taste

Make a depression all along the length of the pork (ham, brisket), salt and lay the hard-boiled eggs in there. Stuff it with the fat and raw carrots. Rub in some salt, sugar, and cayenne, sprinkle with vinegar, let it set for three hours, and roast till done.
Slice the cooled pork and serve with horse-radish sauce.

BAKED PORK

1.5 lb (700 gm) pork, 2.5 glasses flour, $3/4$ glass water; salt and sour-cream sauce with horse-radish to taste

Put the pork, or better, ham in cold water for 1 hour and dry it. Make sufficiently thick dough, preferably from rye flour, and spread it over the pork dipping your hands in cold water. Lay it on a dripping-pan and put it in the oven for 1—1,5 hours. When the crust has browned, moisten it with warm water. When the pork is done take it out of the oven, remove the dough and cool it.
Serve with sour-cream-and-horse-radish sauce.

CHICKEN AND MAYONNAISE SALAD

10 oz (300 gm) boiled chicken, 4 oz (100 gm) boiled pasta, 10 oz (300 gm) marinated or pickled mushrooms, 7 oz (200 gm) tomatoes, 4 hard-cooked eggs, 1.5 cup mayonnaise, 1 tbsp. finely chopped parsley; salt and ground pepper to taste

To make the mayonnaise take *1 egg-yolk, 1 tsp. granulated sugar, about 1 tsp. salt, 7 oz (200 gm) sunflower oil, $2/3$ oz (20 gm) vinegar*

Put the chicken meat sliced like noodles, pasta, cut mushrooms, tomatoes, eggs, and finely chopped parsley in a bowl. Mix it all, add the mayonnaise, and serve.

The mayonnaise

Grate an egg-yolk, add sugar and salt, and put it in a porcelain or enameled bowl. Mix with a wooden spoon. Gradually add (at first drop by drop and then in teaspoons) oil continually stirring the light mass to one side. When you have a compact thick mass, dilute it with vinegar and, if you want a thinner sauce, dilute it with cold broth or vegetable liquid to taste. For a more pungent mayonnaise, add 1 tsp. mustard.

CHICKEN FILLET WITH MAYONNAISE

1 chicken, 5 oz (150 gm) mayonnaise, salt, ground black pepper, radish, and parsley

Cook the chicken, remove the bones and skin. Cut the chilled meat into small pieces, about $3/4$ in (2 cm) each. Lay it in a salad-bowl, add some salt, the mayonnaise, and ground black pepper. Mix thoroughly and decorate with radish flowerettes and parsley.

Meat Hors D'oeuvres and Salads

CHICKEN SALAD
«STOLICHNY»

1.5 lb (600 gm) chicken, 1.5 lb (600 gm) potatoes, 15 oz (400 gm) pickled or marinated cucumbers, 4 oz (100 gm) crayfish meat, 10 eggs, 5 oz (150 gm) tomato sauce, 1.5 lb (700 gm) mayonnaise, 4 oz (100 gm) pickles, and 4 oz (100 gm) olives

Cut boiled or roasted chicken, boiled potatoes, pickled or marinated cucumbers, and hard-cooked eggs into thin slices (2—2.5 cm). Mix and add the mayonnaise and tomato sauce. Mix properly and lay the salad in a mound in a salad-bowl. Top it with rings or slices of hard-cooked eggs, small pieces of pickles, and rings of marinated cucumbers. You can add bits of crab or lobster meat, or shrimp and olives.

MEAT SALAD, À LA RUSSE

4 oz (100 gm) beef, 2 oz (50 gm) mayonnaise, 2 oz (50 gm) marinated onions, 1 clove garlic; salt to taste

Remove the bones and tendons, boil the beef and cut it in long thin slices. Cut the marinated onions the same way. Chop the garlic fine. Mix, salt, and dress with mayonnaise.

«RUSSIAN FOREST» HORS D'OEUVRE

4 oz (100 gm) bear-meat, 2 oz (50 gm) elk-meat, $1/2$ partridge, half a fresh cucumber, a medium size tomato, 4 oz (100 gm) green onions, 1—2 tbsp. of any kind of pungent sauce, butter, 0.9 oz (25 gm) olives, $1/4$ oz (7 gm) greens; salt and spices to taste

Cut the bear- and elk-meat into pieces and keep them in a marinade (vinegar, onions, a dash of pepper, and kvass or beer plus other ingredients as desired). Stew the meat, cool and cut it into thin slices. Cut half the partridge in half, roast it in a small amount of butter till the skin is brown and crisp.
Lay the pieces of meat on a dish, adorn with the olives, marinated fruit, and sprigs of parsley or dill.

«FOREST STORY» HORS D'OEUVRE

4 oz (100 gm) bear-meat, 2 oz (60 gm) venison, $1/2$ ptarmigan, 4 oz (100 gm) fresh tomatoes, 1.5 oz (40 gm) green onions, 1.5 oz (40 gm) mayonnaise, 2 oz (60 gm) marinated plums, one onion, 2.5 oz (70 gm) pickled cucumbers, 0.9 oz (25 gm) olives, $1/4$ oz (7 gm) parsley; salt and spices to taste

Cut the bear-meat and venison in small pieces, put them in a marinade (vinegar, spices, and onions) and leave for 6 hours. Chill the meat for some time and then stew it. Cut the ptarmigan (or some other game) in half and roast it. Lay the meat, game, marinated plums, tomatoes, olives, and green onions on a dish in an eye-pleasing way. Serve with mayonnaise and pickled cucumbers.

MEAT PÂTÉ

1.5 lb (700 gm) fat pork, 1 lb (500 gm) beef, 7 oz (200 gm) liver, 3 eggs, 4 oz (100 gm) roll, 2—3 boiled potatoes, 1 carrot, 1 piece parsley, 1 onion, 2 tbsp. bread-crumbs, 1 bay-leaf, 2—3 black peppercorns, ground pepper, and salt

Wash the meat and peel the carrot, onion, and parsley. Put the ingredients in a pan, pour cold water over them, and then set the pan on a burner. Bring the water to a boil and salt it, add the spices and keep the broth simmering for about 2 hours. Fifteen minutes before they are done put the previously milk-soaked liver in the pan. When the liver is ready strain the broth and soak the roll in it. Put the meat, liver, roll, boiled potatoes and vegetables three times through a meat-grinder, add the eggs, salt, and pepper. Stir the mass properly with a spoon, sprinkle the bread-crumbs in a well-greased oblong pan and lay the mass in it. Bake it in a heated oven (200°C) for 30—40 minutes. Take the pâté out of the pan after it gets cold. Before serving cut it into slices and lay them on a platter. You can decorate the dish with rings or slices of hard-cooked eggs, marinated cucumbers, mushrooms, olives, and parsley.

Appetizers and Salads

HOT HORS D'OEUVRE WITH CHICKEN

7 oz (200 gm) boiled chicken, 3 hard-cooked eggs, 1 apple, sour-cream sauce; 1.5 oz (40 gm) cheese, 2 tbsp. butter

Slice the boiled chicken's flesh. Chop an onion fine and fry it in butter. Chop the eggs fine. Peel the apple, remove the core and cut the apple into thin pieces. Mix the ingredients, lay the mixture in small clay pots or cocottes, pour the sour-cream sauce over it, top it all with grated cheese and bake in the oven at 220°C for 15—20 minutes.

HOT HORS D'OEUVRE WITH LIVER

1 lb (500 gm) beef liver, 6 potatoes, 1 onion, 9 oz (250 gm) sour cream, 5 tbsp. butter, pickled cucumbers; spices, herbs, and salt to taste

Cut the liver into small bits, fry them promptly on high heat, and lay them out in small clay pots. Add the potatoes cut into cubes, chopped onion, salt, spices, and sour cream. Bake it all in the oven. Serve with pickled cucumbers and herbs.

HOT HORS D'OEUVRE, COUNTRY STYLE

10 potatoes, 7 oz (200 gm) salted pork fat; salt to taste

Wash the potatoes well, cut them in half and salt a little. Cut the fat into thin rectangular pieces, 1 in (3×4 cm) each. Take some matches, remove the sulphur, sharpen their ends, and run the sticks diagonally through each piece of fat. Stick a match with a piece of fat into the potato's halves, bake everything in the oven and serve hot.

JELLY FOR JELLIED DISHES

Make a broth from beef and chicken bones, add some carrots, onion, and parsley. Spill some gelatine (1 part of gelatine and 8 parts of water) into cold water stirring it all the while. Let it swell. Pour the soaked gelatine into the hot broth, stir it till fully dissolved. Do not bring it to a boil! This kind of jelly is used for cooking jellied dishes. Congeal the jelly in the refrigerator.

JELLIED VEAL

The bottom chuck of veal, 5 hard-cooked eggs, 2 oz (50 gm) butter, parsley, and salt

The broth: *the bone of the bottom chuck, 1 carrot, 1 piece of parsley, 1 onion, 1 garlic, 2 bay leaves, 3—4 black peppercorns, 1 tsp. gelatine, and salt*

Remove the bones, beat the meat properly, salt, and put chopped eggs on it, fold in a roll and tie it up with a cord. Roast the roll in hot fat, lay it in an oblong pan, cover it with the lid and bring to readiness in the oven adding water. Make broth from the bones, vegetables, and spices in a small amount of salted water and dress it with pounded garlic. Cool the ready roll, remove the cord, cut it in rings $2/3$ in (1.5 cm) thick, lay it carefully out on a dish, ornate it with cooked carrots and leaves of parsley, and pour strained broth with previously diluted gelatine in it. Place the veal in a cold place to let the jelly set.

JELLIED BEEF

2 lb ($1/2$ kg) beef, 3 oz (85 gm) salted pork fat, 3 carrots, 2 onions, parsley, 5 tbsp. grease, 2 oz (50 gm) dried mushrooms, vinegar, ground black pepper, and salt

The broth: *1.5 lb (600 gm) beef bones, 1 carrot, 1 onion, 1 piece parsley, 6 black peppercorns, 4 tsp. gelatine and salt*

Wash the meat, remove the film and beat it. Sprinkle vinegar over it, and leave it for the night. The next day stuff the beef with thin strips of the salted pork fat, add salt and pepper, and brown it off in hot grease. Put it in an oblong cast-iron bowl, add the vegetables and mushrooms (whole). Stew it in the water in which the well-washed mushrooms were soaked for 2—3 hours. Cool the meat, cut it into thin slices across the fibres, lay out in an oval dish together with rings of boiled carrots and minced mushrooms. Make a broth from the beef bones and vegetables in 2 pints (1 litre) of water and add swollen gelatine to it.

Before dissolving the gelatine, strain the broth and skim the grease.

Meat Hors D'oeuvres and Salads

BOILED TONGUE IN JELLY

1 boiled beef tongue, 3 small boiled carrots, 1 marinated cucumber, 3 hard-cooked eggs, 1 marinated red pepper, 2 cups beef-tea, $2/3$ oz (20 gm) gelatine, salt, pepper, vinegar

Make the jelly based on hot broth with spice and vinegar. Pour the liquid mass in a thin layer into round plates and let it thicken. Slice the tongue fine and lay them in a row. Top the slices with rings of the pepper, patterned bits of the cucumber, rings of the eggs and carrots. Pour the jelly over them and take the dish out to the cold.

JELLIED SUCKLING PIG

1 suckling pig (2—2.5 kg), 2 carrots, 1 onion, 1 piece parsley, 3 hard-cooked eggs, canned green peas, black peppercorns, salt, 1 oz (30 gm) gelatine

Chop the pig into pieces, pour water over it, add some salt, spice, and aromatic culinary roots. Boil in a pot. Bring the water to a boil, lessen the heat, skim the froth and keep boiling it for about an hour. Remove the scum. Take out the meat, cover it with a piece of linen cloth, and let it cool. Strain the broth through two-layered gauze (better 2—3 times), make the jelly with the gelatine. Put the suckling pig in a large form. Add the jelly not more than $1/5$ in (0.5 cm) thick, lay out rings of the hard-cooked eggs, chopped carrots, parsley, green peas. Let it congeal and pour the broth over it so that the broth could cover the ingredients. Top it with the meat and take it out to the cold.
Serve on a dish adorning the jellied suckling pig with the vegetables and fresh herbs with grated horse radishes.

PIG'S LEGS' JELLY

2 lb (1 kg) pig's legs, 1 carrot, 1 piece parsley, 2 onions, 1 bay leaf, peppercorns, salt

Singe the pig's legs, remove the hooves, cut the legs lengthwise and keep them in cold water for 2—3 hours; wash and again pour cold water over them, bring the water to a boil on a strong heat. Peel and chop the carrot, add the parsley, onions, bay leaf, and peppercorns; salt and simmer till the legs are done. Take out the legs, remove the meat from the bones, skim the broth's grease, pour the broth over the meat, let it boil for 5—10 minutes, pour it into plates or a special form, and cool.
Serve with grated horse-radishes.

PORK IN JELLY

1.5 lb (600 gm) boiled lean pork, $2/3$ cup tomato juice, $2/3$ oz (20 gm) gelatine, 1 hard-cooked egg-white, herbs, pepper, salt

Heat, salt and pepper the tomato juice; dissolve swollen gelatine in it. Pour the liquid into plates in a thin layer and let it cool. Cut the pork into slices, lay the slices out on the jelly, adorn each slice with squares or rings of the egg-white. Top it with the rest of the jelly. Before serving adorn the dish with the herbs' branches.

ASPIC DISH, NOVGOROD STYLE

10 oz (300 gm) boiled chicken fillet, 5 pickled tomatoes, 1 cup pickles, 1 cup chicken broth, 2 tbsp. gelatine; salt, herbs, and green peas to taste

Soak the gelatine in a cup of cold water and let it swell for $1/2$ hours. Divide it in two parts and make two kinds of jelly: one with the tomato pickles and the other with the chicken broth. Pour the pickled jelly into a form in a layer, let it cool; put a tomato on it, pour another layer of the jelly over it, and let it cool. Lay out thin slices of the chicken fillet on it, top it with a layer of the chicken jelly and let it cool. Before serving dip the form with the jelly ($2/3$ of its height) in hot water for several seconds, shake slightly, and lay it out on a plate. Adorn with the herbs and green peas.

CHICKEN MEAT JELLY

1 chicken, 2 carrots, 2 pieces parsley, 1 onion, black peppercorns, 1 bay leaf, salt

Boil the chicken with culinary roots on a low heat till done. Add condiment. Remove the meat from the bones and cut it into small bits. Lay the parsley, chopped carrots, chicken meat, and canned green peas in small forms. Make a jelly with gelatine with the hot chicken broth as its base, top the prepared ingredients with the jelly, and let it cool. Serve the chicken meat jelly with mayonnaise.

APPETIZER, RUSSIAN STYLE

5 oz (150 gm) ham, 5 oz (150 gm) boiled tongue, 4 eggs, 4 oz (100 gm) meat, pepper, herbs, pickled mushrooms; horse radish to taste

Boil the meat, cut it into small pieces, and adrorn with rings of boiled carrots, egg-white, red peppers, and parsley. Let the broth cool.

Soak gelatine for 40 minutes and beat the egg-white till it gets foamy, put them in the cooled broth, set on the kitchen-range and simmer for 5—7 minutes. Remove the scum and flakes of the egg-white, strain and cool. Pour the jellied meat in layers. Before serving, chop the jellied meat, cut the ham and boiled tongue into slices and roll them in the shape of gramophone tubes. Lay it all out on a large dish together with the pickled mushrooms and horse-radish, soaked in beetroot juice.

MIXED MEAT JELLY

2 lb (1 kg) pigs' haunches, 1 pig's leg, 1.5 lb (600 gm) cow's haunches, $1/2$ rooster (goose or duck) with giblets (without the liver), 1 carrot, 1 piece parsley, 3 onions, 4 bay leaves, 1 garlic, 4 hard-boiled eggs, 7 oz (200 gm) green peas, 5—6 black peppercorns, ground pepper, salt

Chop the leg, haunches, and rooster (goose or duck), put them in a sauce-pan, pour cold water over them, and start heating. Bring to a boil, remove the scum, add the vegetables and condiment, salt and boil on a very low heat till the meat comes off the bones (3—4 hours). When the broth settles, remove and pour out the grease. Put a ring of an egg on the bottom of cups or small tureens. Lay the green peas, pattern-cut carrot, and parsley around it. Remove the meat from the bones. Cut the big chunks into pieces and put them in the cups. Dress the broth with minced garlic, salt and pepper to taste, and bring it to a boil again. Pour the broth into the cups and put it to the cold.

Before serving, circumcise the jelly carefully with a warm knife, take it out from the cups, and lay it out on round plates. Lay the leaves of the parsley in the plates along their edges.

You can arrange the jelly in a different way. Remove the meat from the bones, dress the broth with condiment, put in the meat, and bring the broth to a boil again. Pour it into small eye-appealing ceramic basins, cool and serve.

Fish Hors D'oeuvres

THE ZAGORSK STYLE EGG

1 hard-cooked egg, 1 salted herring, $1/2$ onion, 0.9 oz (25 gm) mayonnaise, $1/2$ carrot, 2 pickled cucumbers, $1/6$ oz (5 gm) butter, salt

Cut the egg in two, remove the yolk. Remove the skin and bones from the herring. Mince the herring, onion, and egg-yolk mix them. Fill the egg-whites with the minced ingredients. Lay the egg's halves on a plate, pour the mayonnaise over them, adorn with the carrot, cucumbers, and onion.

EGGS WITH THE SPICED SPRATS SAUCE

6 hard-cooked eggs, 4 oz (100 gm) butter, 6 oz (170 gm) spiced sprats, 3 tbsp. flour, salt

Lay the eggs in a dish. Melt the butter in a sauce-pan, add the minced floured fillet of the sprats and sieve it. Pour the sauce over the eggs and top it with dill.

SALTED HERRINGS, HOME STYLE

1 lb (500 gm) mildly salted herrings, 1 oz (30—50 gm) diluted mustard, 5 oz (150 gm) vegetable oil

Skin the herrings, remove the fillet, smear them with mustard on both sides. Fold each fillet into a thick roll and put them in a glass jar. Pour the vegetable (sunflower-seed or olive) oil over them and put them in a fridge. Before serving, lay them out in a herring-dish and adorn with branches of herbs. The herring can be served with hot boiled potatoes topped with parsley or dill.

HERRING GARNERED WITH VEGETABLES

9 oz (250 gm) salted herring, 1 beetroot, 1 carrot, 1 potato, 1 onion, 1 salted or pickled cucumber, 1 egg, 1 tbsp. vegetable oil, 1 tsp. vinegar

Boil the potato, beetroot, and carrot in skin. Peel and cut the the boiled vegetables in small cubes. Cut the salted or pickled cucumber the same way. Prepare the herrings according to the previous recipe. Add the vinegar and mustard to the vegetable oil and pour the mixture over the herring. Surround the herring with the vegetables with slices of hard-cooked eggs and rings of onion between them.

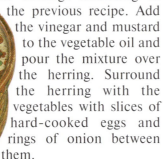

HERRING WITH PICKLED MUSHROOMS

3 herrings, 15 oz (400 gm) pickled mushrooms, 1 onion, 4 oz (100 gm) vegetable oil, 2 tbsp. vinegar, 1/2 tsp. mustard

Remove the skin from the herrings, cut off the heads and tails, and remove the bones. Cut the fillet into pieces, lay in an oval dish, sprinkle with the oil mixed with the vinegar and mustard, adorn with rings of onion. On the side lay the pickled cucumbers cut into cubes. Adorn with herbs.

HERRING IN A SOUR CREAM SAUCE

1 lb (500 gm) herrings, 7 oz (200 gm) apples, 1 onion, 5 oz (150 gm) sour cream; salt, sugar lemon juice to taste

Remove the bones and the skin from the herrings, pour milk over the fillet and put in the fridge (salt herring for 3 hours, slightly salted herring for 1 hour).

The sauce

Peel the apples and onion, grate on a coarse grater. Mix, add salt, sugar, lemon juice, and sour cream.

CHOPPED HERRING

Soak a herring well in milk, water, or drawn tea, remove the skin and fillet, put through the meat-grinder together with white bread soaked in milk, onion browned in vegetable oil, fresh skinned apple without the core and seeds. Dress the mixture with vegetable oil and vinegar. Lay in an oval dish giving it the shape of a roll.

The minced herring can be adorned with slices of a hard-cooked egg, chopped vegetables, and herbs. Instead of vegetable oil you can use slightly melted butter rubbing it thoroughly into the minced herring. In the latter case the onion should best be browned in milk butter too.

FAKE CAVIAR

4 oz (100 gm) and 1 tbsp. vegetable oil, 5 tbsp. manna-croup, 2 tbsp. minced herring, 1 carrot, 1 tsp. vinegar or lemon juice, 2 tbsp. finely chopped green onions, 1.5 cups water; salt to taste

Boil the water with 1 table-spoon of vegetable oil and a pinch of salt; stirring slowly, spill in the manna-croup till set. Let it chill and mix into the minced herring gradually adding the oil, finely chopped boiled carrot and vinegar or lemon juice. Spill in the chopped green onion, lay the mass in a salad-bowl, stick a piece of parsley or a sprig of lettuce in the middle.

PIKE-PERCH'S CAVIAR

15 oz (400 gm) fresh pike-perch's roe, 2 tbsp. chopped green onions, 2 tbsp. vegetable oil, vinegar, salt, pepper, 1 tbsp. finely chopped parsley

Remove the film and scald the roe. After ten minutes pour out the water and let the roe dry a little. Add the vegetable oil, vinegar, finely chopped green onions, salt and pepper. Mix well and stand 1 hour. Before serving strew with parsley. Serve as an appetizer with bread and butter.

PICKLED PIKE-PERCH

1 lb (500 gm) pike-perch, 1 garlic, 5 tbsp. vegetable oil, 1 tbsp. vinegar, salt, 4—5 black peppercorns, 1 cup water

Scale, gut, and wash the fish. Boil in slightly salted water for 15 minutes. Remove the bones and skin and cut into small pieces.

Lay in a herring-dish, add minced garlic, vegetable oil, vinegar, pepper, water, and salt. Cover with the lid and boil for another 5—6 minutes. Serve cold with boiled potatoes, potato salad, or fish sauce.

SMOKED FISH WITH A HORSE-RADISH SAUCE

2 lb (1 kg) filleted cured fish

The sauce: ³/₄ cup sour cream, 3 tbsp. grated horse-radish in vinegar; sugar and salt to taste

Remove the bones, even the thinnest ones, from the fillet, lay the filleted strips in oval plates, and pour the sauce over them.

The sauce

Add the horse-radish, salt, and sugar to the sour cream and mix well. Adorn with fresh cucumbers, radishes, and parsley.

COD AND HORSE-RADISH SALAD

10 oz (300 gm) cod, 5 boiled potatoes, 3 cucumbers, 4 oz (100 gm) horse-radish, ¹/₂ cup mayonnaise sauce, 2 tsp. vinegar, 2 oz (60 gm) green onions

Boil the cod and have it chilled. Cut it into small pieces. Slice the cucumbers and peeled potatoes. Mix well the fish, cucumbers, potatoes, and grated horse-radish, add the mayonnaise, salt, and vinegar; lay in a salad-bowl. You can adorn the salad with rings of cucumbers, parsley, and green onions.

COD LIVER SALAD

1 can cod liver in oil, 2 onions, 2 hard-boiled eggs, 1 tsp. mustard, pepper, and parsley

Chop the eggs fine. Remove the cod liver from the oil, chop, mix with the eggs, add minced onions. Mix well, dress with the mustard, pepper, and minced parsley.

SALAD OF FISH AND TOMATOES

1 lb (500 gm) fish, 3 tomatoes, 3 fresh cucumbers, 4—6 boiled potatoes, 2.5 oz (75 gm) lettuce, 1 pickled cucumber, ¹/₃ cup mayonnaise and vinegar sauce, 2 onions

Boil the fish (sturgeon, sevruga, pike-perch) and have it chilled. Chop it fine. Peel the potatoes. Mix them carefully with sliced fresh and pickled cucumbers and tomatoes, add chopped lettuce. Before serving salt the ingredients a little and mix with the mayonnaise sauce and vinegar. Lay in a salad-bowl in the shape of a mound with the lettuce leaves arranged in the middle of the mound, surround the mixture with rings of tomatoes and cucumbers. You can adorn the salad with pressed, soft or Siberian salmon caviar, slices of salmon, Siberian salmon, sturgeon, and olives with the stones removed.

«STOLICHNY» STURGEON SALAD

15 oz (400 gm) boiled sturgeon, 5 boiled potatoes, 4 oz (100 gm) cucumbers, 1.5 oz (40 gm) canned green peas, 3 oz (85 gm) lettuce, 3 hard-boiled eggs, 9 oz (250 gm) mayonnaise; salt to taste

Take some fish, lettuce, and ¹/₂ egg for adornment. Cut the fish, eggs, and cucumbers into pieces. Wash the lettuce leaves properly and cut them into pieces too. Mix carefully, dress with the mayonnaise and salt, and lay out in a salad bowl.

Adorn the salad with slices of the fish, disks of the eggs, and the greens. For adornment you can use several olives with the bones removed.

SALAD OF STURGEON, FRESH TOMATOES, AND APPLES

15 oz (400 gm) boiled sturgeon, 4 boiled potatoes, 5 oz (150 gm) fresh cucumbers, 4 oz (100 gm) apples, 4 oz (100 gm) tomatoes, 2 oz (50 gm) lettuce, 9 oz (250 gm) mayonnaise, 1 hard-boiled egg

Slice the boiled sturgeon, potatoes, fresh cucumbers, tomatoes, apples, and cut the leaves of lettuce. Add some salt and sugar, dress with the mayonnaise. Mix carefully. Lay out in a salad-bowl in the shape of a mound and adorn with the cut leaves of lettuce, rings of the tomatoes and cucumbers, and slices of the egg.

FISH JELLY

2 lb (1 kg) fresh fresh-water fish (pike-perch, carp, sazan), 1 onion, 1 carrot, several black and aromatic peppercorns, some bay leaves, 1 piece and root parsley, dill, salt, and 1 lemon

Scale, gut, and wash the fish. Cut it into small bits. Pour water over the fish's heads and tails and bring to a boil removing the scum. Add the salt, culinary roots and spices; boil again for $1/2$ hour. Strain the broth, add the bits of fish and boil till done. Make sure the bits do not crumble. Remove the bones carefully and lay out in small forms. Use the strained fish broth as the base for making a jelly with gelatine and a beaten-up egg-white (for colouring). Let the jelly settle and pour into the forms.

Adorn with slices of the lemon and parsley.

JELLIED STERLET, PIKE-PERCH, BURBOT, OR PIKE

2 lb (1 kg) fish, 1 piece parsley, celery, 1 onion, 1—2 bay leaves, 5 aromatic peppercorns, 2 tsp. gelatine

Scale, gut, and wash the fish. Cut it into pieces and boil in a small amount of water with salt, spices, and parsley till done.

Take the ready helpings out from the broth. Remove the gristles from the sterlet. Put the fish in the fridge. Strain the fish broth, set it on a heat, add the gelatine soaked in warm water, stir and bring to a boil till the gelatine is fully dissolved. Chill till normal home temperature. Pour the broth over the pieces of fish. Adorn the jellied sterlet with pieces of lobsters, soft caviar, and lemon rings.

JELLIED STURGEON

2 lb (1 kg) sturgeon, 2 tsp. gelatine, 2 bay leaves, 8 black peppercorns, 1 piece parsley, 1 piece celery, 1 onion

Gut, scale, and wash the fish well. Boil and have it chilled. Remove the skin and cartilages, cut into portions 1 in (3—4 cm) thick, and space in a dish.

Strain the broth, soak the gelatine in warm water and add it to the broth. Bring to a boil stirring it all the while till fully dissolved. Have the broth chilled till home temperature.

Adorn the pieces of sturgeon with disks of carrot, fresh cucumbers, parsley or celery soaked in the setting fish broth. After thirty minutes pour the chilled broth over the helpings with a layer $2/3$ in (1.5 cm) thick. When the layer settles, pour the broth over the portions for the layer above them to be $1/3$ in (1—1.5 cm) thick.

SOUPS

In Russia soups are served as the first course at dinner. In the Russian language the word «soup» was naturalised quite late. Originally, Russian soups were called «*khlebovo*» or «*pokhlyobka*» (soup with cereals).

The typical Russian soups are *schi* (soup with cabbage or sauerkraut), *borsch* (beet and cabbage soup), *rassolnik* (soup with pickled cucumbers), *okroshka* (cold kvass soup), *solyanka* (soup with vegetables, pickled cucumbers, olives, and bits of meat), and *pokhlyobka*.

Meat Soups

THE «FAST» MEAT BROTH

1.5 lb (700 gm) meat (beef, mutton, or chicken), 4 pints (2 litres) water, 1 small onion, 1 carrot, parsley; salt to taste

Remove the bones from the beef, mutton or chicken. Put the meat through the meat-grinder, pour cold water over it, and put it on to boil. When the water starts to boil, salt and put chopped onion, carrot, and herbs in a sauce-pan. Simmer for 20—30 minutes.

BONE-MARROW BROTH

1.5 lb (600 gm) beef or pork bones, 4 pints (1.8 litres) water, 1 onion, 2 small carrots, parsley, peppercorns, 1 bay leaf, salt

Chop the bones into small pieces, put in cold water, bring to a boiling on a low heat removing the scum and grease. Forty minutes before finishing boiling, salt, add the carrots, onion (whole), parsley, and condiment.

BROTH WITH MEAT BALLS

The meat balls: 15 oz (400 gm) chicken or fowl, 2 onions, 3 tbsp. dried white-bread crumbs, 2 eggs, 2 tbsp. sour cream, ground pepper, nutmegs, salt

Put the meat balls in a boiling broth (2 litres) and keep them boiling for 20 minutes.

The meat balls

Put the meat of poultry or fowl and onions twice through the meat-grinder. Mix the bread crumbs with the sour cream and eggs and add them to the meat of poultry or fowl. Dress with the salt, pepper, and nutmegs. Mix well.

BROTH WITH PANCAKES

The broth: 2 lb (1 kg) bones, 6 cups water, 2 carrots, 1 onion; salt, herbs, and spices to taste

The pancakes: $1/2$ cup flour, 1 egg, $3/4$ cup milk, 1 tsp. sugar, 15 oz (400 gm) boneless beef, 4 tbsp. milk butter; spices and salt to taste

Pour cold water over the bones, salt, bring to a boil, and simmer for 3-4 hours, from time to time removing the scum and grease. Put the carrots and onion in the broth 40—50 minutes before finishing boiling. Let the broth set and then strain.

The pancakes

Beat the egg into the milk, add the sugar and salt. Spill the flour gradually, mix till it becomes an even homogenious mass. Bake pancakes browning them on one side. Put the meat twice through the meat-grinder, salt, pepper, and beat well. Lay the raw minced meat on the browned side and fold each pancake in the shape of a pipe.

Lay the pancakes in a frying-pan, sprinkle with the milk butter, and bake in the oven. Before serving lay the pancakes in a plate and pour the broth over them.

MEAT *SCHI* WITH SAUERKRAUT

2 lb (1 kg) beef brisket or pork, 1 lb (0.5 kg) sauerkraut, 1 carrot, 1 onion, 3 tbsp. vegetable oil, 1 piece parsley

Boil meat broth till half done. Brown finely chopped onion and carrot in the frying pan. Add it to the broth and put the sauerkraut in. Before finishing boiling add herbs. Salt to taste.

You can serve the *schi* with sour cream.

SCHI WITH CABBAGE SPROUTS

10 oz (300 gm) beef, 10 oz (300 gm) cabbage sprouts, 1 onion, $1/2$ cup sour cream, salt, pepper, chopped dill

Skald the cabbage sprouts and lay them on a sieve. Let the water drain, chop the onion fine and put it with the cabbage sprouts in the meat broth, bring to a boil and dress with the sour cream, salt, dill, and spices.

SCHI WITH HOG MEAT

10 oz (300 gm) hog meat, $1/3$ oz (10 gm) dried boletusses, 10 oz (300 gm) sauerkraut, 1 piece parsley, 2.5 oz (75 gm) tomato paste (puree), 2 oz (50 gm) wheat flour, 2.5 oz (75 gm) bones of ham, 1.5 oz (45 gm) butter, 1 clove garlic, 1.5 oz (45 gm) granulated sugar; salt, pepper, bay leaf, herbs to taste

Wash the sauerkraut well in cold water, chop it fine, and put in a sauce-pan. Add the ham bones, butter, tomato paste, and granulated sugar. Pour $1/2$ cup of meat broth over them, put the lid on and stew for about an hour. Add the meat, garlic, browned culinary roots, and boil till done. Before finishing boiling add the bay leaf, pepper, salt, and fried flour.

While making the *schi*, put the boletusses in a small sauce-pan, pour $3/4$ cup of water over them, salt and make a mushroom broth. Pour the ready *schi* in a clay pot, add the mushroom broth and finely chopped browned boletuses. Put the lid on and keep in the oven for about 15—20 minutes. Take the *schi* from the oven, top it with the parsley or dill. You can serve the *schi* with buckweat porridge or a cheese-cake, putting it on the pot instead of the lid.

BORSCH, OLD STYLE (WITHOUT TOMATO PASTE)

1 beetroot, 1 small cabbage-head, 2 carrots, 1 onion, 2 tbsp. flour, 3 tbsp. butter, $1/3$ cup cream, 1 tbsp. 3% vinegar, 1 piece parsley or celery; spices to taste

To make this kind of *borsch* peel the beetroot, cut it into thin strips, sprinkle the vinegar over it, add grease, and heat well while stirring. Add some broth (if the *borsch* is made with meat) or water and stew till the beet is softened. Chop the onion, fry it slightly in butter without browning, add thin strips of carrot and again fry the mixture a little. Bring the broth or water to a boil and put shredded cabbage in it. Boil for 10—15 minutes, add the stewed beetroot, slightly fried herbs and onion, condiment, spices, slightly fried flour gruel and keep on boiling till done. At last add some beet infusion and chopped garlic with chopped pork fat.

PEASANT *BORSCH*

3 lb (1.5 kg) beef, 4 carrots, 2—3 tomatoes, 4 pieces parsley, 1 cabbage, 4 pieces celery, 10 oz (350 gm) butter, 75—80 pods haricot, 15 oz (400 gm) sour cream, kvass; salt, pepper, herbs to taste

Make beef-tea, add thin strips of carrot, parsley and celery, and also the pods of haricot cut into 3 or 4 pars. Shred the cabbage. Bring the *borsch* to a boil. Cut tomatoes into slices and fry them (without browning) in butter and a little broth. Remove the sauce-pan from the heat, salt and pepper to taste, add the herbs, let the *borsch* draw for 25—30 minutes, and dress with the sour cream.

Before that you can pour the kvass (1—2 cups) into the *borsch*.

BEETROOT BORSCHOK

1 lb (500 gm) beetroots, 4 oz (100 gm) dried mushrooms, 7 oz (200 gm) haricots, 1 onion, 1 carrot, 15 oz (450 gm) sunflower oil, 0.5 beetroot liquid, 3 pints (1.5 litres) water, 3 cloves garlic, salt, pepper, and 1 bay leaf

Boil the mushrooms. Peel and boil the beetroots. Chop the onion and carrot, put in a sauce-pan, add the oil and 0.5 cup of mushroom liquid. Cook for about 40 minutes. Pour 1 pints (0.5 litres) of betroot liquid and 3 pints (1.5 litres) of water into the sauce-pan. Add the grated beetroots, pepper, and bay leaf. Crush the cloves of garlic together with the salt and put the mixture in the borschok. Add the boiled haricots.

RASSOLNIK WITH KIDNEYS

1 lb (500 gm) kidneys, 4 pints (2 litres) meat broth, 5 potatoes, 1 onion, 3 pickled cucumbers, $^1/_4$ cup pearl-barley, $^1/_2$ cup sour cream, 1 tbsp. flour, 1 piece parsley; dill, parsley, and salt to taste

Remove the film and excessive fat from the kidneys, soak in cold water for 2—3 hours changing the water several times. Put the kidneys in hot water, bring to a boil, lay in a colander, wash with cold water, and cook in meat broth till done. Cut the kidneys into thin slices across the fibres.

Wash the pearl-barley several times in cold water, spill into boiling water, boil till done; wash in cold water and put in the meat broth. Boil well and add the potatoes cut in slices. Brown the herbs, onion, chopped and slightly boiled cucumbers, dress with the flour, add the slices of kidneys, and continue boiling for another 10 minutes.

At last dress with the sour cream, and serve with the herbs.

RASSOLNIK WITH CHICKEN GIBLETS

Singe and wash chicken's heads, necks, and wings. Cut the stomachs in two, take out the stomachs' content, remove the skin and wash well; cut the hearts slightly, drain them of the blood, and wash well; skald the legs, remove the scales, and wash well. Pour broth or water over the giblets, boil for 1.5—2 hours skimming the grease; boil the liver separately.

Strain the broth and make *rassolnik* in it the way you boiled the kidneys (see above). Before serving chop the giblets and put them in the soup.

KALYA WITH CHICKEN

1 lb (0.5 kg) chicken, 2 pickled cucumbers, several pieces parsley, celery, parsnip, 1 onion, 2 tbsp. melted butter, 0.5 cup sour cream, herbs

Boil the chicken and chop it fine, fry the onion in the melted butter without letting it brown. Put the fried onion, parsley, and celery in the chicken broth, bring to a boil, pour slightly fried flour gruel (mixed into the broth) into the chicken broth, add slices of ham, rings of peeled pickled cucumbers, and boil. At last add the herbs, pieces of chicken and dress with pickle to taste.

Serve with the sour cream and minced herbs.

COMBINED MEAT SOLYANKA

The boiled minced meat ingredients: 5 tbsp. veal, 5 tbsp. beef, 5 tbsp. ham, 3 tbsp. sausages, 6—7 tbsp. beef kidneys, 4 onions, 2 pickled cucumbers, 3 tbsp. tomato paste, 3 tbsp. butter, 4 pints (2 litres) buillon, 8 canned black or green olives, 10 black peppercorns, 1 bay leaf, salt, $^1/_2$ lemon, 4 tbsp. sour cream, herbs

Make marrow-bone broth (see above). Shred the onions and fry without letting the onion brown. Add the tomato paste. Remove the skin and seeds from the cucumbers, cut into slices, and boil a little. Cut the boiled meat ingredients (beef, veal, ham, kidneys, tongue, sausages) into fine slices. Put the slightly fried onion and tomato paste, slightly boiled cucumbers, meat ingredients, and herbs and boil for 5—10 minutes. When serving put the olives (without the stones), sour cream, a ring of lemon (peeled), and finely chopped herbs in a plate.

MEAT OKROSHKA

1.5 bread kvass, 4 hard-cooked eggs, 10 oz (300 gm) boiled beef, several green onions (chopped), 2—3 radishes,

2 fresh cucumbers, 3 boiled potatoes, 1—2 tbsp. sour cream, 1 tbsp. sugar, mustard, salt

Grind the egg-yolks together with the sour cream, mustard, salt, and sugar, dilute in cold kvass, add small cubes of the fresh cucumbers, radishes, boiled beef, minced egg-whites, boiled potatoes, chopped green onions.

OKROSHKA, URAL STYLE

It is made like meat *okroshka* with sauerkraut drained of the pickle instead of cucumbers.

GREEN NETTLE SOUP

7 oz (200 gm) beef, 10 oz (300 gm) new nettle, 3—4 sprigs green onions, 1 onion, 1 carrot, 3 potatoes, 3 eggs, and sour cream

Cook the beef with the addition of the onion and cut can carrot. Cut the meat into small pieces and put it back in the broth. Sort out, wash, scald, and chop the nettle. Peel and slice the potatoes. Put the nettle and potatoes in the broth and boil until done. Salt the soup and add a little citric acid. Make the dressing. Chop 3 hard-boiled eggs and green onions. Add the sour cream. Serve the soup with the dressing.

GREEN SOUP WITH EGGS

1 chicken (700—900 gm), 4 oz (100 gm) beef with bones, 4 pints (2 litres) water, 9 oz (250 gm) sorrel, 1 piece parsley, 1 carrot, 3 eggs; salt and pepper to taste

Boil pieces of the chicken and beef in slightly salted water, remove the scum. Strain the broth. Wash the herbs well, chop fine, skald, and put in a strainer. Mince the parsley and carrot and put in the broth adding the pieces of chicken and beef, spices, and the halves of the hard-boiled eggs.

RUSSIAN SOUP IN A CLAY POT

4 oz (120 gm) beef, 5 oz (150 gm) beef bones, 9 oz (260 gm) potatoes, 2 oz (60 gm) fresh mushrooms, $2/3$ oz (20 gm) buckwheat, 1 carrot, 1 onion, 0.9 oz (25 gm) tomato paste, 1 tbsp. butter, 1 tbsp. chopped herbs; spices and salt to taste

Boil the meat and bones. Cut the vegetables into slices and the potatoes into cubes, sort out and fry the buckwheat and vegetables (except the potatoes), boil the mushrooms in a separate sauce-pan. Pour the beef-tea into a clay pot and bring to a boil. Spill the buckwheat into the pot, let the broth boil for 5—10 minutes, put in the potatoes and (after another 10—15 minutes) vegetables. Before serving put the meat and boiled mushrooms in the pot and strew the soup with the chopped herbs.

POKHLYOBKA

7 oz (200 gm) turkey or chicken, 4 oz (100 gm) potatoes, 1.5 oz (45 gm) millet, 1 onion, $2/3$ oz (20 gm) salted pork fat, $2/3$ oz (20 gm) dried mushrooms, 1 bay leaf; herbs and salt to taste

Sort out and wash the millet. Soak the mushrooms in advance and peel the potatoes. *Pokhlyobka* is best made in a clay pot or, if you don't have one, in a sauce-pan. Pour some water into the pot, add the millet, turkey, mushrooms, and bay leaf. Cut the potatoes into cubes. When the turkey is half cooked, put the potato cubes in the soup. Boil for another 10 minutes. Chop the onion and brown it in the pork fat. Put it in the soup right before you finish cooking. Boil thoroughly. Salt and strew with the herbs (minced).

POKHLYOBKA, ARKHANGELSK STYLE

1 pints (0.5 litre) meat broth, 7 oz (200 gm) beef brisket, 1 oz (30 gm) dried boletuses, 2 tomatoes, 3—4 potatoes, 1 onion, $1/2$ oz (15 gm) butter, $1/2$ oz (15 gm) herbs; salt and pepper to taste

Put small pieces of the brisket in a clay pot, pour meat broth over them, add some peppercorns, chopped boiled mushrooms, potatoes, sliced onion and start boiling. In the meantime slice the tomatoes and cook some mushroom broth.

When the potatoes are boiled, add the sliced tomatoes and pour in the mushroom broth.

RUSSIAN *POKHLYOBKA*

½ chicken, 2 potatoes, ½ onion, half a piece parsley, 1 tbsp. sour cream, 1 clove garlic, 1 carrot, 1 peppercorn, 1 bay leaf, ½ oz (15 gm) milk butter, dill, celery; salt to taste

Cook some broth, peel the potatoes and cut them into slices. Fry the carrot, parsley, and onion till golden brown. Shred the garlic, parsley, dill, and celery. Take the chicken out from the broth, cut it into small pieces and put in the broth again.

Add the sliced potatoes, boil thoroughly and put the browned carrot, onion, parsley, and also the bay leaf, the peppercorn, garlic and herbs in the broth. Boil thoroughly again. Ladle the ready *pokhlyobka* out into plates, add the sour cream to taste, and serve.

GIBLET SOUP

2 lb (800 gm) veal, 15 oz (400 gm) beef, 10 oz (300 gm) goose giblets, 2 tbsp. milk butter, 2 tbsp. flour, ½ onion, 1 piece parsley

Skald the goose giblets, legs, and head, wash the necks, liver, and kidneys. Put the meat in a sauce-pan and bring to a boil. Remove the scum, put on the lid, and boil till done. Strain the broth, let it draw for thirty minutes. Sort out and wash the giblets, dilute the butter and flour in the sauce-pan, brown and dilute in the broth. Shred the parsley, put it in the broth with chopped onion and giblets. Bring to a boil and remove the scum. Before serving add two table-spoons of lemon juice and strew with the parsley.

CHICKEN SOUP WITH MORELS

3 chickens, 7 oz (200 gm) pearl-barley, 4 onions, 1 tbsp. butter, 2 pieces parsley, 7 oz (200 gm) morels

Wash and gut the chickens, put them in a sauce-pan and pour cold water over them. Bring to a boil. Remove the scum, add the pearl-barley, 1 table-spoon of butter, minced onions, and two pieces of parsley. When the soup has thickened, add the morels, minced parsley, a ladleful of the broth, and pepper. You can also add some ground nutmegs.

SOUP FROM HARICOTS AND SAUERKRAUT

2 cups haricots, 9 oz (250 gm) sauerkraut, 1 onion, 3 tbsp. sunflower oil, 4 pints (2 litres) water, salt, and pepper

Boil the haricot beans. Chop and brown the onion in the sunflower oil. Add it to the boiled haricots. Have it chilled. Put the sauerkraut in the chilled soup, salt and pepper to taste. Serve cold.

Fish Soups

JOWL BROTH

2 lb (1 kg) jowl, 1 onion, 1 piece parsley, celery; salt to taste

Wash the heads of sturgeon fishes thoroughly and cut them in two or into four parts. Skald and again wash them with cold water. Put the heads in a sauce-pan and pour cold water over them. Bring to a boil, remove the scum, and add the salt, chopped onion, the root of parsley, and also the celery and the leaves of parsley. Put on the lid, lower the heat, and boil the heads for about one hour. Take them out from the sauce-pan, remove the meat and set it aside. Put the left-overs in the sauce-pan again and keep boiling for about one hour. Remove the broth from the burner, have it chilled for about 30 minutes, remove the surfaced grease and strain the broth. It is preferable to use the flesh and gristles of the jowl to fill patties which are good to be served with this broth.

THE ASTRAKHAN FISH SOUP

2 lb (800 gm) sturgeon jowl, 10 oz (300 gm) sturgeon, 2 tomatoes, 3 onions, 1 tbsp. rice, 1 egg-yolk,

3 tbsp. sour cream; parsley, dill, bay leaves, peppercorns, and salt to taste

Cut the sturgeon jowl into several parts, put them in a sauce-pan, pour cold water over them, add salt, pepper, bay leaf, onion and boil on a low heat till the gristles are softened. Strain the broth, add the rice and sliced tomatoes, and boil for about 10 minutes. Add pieces of the sturgeon, boiled gristles, the jowl's flesh and boil over a gentle heat till done.

Dress the soup with the sour cream grated with the egg-yolk and strew it with minced herbs.

THE TRIPLE FISH SOUP

15 oz (400 gm) fresh Caspian roach (vobla), 10 oz (340 gm) pike-perch, 10 oz (300 gm) sevruga, 15 oz (400 gm) potatoes, 1 onion, 3—4 bay leaves; pepper and salt to taste

Scale, gut, and wash the fish thoroughly. Sink the Caspian roach into hot water (previously removing the eyes). Add some salt, pepper, and bay leaves. Remove the scum.

Take the fish out when it's done. Put the scaled, gutted, and boiled sliced pike-perch in the broth. When the pike-perch is cooked, lay it out in separate dishes and strain the broth. Boil the broth again. After it has boiled, add the potatoes cut into cubes, and the sevruga cut into small bits, minced onion and boil till done. Before serving dress the fish soup with the herbs.

The triple soup can be cooked with any other kind of fish.

FISH SOUP, CASPIAN STYLE

15 oz (400 gm) spiced sprats, 4 oz (100 gm) potatoes, 1 onion, 2 pints (1 litre) water; herbs, spices and salt to taste

Scale and gut the fresh sprats (excepting the roe). Do not remove the heads and tails. Boil in a cast-iron bowl or stainless-steel sauce-pan. Remove the scum. Cut the

onion into thin strips, add the greens, salt, pepper, and bay leaves. Boil the fish soup till done (till the sprats are boiled soft). Strain the broth through a fine colander into a separate dish. Boil the potatoes till softened. Do not dress the soup with fat since the sprat's grease is sufficient. Serve the fish soup hot with brown bread.

FISHERMEN'S SOUP

15 oz (400 gm) river fish (ruff, gudgeon, perch), 4 potatoes, 3 onions, 1 root parsley, ground black pepper, salt, 1 bay leaf, 1 piece parsley or dill

Gut the fish, remove the gills, wash thoroughly and cut into bits. Pour cold water over the prepared fish and boil on a low heat for 30—40 minutes. Twenty minutes before finishing cooking add the remaining ingredients.

RICH FISH SOUP

2 lb (1 kg) small fry, 1 lb (500 gm) big fish, 1 piece parsley, 1 onion, 6 black peppercorns, 1—2 bay leaves, half a lemon; salt to taste

Boil the small fry for about an hour till boiled soft. Gut, scale, and wash the bigger fish, remove the skin and bones, and cut into helpings. Strain the spicy broth, put it again on the burner. Bring to a boil again. Add the helpings of the big fish. Boil for 15—20 minutes.

Before serving strew the broth with the herbs. Put each helping in a separate plate with several lemon slices with the seeds removed.

FISH SOUP WITH POTATOES AND TOMATOES

2 lb (1 kg) fish, 1 piece parsley, 3 onions, 1 lb (500 gm) potatoes, 15 oz (400 gm) tomatoes, 2 tbsp. butter, 1—2 bay leaves, 3—5 black peppercorns; salt to taste

Gut and scale the fish. Remove the fillet together with the skin, cut into helpings, salt and put in the refrigerator.

Make a broth from the heads, fins, and bones. Strain the broth, bring to a boil, add cut potatoes, onions, and parsley. Boil for about 20 minutes, add the fish, condiment, fresh sliced tomatoes and boil for another 30 minutes. Remove from the burner, dress with the butter.

Before serving put each helping in a plate and strew with minced herbs.

FISH SOUP WITH HARD-COOKED EGGS

1.5 lb (600 gm) hake or some other kinds of sea fish, 10 potatoes, 1 carrot, 2 onions, 3 tbsp. milk butter, 2 hard-boiled eggs; pepper, salt, bay leaves, and herbs to taste

Make some fish broth, strain it, add the potatoes sliced into small cubes, and boil for 15 minutes. Brown the onions and carrot in the butter, salt, pepper, and boil till done on low heat without stirring for the potatoes to keep their shape.

Before serving add the fish, minced hard-cooked eggs, and strew with the herbs.

FISH SOUP WITH MUSHROOMS

1 lb (500 gm) fish, 5 potatoes, 10 oz (300 gm) fresh mushrooms, 2 onions, 1 piece parsley, 5 tbsp. butter, 5 cloves garlic; herbs, salt, and pepper to taste

Boil the mushrooms, take them out of the mushroom liquid, slice into cubes, and brown together with the finely chopped onions and sprig of parsley. Put the potato cubes in the broth, bring to a boil and put in small pieces of the fish. Boil for 15 minutes, then add the browned mushrooms, onion, and parsley and simmer till done. Before serving add the finely chopped garlics.

POKHLYOBKA WITH FISH DUMPLINGS

7 oz (200 gm) dried mushrooms, 3 onions, 3 tbsp. vegetable butter, 4 tbsp. sour cream; herbs and salt to taste

The fish dumplings: *1 cup flour, 1 egg, 2—3 tbsp. water, 10 oz (300 gm) fish flesh withiout the bones, 1 onion; salt and pepper to taste*

Soak the dried mushrooms and make a mushroom broth. Cut the boiled mushrooms and onion into strips and brown in butter.

Pour the boiling broth with the onion and mushrooms into clay pots, put in the fish dumplings and boil till done. Before serving add 1 table-spoon of sour cream to the content of each pot and strew with herbs.

The fish dumplings

Sift the flour, spill it in the shape of a mound, make a depression in the middle, pour water mixed with the egg and salt into it, knead the mixture till you have thick dow, cover it with a piece of cloth (napkin) and leave for 30 minutes. Put the fish flesh and onion through a meat grinder, salt, pepper, and mix well. Make a flat thin cake from the unleavened (3 mm thick), put the ingredients on it and fold in the shape of a dumpling.

POKHLYOBKA À LA SUVOROV (THE RUSSIAN COMMANDER)

4 oz (100 gm) filleted sturgeon, a little fish broth, 2 potatoes, 1 onion, 1 carrot, 2 oz (50 gm) fresh mushrooms, 2 tbsp. tomato paste, 2 fresh tomatoes, 1 garlic, vegetable oil, 1 lemon

Cut the sturgeon (or some other fish) into slices, slightly brown both sides in butter, put it in a clay pot, cast-iron pot or saucepan, pour some fish broth into it, add slices of raw potatoes, brown the onion, mushrooms, and carrot. Put them in the clay pot and boil until done.

Mince some herbs and garlic, slice the tomatoes and lemon, put it in the *pokhlyobka* and serve.

RASSOLNIK (SOUP WITH PICKLED CUCUMBERS) WITH STURGEON

1.5 lb (700 gm) sturgeon, 1 piece parsley, celery, 1 onion, 4 oz (100 gm) sorrel, 2 oz (50 gm) spinach, 2 pickled cucumbers, 1.5 tbsp. butter, 5 oz (150 gm) sour cream

Pour cold water over the gutted and washed sturgeon, salt and put on a burner. While the fish is boiling, mince the parsley, celery, and onion and brown in butter. When the fish is done, take it out, transfer into another dish, and pour some broth over it. Bring the remaining broth to a boil, put in strips of the peeled cucumbers, browned culinary roots, and condiment. Boil for another 20—25 minutes. Add the minced spinach, sorrel, and strained cucumber pickle. Cut the sturgeon into portions and heat them. Lay each helping on a separate plate. Dress the *rassolnik* with the sour cream and strew it with the minced parsley.

SOLYANKA, CASPIAN STYLE

15 oz (400 gm) sevruga, 15 oz (400 gm) gristles, 1 carrot, 2 onions, 4 potatoes, 2 pickled cucumbers, 15 oz (400 gm) margarine, 3—4 bay leaves, 1 tbsp. tomato paste; salt and pepper to taste

Gut the fresh fish, remove the gristles and bones. Make a thick broth from the gristles. Cut the potatoes into cubes. Put the potato cubes, sliced sevruga, pepper, salt, and bay leaves in the broth and simmer for 20 minutes. Brown the onions, carrot, and cucumbers. Add the tomato paste. Dress the broth with it. You can add vinegar or dry wine to taste.

SOUR *SCHI* WITH FRIED FISH

15 oz (400 gm) fish, 10 oz (350 gm) chopped sauerkraut, 3 onions, 4 oz (100 gm) sunflower oil, 2 oz (50 gm) tomato paste, 6 pints (3 litres) water, 2 tbsp. flour, 1 tbsp. minced herbs; bay leaves, salt, and pepper to taste

Cut and wash the fish. Remove the back bone, cut the fish into portions, roll in flour, brown in the sunflower oil, put in a pan, pour cold water over them, and boil till done. Brown the onions and sauerkraut in the sunflower oil and cook them from time to time adding the fish broth. Dress the sauerkraut with the tomato paste diluted in the sunflower oil, add the pepper and bay leaves. Take the fish out of the broth and pour the broth over it. Boil the *schi* for another 30 minutes. Before serving, put the boiled fish in the *schi* and strew with the herbs.

SOUP BELLE, SUZDAL-CITY STYLE

7 oz (200 gm) dried mushrooms, 1 small piece celery, 1 carrot, 1 sprig parsley, 3—4 big onions, 6 freshwater fishes (ruff, tench, perch), 4 oz (100 gm) macaroni or noodles, 1 tsp. black peppercorns, several cloves, a pinch of ground nutpegs, herbs and salt

Wash the mushrooms well, soak them in cold water for 2—3 hours, and boil in the same water. Put the celery, carrot, unpeeled onions (cut in half), peppercorns, cloves, nutpegs, and salt in the same saucepan. Without bringing the soup to a boil, add bits of the gutted fish. Boil till the broth is thick. Strain the broth through a strainer and then through double gauze. Add the macaroni or noodles making sure the broth is not too thick. Mince the herbs and serve with the soup.

Vegetable, Mushroom, and Milk Soups

CABBAGE SOUP WITH SOUR CREAM

2 lb (800 gm) fresh cabbage, 1 bay leaf, 1 onion, 3 tsp. flour, butter, 1/2 cup sour cream, dill, and parsley

Chop 2 lb (800 gm) of fresh cabbage, salt and cook in the butter. Pour boiling water over it, add the bay leaf, minced and browned onion, 3 teaspoons of flour browned in the butter. Bring to a boil, add a table-spoon of butter, 1/2 cup of the sour cream, and heat without bringing it to a boil. Add the minced dill and parsley. Serve with the sour cream.

SCHI, VALAAM STYLE

2 lb (1 kg) cabbage, 2 onions, 1 large bay leaf, 3—4 sprigs parsley, 8-10 black peppercorns, 1 lb (500 gm) mushrooms, 1 tbsp. flour, 2 tbsp. sour cream; herbs to taste

Cook the cabbage, chopped onions, bay leaf, parsley, and peppercorns with the addition of the water.
Boil the finely chopped mushrooms in a separate pan. Take the mushrooms out of the mushroom liquid and brown them slightly.
When the cabbage is semi-soft, add some browned flour.
Put all the ingredients, fresh herbs, and sour cream in the mushroom liquid.
Simmer the *schi* for quite a time without bringing it to a boil until it has a mushroom-and-cabbage flavour.

SCHI WITH SAUERKRAUT

4 oz (100 gm) dried mushrooms, 1 onion, 1 carrot, 1 lb (0.5 kg) sauerkraut, 1 turnip, herbs, and salt

Sort out the sauerkraut and shred the large pieces. Mince and slightly brown the carrot, turnip, swede, and onion constantly stirring them. Add the tomato paste and brown all the ingredients again.
You can make this kind of *schi* without tomato paste. Put the sauerkraut in a sauce-pan or cauldron, add the vegetable oil, and cook for about an hour. Add the roots browned in tomato paste and cook everything for another half hour. Heat the flour in a frying-pan stirring it with a spoon, dilute with water, put in the *schi*, add some ground garlics, and boil for 5—7 minutes. Before serving strew the *schi* with herbs.

SCHI WITH SAUERKRAUT AND MUSHROOMS

10 oz (300 gm) sauerkraut, dried mushrooms, 2 carrots, parsley, 1 onion, 1 swede, 1 turnip, 2 tbsp. tomato paste, 4 tbsp. vegetable oil, 1 tbsp. flour

Cook the *schi* in mushroom liquid with the addition of the vegetables diluted in vegetable oil. Chop the boiled mushrooms fine, brown slightly with the onion, and put it in the *schi*. Boil for 5—10 minutes.

SELYANSKIYE (VILLAGE) SCHI

5 oz (150 gm) shoots of stinging nettle, potatoes, 2 oz (50 gm) sourgrass, 1/6 oz (5 gm) carrot, 2/3 oz (20 gm) onion, 1/2 oz (15 gm) green onions

Pour boiling water over the shoots of stinging nettle, chop them, add sourgrass, carrot, parsley, onion, and green onions.
Boil the nettle and brown the vegetables in oil. Put all the ingredients in boiling water and boil for another 20—25 minutes. Ten minutes before it is done add a bay leaf, pepper, clove, and grated potatoes. Before serving dress with sour cream and add several slices of a hard-boiled egg.

GREEN SCHI

1 carrot, 1 turnip, 1 sprig celery, 1 sprig parsley, 3 tsp. flour, 7 oz (200 gm) canned spinach puree, 7 oz (200 gm) canned sorrel puree, dill, 1/2 cup sour cream, and butter

Chop the carrot, turnip, celery, and parsley,

boil them in slightly salted boiling water, and grate. Slightly brown 3 tea-spoons of flour in butter, put it in the grated vegetables, dilute with the broth, and bring to a boil. Add 7 oz (200 gm) of canned sorrel puree and 7 oz (200 gm) of canned spinach puree, 1 tablespoon of butter, 1/2 cup of sour cream, salt and heat without bringing to a boil. Strew with the minced dill and parsley. Serve with the sour cream.

SORREL *SCHI*

5 oz (150 gm) sorrel, 1 onion, 1 tbsp. butter, 2 eggs, dried bread-crumbs, sour cream, and dill

Sort out the sorrel, wash well, cook half of it in butter, put through a sieve, put in the boiling broth, add the finely chopped and slighlty browned onion and white roots, diluted and browned flour, and boil for 15—20 minutes. Cut the remaining sorrel into small bits, put them in the *schi*, add spices, and bring to a boil.

Before serving, mix an egg into milk, heat the mixture till it gets thick, pour it into a plate, add a hard-boiled egg, and pour the *schi* over it; serve with the sour cream, dried white bread-crumbs, and dill.

BEET AND SOUR-CREAM SOUP (*BORSCH*)

1 red beetroot, 1 tbsp. butter, 4 oz (100 gm) sour cream, dill, and parsley

Chop the beetroot, pour cold water over it, boil till soft, strain through a sieve. Add the juice of the raw beetroot, 1 table-spoon of butter, 4 oz (100 gm) of sour cream, and salt. Heat without bringing to a boil. Strew with the chopped dill and parsley.

LEAN *BORSCH* (BEET AND CABBAGE SOUP)

1.5 lb (600 gm) beetroot, 10 oz (300 gm) carrots, 1 piece parsley, 2 onions, 2 lb (800 gm) tomatoes or 1 tbsp. tomato paste, 10 oz (300 gm) fresh cabbage, 4 big potatoes, 1/2 cup sunflower oil, 5 green (not hot) peppers, 10 black peppercorns, 2 bay leaves, 2 tbsp. minced parsley, 1 garlic; salt to taste

Mince the onions, beetroots, carrots, parsley, and three green peppers, put them in a sauce-pan and top them with the ground tomatoes and sunflower oil. Salt and add the bay leaves and peppercorns. Boil on low heat with the lid on. When the juice is evaporated with only red oil left over, add 6 pints (3 litres) of water, let it boil for about 20 minutes, and put in the cabbage.

Boil the potatoes whole in a separate pan and then put them in the *borsch* when the cabbage is done. You cannot boil raw potatoes in the *borsch* since the tomatoes will prevent them from boiling soft. Add the ground garlic, finely chopped peppers, and parsley to the cooked *borsch*. Leave for 20 minutes and serve.

The *borsch* tastes better the following day. You can serve it cold.

VEGETARIAN *BORSCH*

4 medium-size beetroots, half a medium-size cabbage, 1 carrot, 2 white culinary roots, 5—6 medium-size potatoes, 2 tbsp. tomato paste, 3 tsp. minced herbs, 2 tbsp. butter, 4 tbsp. sour cream, 2 tsp. granulated sugar, 2 tsp. flour, 2 tsp. 3% vinegar, 6 cups vegetable broth, and 1 tsp. salt

Chop the beetroots into thin strips. Cook them in a vegetable broth together with the roots, tomato paste, and butter in a sauce-pan with the lid on. Add some vinegar for red-beet colouring. Shred the cabbage and boil it in the boiling vegetable broth until semi-done. Add the potatoes and, after some time, the boiled beetroots and culinary roots. Add the flour, salt, and granulated sugar.

BORSCH WITH SAUERKRAUT

1.5 lb (600 gm) beetroots, 15 oz (400 gm) sauerkraut, 3 onions, 1 carrot, 1 tbsp. tomato paste, 4 oz (100 gm) sunflower oil, 6 pints (3 litres) water, 10 black peppercorns, 1 bay leaf, 1 clove garlic; salt to taste

Chop the beetroots into strips and boil them in an uncovered enamel sauce-pan till soft. Chop the onions fine, cut the carrot into thin strips, and brown them slightly. Add the sauerkraut and cook till soft adding some oil and water. Add the cooked sauerkraut, bay leaf, peppercorns, carrots, and onions to the boiled beetroots and boil until done. Serve with the ground garlic and grated boiled beetroots.

LEAN MUSHROOM *BORSCH*

1 beetroot, 4 oz (100 gm) mushrooms, 1 carrot, 1 onion, 2 tbsp. tomato paste, 1 lb (0.5 kg) cabbage, 5—6 prunes

Boil the beetroot, peel it and cut into strips. Soak the mushrooms for 3—4 hours, then boil them and strain the broth. Cut the mushrooms into slices and brown in vegetable oil. Chop the carrot and onion fine, brown them slightly in vegetable oil (without letting them change their colour), add the tomato paste or skinned tomatoes, and heat for 5—10 minutes.

Boil the soaked prunes, remove the stones, and cut into slices.

Put the chopped cabbage in the boiling mushroom liquid and boil for 10—15 minutes. Add the browned mushrooms, carrot, culinary roots, and prunes and bring to a boil. Add vinegar, salt, and sugar to taste.

SOUR *SCHI* WITH BOLETUSSES

2 oz (50 gm) dried boletusses, onions, butter, 1.5 lb (600 gm) chopped sauerkraut, 1 bay leaf, 3 tsp. flour, parsley, and sour cream

Boil the dried boletusses, strain the mushroom liquid, and shred the boletusses. Chop the onion fine and slightly brown in butter. Boil the chopped sauerkraut together with 2 small onions and bay leaf. Add 1 tablespoon of butter and bring to a boil. Add the boletusses, 1 table-spoon of butter, 4 oz (100 gm) of sour cream, and browned onion and pour the mushroom liquid over the ingredients. Heat the *schi* without bringing it to a boil and strew with minced dill and parsley.

«LAZY» *SCHI* À LA GRIBOYEDOV

2 oz (50 gm) dried boletusses, cabbage, 1 onion, 1 turnip, 1 carrot, potatoes, 3 tsp. flour, butter, dill, parsley, and sour cream

Pour cold water over the boletusses, add some salt, boil, strain the mushroom liquid, and chop the boletusses fine. Cut the cabbage into small pieces, cook in slightly salted boiling water, add the sliced onion, turnip, carrot, parsley, and potatoes. When the *schi* is done, add the boletusses with the mushroom liquid, 3 tea-spoons of slightly browned flour and bring to a boil. Add 1 table-spoon of butter, 4 oz (100 gm) of sour cream, heat the *schi* without bringing it to a boil, strew with the chopped dill and parsley. Serve with the sour cream served separately.

«MONASTERY» SOUP

2 oz (50 gm) dried boletusses, 1 onion, 5 pickled cucumbers, 6 potatoes, 1 turnip, 1 leek, 1 carrot, 1 swede, 1 bay leaf, butter, and sour cream

Boil the boletusses, strain the liquid, and mince the boiled boletusses. Shred and brown the onion in the butter. Peel six potatoes. Cut the potatoes, big pickled cucumbers, a medium-size turnip, leek, carrot, and swede into long slices. Boil them with the addition of one bay leaf. Add the boletusses with the mushroom liquid, browned onion, 2 oz (50 gm) of butter, 4 oz (100 gm) of sour cream and heat without bringing it to a boil. Serve the sour cream.

MUSHROOM SOUP WITH «EARS»

7 oz (200 gm) dried mushrooms, 5 oz (150 gm) sunflower oil, 5 oz (130 gm) rice, 3 onions, 8 pints (4 litres) water; salt and pepper to taste

Vegetable, Mushroom, and Milk Soups

The dough: *7 oz (200 gm) flour, 1 tbsp. sunflower oil, 1 egg, 1 cup water; salt to taste*

Cook a mushroom broth. Take the mushrooms out of the broth, mince them and brown with the finely chopped onions. Mix with the boiled crumbly rice, salt and pepper.

To make thick unleavened dough spill the flour on a board in the shape of a mound. Make a depression in the middle, pour some water, one uncooked egg, and the sunflower oil into the depression. Salt and knead carefully. Keep kneading until the dough is even and not gluey. Put the dough on the board, cover it with a heated saucepan, and leave for about ten minutes until the gluten is sufficiently swollen. Roll the dough into a thin layer, cut into small square-shaped pieces, lay the minced mushrooms and rice on each of them, fold the squares in the shape of triangles, moist the edges and paste them together. Wrap each triangle's base around the index finger of your left hand and join its opposite corners together with your right hand to make it look like an ear. Boil the resulting «ears» separately in salted boiling water and transfer onto a colander. Before serving, lower in the previously strained broth.

POTATO SOUP WITH PICKLED SAFFRON MILK CAPS

15 oz (400 gm) pickled saffron milk caps, 8 cups milk, 1 onion, butter, potatoes, 1 bay leaf, 2 egg-yolks, sour cream, dill, and parsley

Mince the pickled saffron milk caps, boil in 2 cups of milk with the addition of the bay leaf. Cut the onion fine and brown in butter. Peel the potatoes, boil them in slightly salted milk, and strain the broth. Bring 6 cups of milk to a boil, add the mushrooms in their liquid and milk, onion, potatoes, 1 table-spoon of butter, 4 oz (100 gm) of sour cream mixed with two egg-yolks, and salt. Heat without bringing to a boil. Strew with the minced dill and parsley. Serve with the sour cream served separately.

POTATO SOUP WITH MUSHROOMS

2 oz (50 gm) dried mushrooms, 1 onions, 0.5 cup milk, 8 potatoes, pepper, salt, and butter

Put six well-boiled and slightly salted potatoes through a sieve. Dilute the potato puree with milk and mix till smooth. Dilute the puree with water till the soup is set properly. Cook the previously boiled and chopped dried mushrooms separately in butter with the addition of salt, pepper, and onion. Put all the ingredients in the soup, bring it to a boil and serve with browned toasts.

MUSHROOM *SOLYANKA* (VEGETABLE SOUP)

1 lb (500 gm) boletusses, 4 onions, 2 fresh cucumbers, 4 tbsp. butter, 2 tbsp. tomato paste; capers, olives, sour cream, salt and herbs to taste

Peel, wash, and boil the fresh boletusses. Mince the boiled boletusses and put them in the strained broth, add the chopped and browned cucumbers, the onions browned with the tomato paste, capers, and salt and simmer for ten minutes.

Before serving, add the olives, herbs, and sour cream.

MUSHROOM *POKHLYOBKA*

7 oz (200 gm) rye bread, 10 oz (300 gm) fresh or 1 oz (30 gm) dried mushrooms, 2 pints (1 litre) mushroom liquid, 2 medium-size onions, 2 tbsp. butter, 4 tbsp. sour cream; salt and pepper to taste

Make a mushroom broth. Grate the rye bread. Mince and brown the onions. Mix them with the grated rye bread and cook. Add the mixture to the mushroom liquid; add some salt, pepper, and sour cream to taste.

MUSHROOM *RASSOLNIK*

2 oz (60 gm) dried mushrooms, 6 pickled cucumbers, 4 potatoes, 1 carrot, 1 piece parsley, 2 onions, 1 tbsp. rice, 2 oz (50 gm) tomato paste, 2 tbsp. flour, 4 oz (100 gm) sunflower oil and 6 pints (3 litres) water

Boil the mushrooms separately in slightly salted water till soft. Put the pickled cucumbers, onion, carrot, and parsley in a sauce-pan. Add the oil, half a cup of water, one bay leaf, and eight black peppercorns and stir till done. Brown the boiled mushrooms together with the finely chopped onions, mix the flour into it, and dilute with cold mushroom liquid. Boil the rice and potato cubes in separate pans. Put the cooked vegetables, mushrooms, and rice in a sauce-pan, pour salted boiling water over them, mix well, dress with the flour and browned onions, let it boil a little, and serve.

MUSHROOM SOUP WITH PEARL-BARLEY AND POTATOES

2 oz (50 gm) dried boletusses, 2 oz (50 gm) butter, potatoes, 1 onion, sour cream, and 4 oz (100 gm) peal-barley

Boil the dried boletusses, strain the liquid, and chop the mushrooms fine. Boil the pearl-barley in water. Put the peeled and sliced potatoes, minced boletusses, slightly browned oion, 4 oz (100 gm) sour cream, 2 oz (50 gm) butter, and salt in the broth. Heat without bringing to a boil. Serve with the sour cream, served separately.

MUSHROOM SOUP WITH NOODLES

2 oz (50 gm) dried boletusses, 1 onion, home-made noodles, 2 tbsp. butter, and sour cream

Boil the boletusses, strain the liquid, and mince the boletusses. Make $1/3$ of home-made noodles' helping and cook in the mushroom liquid. Add 1 table-spoon of butter, slightly browned chopped onion, 4 oz (100 gm) of sour cream, and heat without bringing to a boil. Serve the sour cream.

HOME-MADE *RASSOLNIK*

10 oz (300 gm) fresh cabbage, 15 oz (400 gm) potatoes, 7 oz (200 gm) carrots, 1 piece parsley, 1 piece celery, 2 onions, 4 pickled cucumbers, 2 tbsp. vegetable oil, 2 tbsp. sour cream, herbs, salt, and spieces

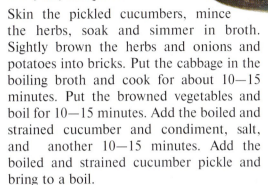

Skin the pickled cucumbers, mince the herbs, soak and simmer in broth. Sightly brown the herbs and onions and potatoes into bricks. Put the cabbage in the boiling broth and cook for about 10—15 minutes. Put the browned vegetables and boil for 10—15 minutes. Add the boiled and strained cucumber and condiment, salt, and another 10—15 minutes. Add the boiled and strained cucumber pickle and bring to a boil.

RASSOLNIK WITH BUCKWHEAT

8 big pickled cucumbers, $1/2$ swede, 1 carrot, 1 leek, 1 turnip, 1 onion, $1/2$ sprig parsley, $1/2$ sprig celery, 6 potatoes, 2 oz (50 gm) buckwheat, 1 bay leaf, dill, 1 tbsp. butter, and 5 oz (150 gm) sour cream

Skin and slice 8 pickled cucumbers, 1 medium-size turnip, swede, carrot, leek, turnip, onion, parsley, celery, and 6 potatoes. Add the buckwheat, bay leaf, and boil. Before serving add the minced dill, parsley, 5 oz (150 gm) of sour cream, butter, and cucumber pickle. Heat without boiling. Serve with the sour cream served separately.

LENTEN *BOTVINNIA* (FISH AND VEGETABLE SOUP)

1 plate sorrel, 1 plate spinach, 1 pints (0.5 litres) kvass, sugar, and lemon

Sort out the sorrel, boil in a small amount of water. Sort out the spinach and boil it separately in a small amount of water. Grate the sorrel and spinach fine. Chill the puree, dilute with the kvass, add the sugar and dried lemon peel. Leave in the cold.
Pour the *botvinnia* into plates, add slices of cooked or smoked fish, minced green onions, dill, fresh cucumbers, grated horse-radish, and some other spices.

Vegetable, Mushroom, and Milk Soups

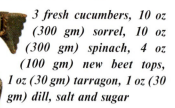

RUSSIAN *BOTVINNIA*

3 fresh cucumbers, 10 oz (300 gm) sorrel, 10 oz (300 gm) spinach, 4 oz (100 gm) new beet tops, 1 oz (30 gm) tarragon, 1 oz (30 gm) dill, salt and sugar

Slice the peeled cucumbers, boil the sorrel in slightly salted water and grate them fine. Skald the new spinach and beet tops till soft and mince. Before serving dilute with sour *schi*, add the salt, sugar, tarragon, and dill.

Normally the *botvinnia* is served with cold boiled fish.

BOTVINNIA, NOVGOROD STYLE

2 pints (1 litre) kvass, 10 oz (300 gm) spinach, 10 oz (300 gm) sorrel, 1 tsp. sugar, 4—5 green onions, 3 tbsp. grated horse-radish, a little dill and 9 oz (250 gm) any boiled fish; salt (you can substitute the spinage for new nettle)

Boil the spinach in slightly salted water, making sure it is not too soft. Cook the sorrel in a separate sauce-pan. Grate the ingredients fine to have some kind of green paste (puree). Add the sugar, salt, and, possibly, a little mustard and dilute with the kvass. Shred the green onions and dill. Put them in a sauce pan. This kind of *botvinnia* is served cold. Put the grated horse-radish and slices of boiled fish in each plate.

«*POLEVITSA*» (SPEAR GRASS) SOUP

15 oz (400 gm) herbs, 2 roots parsley, 1 onion, 3 potatoes, condiment, sugar, and sour cream

In spring, when there is no kitchen-garden herbs and vegetables, you can make a soup from wild plants: stinging nettle, white edible goose-foot, sorrel, plantain, clover, etc. (Sorrel and some other sour plants should not make more than one third of the whole amount of the ingredients). Use only young plants. Skald the sorrel and nettle only one time and the goose-foot two times.

Wash the herbs properly. Cut them fine and pour boiling water or mushroom liquid over them. Slightly brown the roots and onion, put the herbs in the broth, add the potatoes cut into cubes, and boil till done. 5—10 minutes before the cooking is finished add a bay leaf, salt, pepper, and 1 tea-spoon of granulated sugar. Add the sour cream or clotted sour milk and serve.

SOUP WITH YOUNG NETTLE

1 lb (500 gm) nettle leaves, 3 tsp. flour, 4 oz (100 gm) sour cream, 2 egg-yolks, 2 oz (50 gm) butter, dill, and parsley

Boil the nettle in slightly salted water, strain the broth, and grate the nettle fine. Chill half a glass of the broth. Bring the remaining broth to a boil, trickle half a glass of the cold broth mixed with 3 tea-spoons of flower. Bring to a boil. When the broth sets, add the grated nettle, 4 oz (100 gm) of sour cream mixed with 2 beaten egg-yolks, 2 oz (50 gm) butter, minced dill, parsley, and salt. Heat without boiling. Serve the sour cream.

BEET SOUP WITH SORREL AND SOUR CREAM

1.5 lb (700 gm) beet tops, 7 oz (200 gm) sorrel, 4 tsp. flour, butter, 2 egg-yolks, 1—2 beetroots, dill, parsley, and sour cream

Separately cook the young beet tops and sorrel in slightly salted boiling water. Strain the broth and chop the ingredients. Slightly brown the flour in the butter, add it to the beet broth, sorrel and their liquid. Bring it to a boil. Add 1 table-spoon of butter, 4 oz (100 gm) of sour cream mixed with the beaten egg-yolks, and raw red beetroots with their juice. Heat without boiling, strew with the minced dill and parsley. Serve the sour cream.

SOUP WITH GREEN PEAS AND CEREAL

1 cup green peas, 1/2 cup pearl-barley, 1 onion, and a little salted pork fat and salt

Sort out the green peas and pearl-barley. Wash them well, pour cold water over them,

and boil. Chop the onion fine, brown it in the pork fat, and add to the soup 10—15 minutes before done.

GREEN-PEAS SOUP WITH TOASTS

15 oz (400 gm) hulled green peas, 3 oz (80 gm) sunflower oil, 1 tbsp. flour, 1 onion, 1 loaf white bread, 4 oz (100 gm) pungent cheese, 6 pints (3 litres) water; salt to taste

Wash the green peas well. Pour cold water over them and boil till soft. Put them through a colander together with the broth. Salt the soup, add the browned onion and flour, and dilute with the cold broth. Let it boil a little and lift from the burner.

Serve the green-peas soup with toasts with cheese browned in vegetable oil. For this remove the crust from the loaf, cut it into slices and then into cubes, lay the cubes on a dripping-pan, pour some oil over them, strew with the grated cheese, and put in a heated oven.

MOSCOW *OKROSHKA* (KVASS SOUP)

2 pints (1 litre) kvass, 4 oz (100 gm) potatoes, 3 oz (80 gm) beetroots, 2 oz (60 gm) fresh cucumbers, 1 oz (30 gm) apples, $^2/_3$ oz (20 gm) parsley, $^2/_3$ oz (20 gm) sugar, 1 tsp. mustard, green onions, 2 hard-boiled eggs, about 1 cup sour cream; salt and pepper to taste

Chop one hard-boiled egg, boiled vegetables, and apple into cubes. Grate the egg-yolk together with the mustard, sour cream, and green onions. Add salt and pepper to taste. Join the ingredients and dilute them with the kvass.

OKROSHKA, VYATKA-CITY STYLE

1 radish, 3 potatoes, 1.5 pints (0.75 litre) kvass, horse-radish; herbs and salt to taste

Grate one radish. Slice some unpeeled boiled cold potatoes. Mix the radish with the potatoes. Salt the mixture and leave it for about 40—50 minutes. Add cold kvass and grated horse-radish. Serve with herbs.

HORSE-RADISH SOUP WITH KVASS, THE URALS STYLE

1 cup kvass, 1 medium-size radish, 2 oz (50 gm) potatoes, 1 egg, several sprigs green onions, 1 tbsp. sour cream; herbs and salt to taste

Peel and grate the radish coarse, and mix it with the kvass. Add the minced hard-boiled egg, cubes of boiled potatoes, and minced green onions. Add the sour cream, salt, and strew with parsley or dill.

CLOTTED SOUR-MILK- AND-BEET-TOP COLD SOUP

1 cup sour milk, 1 cup sour cream, 7 oz (200 gm) fresh cucumbers, 2 pints ($^1/_3$ litre) kvass, 10 oz (300 gm) beet tops, 2 hard-boiled eggs, 2 tbsp. chopped dill and green onions; salt, sugar, lemon juice, and 6% vinegar to taste

Wash the beet tops well, chop into strips, and boil in a sauce-pan with the lid on in a small amount of water (with the addition of lemon juice or vinegar). Chill the beet tops, peel and cut the cucumbers into cubes. Mix the clotted sour milk with the sour cream, add the beet tops, cooked cucumbers, rings of eggs, dill, and green onions. Pour the kvass into it and mix well. Serve cold.

MILK SOUP WITH VEGETABLES

2 pints (1 litre) milk, 7 oz (200 gm) cabbage, 5 potatoes, 4 oz (100 gm) celery, 2 turnips, 1 carrot, 4 tbsp. sour cream; salt to taste

Cut the turnips, celery and carrot into thin slices. Brown and put in boiling milk. Add the sliced potatoes, cabbage (chopped into squares), salt, and simmer till done. Serve with the sour cream.

MILK SOUP WITH NOODLES

3 pints (1.5 litres) milk, 1 pints (0.5 litres) water, 8 tbsp. noodles, 1 egg-yolk, 1.5 oz (40 gm) butter; salt and sugar to taste

Put the noodles in boiling water and transfer onto a colander. Boil the slightly

Vegetable, Mushroom, and Milk Soups

salted milk to a boil. Add the boiled noodles and heat. Before serving, add the egg-yolk mixed in milk, butter, and sugar.

BREAD SOUP, COUNTRY STYLE

10 oz (300 gm) dried bread crust, 4 oz (100 gm) fat, 2 eggs, 2 onions, salt, parsley, a pinch of ground red fragrant cayenne

Brown small pieces of dried white bread crust in the fat together with the minced parsley and onions. Pour 3 pints (1.5 litres) of water over them, salt, pepper, and bring to a boil. Pour in the ground eggs, stirring all the while. Serve immediately.

VEGETABLE MARROW- AND-MUSHROOM SOUP

7 oz (200 gm) wheat bread, 4 pints (2 litres) water, 15 oz (400 gm) vegetable marrows, 10 oz (300 gm) fresh mushrooms, 2 tbsp. vegetable oil, 1 tbsp. flour, salt to taste

Peel the vegetable marrows, remove the seeds, cut into rings or cubes, roll in the flour and brown, in the vegetable oil. Boil the mushrooms, wash them well, pour boiling water over them, boil well, remove the scum, add the grated white bread (soak it in hot water, press out, and rub through a sieve).

Mince an onion and brown it in the vegetable oil. Add it to the vegetable marrows, salt, put in the soup, and boil till done (20—25 minutes).

BILL-BERRY SOUP

1 lb (500 gm) bill-berries, $2/3$ oz (20 gm) sugar, 7 oz (200 gm) sour cream, $1/3$ oz (10 gm) potato powder and salt

Strew the frozen bill-berries with sugar and then defrost them. Strain the juice. Put the berries in boiling water, boil well, strain, rub through a sieve, add the potato powder diluted in a small amount of water, and bring to a boil. Have it chilled, pour the sour cream and strained juice into it, salt to taste, and mix well. Serve with toasts or noodles.

HOT MEAT DISHES

Russian cuisine has always been rich in meat dishes. Until the 11th century, horse meat was the main meat dish, whereas veal was not welcomed. To kill a calf was thought to be next to a crime. Beef, too, was eaten comparatively seldom.

In time, Russian cuisine underwent changes. The following recipes deal with dishes of beef, pork, mutton, poultry, game, and wild animals.

As a rule, meat dishes are served with vegetables, noodles, and cereal.

Dishes with Beef

BEEF WITH HORSE-RADISH SAUCE

1 lb (500 gm) beef, 1 onion, 1 clove garlic, 2—3 tbsp. butter or margarine, 1 horse-radish, herbs, 1 bay leaf, clove garlic, sugar, and salt

Pour hot water over the beef, add the herbs, bay leaf, onion, clove, garlic, sugar, and salt and boil until done.

The sauce

Melt the butter, brown some flour in it, add the beef-tea and cream (as desired) and mix with the grated horse-radish. Cut the beef into portions and serve with boiled potatoes and the horse-radish sauce.

RUSSIAN ROAST BEEF

1 lb (0.5 kg) beef, 2 potatoes, 1 onion, 1 root parsley, black pepper, 1 bay leaf, salt, sour cream, dill, and parsley

Peel the potatoes, wash them, cut into cubes, and brown in butter. Cut the onion into rings and fry until golden-brown. Cut the beef into small pieces and brown on both sides until they are covered in pink crust. Put the meat, potato cubes, onion, and culinary roots into a clay pot, add some salt, pepper, bay leaf, and a little broth. Cook in the oven for 30 minutes. Ten minutes before finishing cooking, pour some sour cream over the roast beef, strew with minced dill and parsly. Serve the roast beef with a salad of fresh vegetables, pickled cucumbers, sauerkraut, and herbs.

ROAST BEEF WITH RAISINS

1.5 lb (600 gm) beef (fillet, thick side), 3 tbsp. rice, 4 tbsp. raisins, 3 onions, 8 tbsp. vegetable oil, 0.5 cup red table wine, 1 root celery, 1 bay leaf, ground black pepper, and salt

Cut the beef into relatively flat helpings, pound and salt them. Shred the onions, grate the root of celery, wash the rice and raisins well. Mix all the ingredients, then salt and pepper them. Spread the resulting mass over the beef helpings. Fold each helping into a roll, tie up with a length of thread, put in boiling vegetable oil and brown on both sides. Pour red table wine over them, add the bay leaf, clove, and nutmegs. Cook for about 50 minutes. Before serving remove the thread.

ROAST MEAT, HOME STYLE

10 oz (300 gm) beef, 7 oz (200 gm) potatoes, 1 onion, $2/3$ oz (20 gm) butter or melted butter, 1 root parsley, 1 carrot, $1/2$ oz

(15 gm) tomato paste, 3 cloves garlic, 2 tbsp. sour cream, herbs, 1 tbsp. flour; salt and pepper to taste

Cut the beef into two pieces, salt, pepper, and brown. Put the meat in a frying-pan, add the minced onion, roots, carrot, tomato paste, and browned flour. Cook until the vegetables are done. At last add the sour cream.

While the beef is cooking, peel the potatoes, cut them into cubes, and slightly brown in another frying-pan until they are covered in golden crust. Transfer a layer of potatoes, then a layer of beef, and again a layer of potatoes and a layer of beef into a clay pot. Pour some sauce over the roast beef, strew with the herbs and minced garlic. Put the pot in an oven and keep it there for 20 minutes.

MEAT IN A CLAY POT

5 oz (150 gm) beef fillet, 3 potatoes, 2 oz (50 gm) onions, 2 oz (50 gm) fresh mushrooms or $2/3$ oz (20 gm) dried mushrooms

The sauce: $1/3$ oz (10 gm) melted butter, 2 oz (50 gm) sour cream, $1/3$ oz (10 gm) parsley, 4 oz (100 gm) mushroom liquid, $1/2$ tbsp. flour

Roast the fillet on a skewer until semi-done. Cut the potatoes into cubes or slices and fry in melted butter in a frying-pan. Cut the onions into rings and fry until golden brown. Slightly brown the mushrooms. Brown the ingredients separately. Put the meat, potatoes, onions, and mushrooms in the clay pot. Pour the sauce in it, put the lid on, and stand in an oven. Stew the meat for about an hour.

The sauce

Fry the flour in the boiled butter until light brown. Dilute it with mushroom liquid until liquified and add the sour cream. Bring to a boil. Strain the sauce through a piece of cloth, pour it into a sauce-pan, and simmer. Keep evaporating the sauce for about an hour.

Strew the cooked beef with the herbs and set the clay pot on a small plate. The meat can be served in a plate.

ROAST MEAT À LA RUSSE

4 oz (100 gm) beef fillet, 0.9 oz (25 gm) fried mushrooms, 1 onion, $1/3$ cup sour cream, 3 tbsp. melted butter, 4 oz (100 gm) fried potatoes, herbs, 1 fresh tomato or the equivalent amount of tomato paste

Cut the fillet into strips, salt and pepper to taste, and brown in the butter. Add the sour cream, tomato paste, and the slightly browned onion and mushrooms. For a garnish, serve the fried potatoes, fresh tomato, and herbs. Serve the roast beef in a frying-pan.

ROAST BEEF WITH SAUERKRAUT

2 lb (1 kg) beef, 2.5 oz (75 gm) lard, 4 tbsp. lard, 3 onions, 3 carrots, 1 root parsley, 3 lb (1.5 kg) sauerkraut, $1/2$ tbsp. flour, 2 cups broth or water, salt, pepper, and 1 bay leaf

Lard large pieces of beef, put them in a lard-greased pan, brown until pink, add the preliminarily boiled minced onions, carrots, parsley, some broth or water, and cook until done. Cut the cooked meat into small pieces. Boil the flour in a small amount of water, dilute it with beef-tea, add some hot broth or water, boil well and rub through a sieve together with the vegetables.

Press out the sauerkraut, cook it with the addition of lard until done, and add the browned onions, pepper, bay leaf and part of the cooked gravy.

Lay slices of the lard on the bottom of a stew-pan, put the sauerkraut and meat (layer upon layer) on top of them, pour the remaining gravy over it, and cook for 15—20 minutes.

ROAST BEEF À LA ARKHANGELSK

6 oz (180 gm) beef fillet, 3 potatoes, $1/2$ oz (15 gm) dry boletusses, 1 onion, 0.9 oz (25 gm) butter, 4 oz

46 Hot Meat Dishes

(100 gm) cheese, 4 oz (100 gm) sour cream, parsley, and 1 fresh tomato; salt and pepper to taste

Remove the meat's film, cut into small pieces, salt, pepper, and brown both sides on a red-hot frying-pan. Separately brown the chopped mushrooms, onion, and tomato. Boil and brown the potatoes, lay the pieces of meat on the frying-pan, put the boletusses, onion, and tomato on them with the potatoes at the side; pour sour cream over it and strew with the grated cheese. Put the frying-pan in an oven and keep it there till the roast beef is done. Before serving strew with the parsley. Serve in the frying-pan.

FRIED MEAT WITH A GARNISH

15 oz (400 gm) beef (pork, mutton), 3 onions, 5 tbsp. butter, 4 tbsp. tomato paste, ground black pepper, salt, and herbs

Cut the meat into bars, salt, pepper, and brown it. Mince the onions and boil them in a little water. Add the onions and tomato paste to the browned meat and brown until done. Strew with the herbs and serve with fried or boiled potatoes and boiled vegetabels.

HOT ROAST WITH MUSHROOMS

1.5 lb (600 gm) beef, 4 oz (100 gm) smoked brisket, 1—2 onions, 2 tbsp. fat, 3 tbsp. tomato paste, 1 tbsp. flour, 7 oz (200 gm) mushrooms, 1 bay leaf, pepper, and salt

Cut the beef's flesh into pieces (1 or 2 for each helping) and the lean smoked brisket into small cubes. Brown them together with the onions, put in a sauce-pan, pour some broth over it, add the tomato paste and condiment, put the lid on, and cook on low heat until done. Cook a sauce in the meat broth, with the addition of finely chopped browned boletusses or field-mushrooms. Put the cooked meat in the sauce and boil well. Serve with the boiled potatoes or macaroni.

You can make the dish without a brisket, with a bigger amount of beef.

ROAST BEEF WITH MUSHROOM SAUCE

1 lb (500 gm) boiled beef, 5 oz (150 gm) salted pork fat, 2 tbsp. butter, 2 tbsp. flour, 5 oz (150 gm) pickled mushrooms, 1 tbsp. lemon juice or vinegar, 1 onion, salt, and pepper

Lay the boiled beef, quartered onion, several slices of pork fat, and butter on a frying-pan put the lid on, and fry on low heat. When the meat is evenly browned, sprinkle it with the flour, pour two cups of boiling water over it, boil well, and transfer into a sauce-pan. Strain the sauce and pour it into the same pan.

Wash the mushrooms with cold water, cut into slices, brown in the butter, and pour the lemon juice or vinegar over them. Put it in the pan with the meat inside and stew.

MEAT WITH VEGETABLES

2 lb (1 kg) beef, 3 oz (80 gm) salted pork fat, 3 tbsp. vegetable oil, 1/2 cup meat broth, 1/2 cup water, 1 big onion and 4 oz (100 gm) small onions, 2 carrots, 1/2 tsp. ground pepper, salt to taste, and 1 tsp. granulated sugar

Remove the bones, pound the meat with a wooden hammer, stuff with the pork fat, pepper and salt on both sides, fold in the shape of a roll, tie up with cord, put in a sauce-pan with the heated vegetable oil in it, put the lid on, brown the meat evenly until pink, pour in the white wine, 1 cup of broth and some water, add one big onion, chopped carrots, and pepper, lower the heat, and stew with the lid on. When the onion and carrots are soft and the meat is done, take it out of the pan, remove the cord, cut the meat with a sharp knife into slices across the fibres, lay on a dish, adorn with the carrots and small onions, and pour the stewed meat liquid over it.

For the garnish peel several small onions, pour boiling water over them, and boil for ten minutes. Take the onions out and boil in

Dishes with Beef

another sauce-pan in one cup of broth with the addition of sugar and salt until done. While boiling, keep stirring the onions not to overdo them.

BEEF BRAISED WITH KVASS

7 oz (200 gm) beef, 1 oz (30 gm) melted fat, 1 carrot, 1 onion, 5 oz (150 gm) kvass, dried bread-crumbs, and condiment

Cut the beef into helpings, chop the carrot and onion fine and brown them in the fat in a frying-pan. Lay the meat helpings on the same frying-pan, salt and pepper them, and brown the ingredients together. At last add tomato paste. Transfer the meat into small clay pots or some other vessels, add the kvass, dried bread-crumbs, and condiment and cook until done.

POT-ROAST BEEF

7 oz (200 gm) beef, $1/3$ oz (10 gm) melted fat, 3 potatoes, 1 carrot, $1/2$ turnip, $1/2$ swede, 1 onion, 3 tbsp. tomato paste or thin sour cream, 2 tbsp. flour

Cut the beef into helpings, pound slightly, brown in the fat together with the onion. Slice the carrot, turnip, swede, and potatoes. Brown the beef helpings, put them in a clay pot, add the resulting meat liquid, a little broth, salt and the prepared vegetables and braise until done. Pour off part of the liquid, dilute the browned flour with it and pour it back in. Add the tomato paste or thin sour cream, condiment (1 bay leaf, pepper, clove, cinnamon, mint) and cook until done.

BAKED MEAT

15 oz (400 gm) beef, 1 lb (0.5 kg) potatoes, 4 oz (100 gm) cheese, sour cream and 1 onion for the sauce

Cook the meat in a little water. Cut the potatoes into rings and brown them. Lay the browned potato rings along the edges of a large metal dish. Cut the cooked meat into slices, put them in the middle of the dish, pour the onion sauce over them, sprinkle with the grated cheese, and bake.

BEEFSTEAKS WITH CABBAGE

2 lb (850 gm) beef fillet, 1 medium-size cabbage, 5 oz (150 gm) margarine, 1 egg, 1 cup buillon, 5 oz (150 gm) cottage cheese, 4 oz (125 gm) Swiss cheese, 1 cup flour; salt to taste

Brown small fillet beefsteaks. Cut the cabbage into slices, boil in slightly salted water, and dry in a colander. Put the boiled cabbage in an enameled sauce-pan, add the browned beefsteaks, cover the pan with the puff dough, spread the egg all over it, and top with the grated cheese. Make a hole in the middle and stand in a not very heated oven. When the dough is sufficiently coloured and baked, take the dish out of the oven, pour one cup of hot broth into the hole, and serve hot.

The puff dough

Chop the margarine together with the cottage cheese and flour in an enameled sauce-pan so you will have oily granular stuff. Nead it without adding the flour and put the resulting dough in a refrigerator for half an hour. Grate the cheese. Roll the chilled dough into a relatively thin layer, sprinkle with the grated cheese, fold in two, and roll into a layer corresponding to the circumference of the enameled pan; lay the dough on top of the browned beafsteaks.

BEEF GOULASH

1.5 lb (700 gm) meat with a bone (bottom chuck, beef leg), 2 oz (60 gm) fat, 1 tbsp. flour, 1 big onion, $1/2$ tsp. hot red peppers, 2 oz (50 gm) tomato paste, and salt

Remove the bone and cut the beef into 6—8 pieces per helping. Salt and sprinkle with the flour. Brown the meat pieces evenly in some of the strongly heated fat and transfer into a sauce-pan. Cut the onion into rings and brown them in the remaining fat. Transfer them (together with the fat) into the sauce-pan with the meat inside. Add some water and cook with the lid on. Brown the tomato paste and the red peppers, add the resulting sauce to the meat and continue cooking for several minutes more.

Serve the goulash with *klotskas* (kind of dumplings).

BOEUF STROGANOFF

1.5 lb (700 gm) beef fillet, 2 oz (60 gm) fat, 2 tbsp. flour, 1 medium-size onion, $^1/_2$ cup sour cream, some hot red peppers or ground fragrant red pepper (to taste), 1 oz (30 gm) tomato paste, 1 tsp. minced parsley, and salt

Cut the fillet into strips $^1/_5$ in (0.5 cm) thick each. Cut the onion into rings, brown them in the fat until pink, and transfer into a large sauce-pan. Then brown the meat in the strongly heated fat stirring the strips in the process and add the flour at last. After that transfer the browned meat into the sauce-pan with the rings of onion in it, add the tomato paste and pepper, salt to taste, pour in the sour cream, and bring to a boil on low heat.

BOILED TONGUES

2 beef tongues, 3 carrots, 3 roots parsley, 3 onions, 10 black peppercorns, 2 bay leaves; and salt

The sauce: 1 root horse-radish, 3—4 hard-boiled eggs, 1 cup sour cream, $^1/_2$ tsp. mustard, 1 tsp. lemon juice, sugar, and salt

Wash the tongues well using a special brush, pour hot water over them and start heating. Bring to a boil, put in the vegetables, bay leaves, peppercorns, and salt. Boil for 1—1.5 hours. Then take the tongues out, pour cold water over them, and remove the skin. Cut the tongues crosswise into thin slices, lay on an oval dish, and pour the sauce over them.

The sauce

Wash, peel, and grate the horse-radish root fine. Grate the egg-yolks and mix them with the mustard and lemon juice, add the sour cream, horse-radish, minced egg-whites, add the salt and sugar to taste, and mix well.

BEEF TONGUE IN A SPICY SAUCE

1 beef tongue, 1 onion, 1 carrot, 1 root and 1 sprig parsley, 1 bay leaf, 2—3 black peppercorns, and salt

The sauce: 9 oz (250 gm) mayonnaise, 2—3 tbsp. sour cream, 2 oz (50 gm) marinated mushrooms, 2 oz (50 gm) pickled cucumbers, 1 tsp. mustard, sugar, vinegar or the juice from half a lemon, and salt

Wash the tongue well, pour boiling water over it, and boil for about an hour. Then take it out, keep in cold water for several minutes, and remove the skin. Put the vegetables and condiment in the broth, salt the tongue, and boil until done. When the broth gets cold, take out the tongue, cut it into thin rings, and lay on a round dish.

The sauce

To make the sauce, mix the mayonnaise with the sour cream, add the chopped (cubes) mushrooms and cucumbers, salt, add the mustard, sugar, vinegar or lemon juice, and mix well. Pour the sauce over the tongue and strew with the minced parsley.

MEAT «HEDGEHOGS»

1 lb (500 gm) minced meat, 1 onion, 1 cup boiled rice; salt and ground black pepper to taste

Sort out the rice, wash well, pour hot water over it, boil until semi-done, transfer into a colander, chill a little, add the minced meat, chopped onion, salt, pepper, mix well, shape into balls, roll in the flour, slightly brown in butter, put in a sauce-pan, pour a little broth over them, put the lid on, and stand in an oven for 20 minutes. Shortly before taking it out from the oven, lift the lid and let the «hedgehogs» brown a little.

Serve the «hedgehogs» with fried potatoes, pickled cucumbers, cauli-

flower, and canned green peas. Serve the sour cream separately.

MEAT «HEDGEHOGS» IN A WHITE SAUCE

10 oz (300 gm) minced meat, $1/2$ cup rice, 1 egg, 2 oz (50 gm) margarine, 1.5 cups milk, 1 tsp. flour, 1 tbsp. vegetable oil, 1 onion; salt and pepper to taste

Mix the minced meat with the boiled rice, add the minced and browned (in the vetetable oil) onion, and raw egg, salt, pepper, and mix well. Shape the mass into small balls, roll them in the flour, and quickly brown on all sides in the sizzling margarine. To make the sauce, grind the margarine with the flour, salt, and gradually dilute with the milk. Bring the sauce to a boil. Put the browned meat-balls in it and heat well.

TEFTELI (MEAT-BALLS) IN TOMATO PASTE

1.5 lb (600 gm) beef, 1 egg, $1/3$ bread-roll, 1 tbsp. vegetable oil, 2 tbsp. dried and finely ground bread-crumbs, 1 tsp. minced parsley or dill, 1 tsp. salt; pepper to taste

The sauce: *2 tsp. flour, 1 tbsp. margarine, 1 cup broth, 2 tbsp. tomato paste, 1 tsp. granulated sugar; salt to taste*

Put the raw beef through a meat-grinder, add the preliminarily soaked and pressed out white-bread roll, salt, a little pepper, parsley or/and dill, mix well, put through a meat-grinder, shape the mixture into small balls, put in a deep frying-pan, pour the sauce over them, strew with the dried and finely ground bread-crumbs, and top it all with the finely sliced margarine; stand it in a moderately heated oven for about 20 minutes. Serve the meat-balls hot.

The sauce

Slightly dilute the vegetable oil in a sauce-pan, mix with the flour, bring the mixture to a boil, add some broth and tomato paste, mix well, salt to taste, pour the granulated sugar into it, and boil well.

RUSSIAN TEFTELI

4 oz (100 gm) meat fillet, 1 oz (35 gm) salted pork fat, 2/3 oz (20 gm) dried mushrooms, 2 oz (50 gm) sour cream, 0.9 oz (25 gm) tomato paste, $1/2$ oz (15 gm) water, 1 tbsp. flour, 1 tbsp. vegetable oil, $2/3$ oz (20 gm) butter, $1/8$ lemon, $1/2$ onion, parsley or celery to taste

The garnish: *potatoes, carrots, canned green peas, 1 onion, 1 bay leaf; salt and pepper to taste*

Put the meat fillet and pork fat through a meat-grinder. Remove the lemon's peel and grate it. Salt and pepper the force meat, add some water and the prepared dried lemon peel. Mix and pound the mass, and stand in the cold for about two hours.

Boil the dried mushrooms. Chop them fine and brown in the vegetable oil together with the onion. Have it chilled a little and add the butter and minced herbs. Salt and mix well.

Transfer the force meat onto a board and shape it into small balls. Then shape the balls into flat cakes, put the minced mushrooms in the middle of the cakes, and again make them into small balls. Roll the *tefteli* in the flour or pounded dried bread-crumbs and brown them evenly in a frying-pan. Put them in a sauce-pan or deep frying-pan and pour the sour cream or thinned tomato paste over them. For pungency, add the granulated sugar and ground pepper to the paste. Top it all with the preliminarily browned potato slices, rings of boiled carrot, canned green peas, browned onion, and bay leaf. Cook it all on low heat for 15 minutes.

RISSOLES OF VEAL (*KOTLETI*) WITH MUSHROOMS

15 oz (400 gm) fresh mushrooms, 1 lb (500 gm) veal, 2 slices stale bread, 1 onion, 3 eggs, dried and finely ground bread-crumbs, black pepper, and salt

Wash the mushrooms well, cut them into large pieces, boil in a little water until soft, transfer into a colander, and chop fine. Put the veal through a meat-grinder, add the force meat soaked in water, pressed out bread-crumbs, grated onion, 2 eggs, salt and ground black pepper to taste. Mix the resulting mass well, shape it into rissoles, soak in the egg, roll in the bread-crumbs, and brown. Serve with a salad or pickles.

ROUND RISSOLES, COUNTRY STYLE

1.5 lb (600 gm) beef, 2 tbsp. margarine, 6 onions, 8 fresh mushrooms, 2 tbsp. flour, 1 tbsp. tomato paste, 8—10 potatoes, ground black pepper, and salt

Put the beef through a meat-grinder, add some water and minced onion; salt, pepper, and mix well. Shape the resulting mass into round rissoles, roll them in the flour and brown. Cut the boiled mushrooms fine and brown them together with the onions and tomato paste. Put the rissoles in a vessel, add the onions, mushrooms, and tomato paste, add some hot water and cook.
Serve with the boiled potatoes.

CHOPPED BEEF WITH HORSE-RADISH

3 lb (1.5 kg) beef, 4 oz (100 gm) grease, 5 oz (150 gm) grated horse-radish, 2 oz (50 gm) mustard, 10 oz (300 gm) bread, 4 oz (120 gm) butter or margarine, and 3 lb (1.5 kg) potatoes for a garnish

Put the beef through a meat-grinder, salt, pepper, and slightly dilute it in water. Shape it into *zrazy* (oblong rissoles). Mix the grated horse-radish with the mustard, ground dried white-bread crumbs, roll the rissoles in the mixture, fry them in a frying-pan, add a little broth, put the lid on, and cook till done.

CABBAGE ROLL

1 medium-size cabbage, 7 oz (200 gm) meat, 3 tbsp. butter, 1 cup milk, 2 tbsp. manna-croup, $1/2$ cup flour, $1/2$ cup sour cream, 1 onion, 1 egg, 1 piece parsley, and salt

Chop the cabbage fine, put it in a saucepan, add the milk and butter and cook for some time. Trickle the manna-croup into the pan and mix thoroughly. Put the lid on and boil for ten minutes, then add the raw egg. Slightly brown the meat with the minced onion and put them through a meat-grinder.
Lay a thin layer of minced cabbage («cabbage dough») and then the minced meat on a greased dripping-pan and «clip» (fold) the edges of the «dough». Spearead the sour cream over the roll's surface, add 2 tea-spoons of flour, and put in an oven.

MACARONI, NAVAL STYLE

9 oz (250 gm) macaroni, 1 lb (500 gm) boneless meat, 2 onions, 4 oz (100 gm) butter; salt and pepper to taste

Boil the macaroni in salted boiling water until done and then transfer into a colander. Put the meat through a meat-grinder, salt, and brown, stirring, until done. Separately brown the minced onions. Mix the meat and onions and again put through the meat-grinder; mix it with the macaroni on a frying-pan and heat well.

NOODLE PUDDING WITH MEAT

4 oz (100 gm) beef flesh, 3 oz (80 gm) cow's heart, 3 oz (80 gm) lung, 3 oz (80 gm) liver, 4 oz (100 gm) home-made noodles, 1 onion, 1 egg, 2 tbsp.

butter, 2 tbsp. dried bread-crumbs, and $1/2$ cup sour cream

Boil the noodles in slightly salted water, chill to about 70°C, add some fat and the beaten egg.

Boil the lung, heart, and liver. Cut the meat into small pieces and brown. Pour the noodles' broth over the meat ingredients and cook. Chop the prepared ingredients fine or put them through a meat-grinder and add the browned onion, pepper, and salt. Put a layer of the dressed noodles, a layer of the meat stuffing, and one more layer of the noodles in a greased dripping-pan, sprinkle with the bread-crumbs, top with the sour cream and bake.

CABBAGES-ROLLS STUFFED WITH MEAT

5 oz (150 gm) beef flesh, $1/2$ cabbage, $1/2$ cup rice, 1 onion, 2 tbsp. butter, $1/2$ cup sour cream, and 3 tbsp. dried bread-crumbs

Remove the outer leaves from the cabbage, cut out the cabbage-stump, boil in slightly salted water until semi-done, and separate every leaf. Pound the leaves' thick ribs. Put the beef through a meat-grinder, make a stuffing from the minced meat, boiled crumbly rice, and browned onion, and wrap it in the leaves in the shape of cylinders. Put the cabbage-rolls in greased dripping-pans and brown in an oven. Pour the sour cream over them, add the ground bread-crumbs, and cook. When the cabbage leaves get soft, top with the bread-crumbs and bake.

LIVER FRIED IN SOUR CREAM

4 oz (125 gm) liver, 3 tbsp. flour, 1 onion, 1 carrot, 4 oz (100 gm) sour cream, 4 tbsp. butter or fat; salt to taste

Slightly pound the liver, remove the film and tendons, cut into slices, add the flour, salt and pepper. Mince the onion and carrot, put them in a sauce-pan together with the liver, and fry. When the liver is done, add the sour cream and bring to a boil. Serve with boiled or mashed potatoes.

MUSHROOMS WITH LIVER

1 oz (30 gm) dried boletusses, $2/3$ oz (20 gm) butter, 4 oz (100 gm) cow's or calf's liver, 2 tbsp. wheat frour, 1 onion, 1.5 oz (40 gm) sour cream, 2 tbsp. grated cheese; salt to taste

Sort out the mushrooms, wash in running water, have them boiled, wash again, and cut into strips. Remove the liver's film, wash in water, and cut into thin strips. Mince the onion, brown it in the butter, add the liver and mushrooms, sprinkle with the flour, brown again, add the sour cream, and salt. Lay the dish into small cocottes, sprinkle with the grated cheese, and put them in an oven. Cook until covered in brown crust.

Dishes With Pork

PORK CHOPS IN DOUGH

15 oz (400 gm) pork brisket, 1 tbsp. butter, 1 tbsp. flour

The dough: *2 tbsp. flour, 1 egg, 1 tbsp. milk, and a pinch of sugar*

Cut the brisket into chops with a rib bone per portion, pound slightly, cut the tendons, remove the skin from the bones, and shape each chop oval. Roast the meat on a grill installed on a dripping-pan until done. After that make the dough. Dip each chop in the dough and brown in the butter. Serve with fried potatoes, canned green peas, and rings of boiled carrots.

ROAST PORK WITH KVASS

7 oz (200 gm) pork, 5 oz (150 gm) kvass, 1 onion, 4 cloves garlic, 3 potatoes, 2 pickled cucumbers, and condiment

Put big chunks of pork in a clay vessel, add

a bay leaf, peppercorns, clove, shredded onion, and garlic, pour the kvass over them and keep in the cold for about an hour. Take out the meat, dry and rub salt in it, and roast in an oven pouring the meat liquid and fat over it. Lay the prepared meat on a frying-pan, pour the used kvass, bring to a boil, and dress with fried potatoes. Serve grated horse-radish and the pickled cucumbers as a garnish.

PORK IN DOUGH

1.5 lb (600 gm) pork, 1.5 onion, 0.07 oz (2 gm) citric acid, 4 oz (100 gm) fat; parsley and salt to taste

The dough: 1/2 cup flour, 2/3 cup milk, 4 eggs, 2 tbsp. vegetable oil; salt to taste

Cut the pork into small pieces, pound slightly, add the shredded onion and parsley, dilute the citric acid with water or lemon juice, pour it over the ingredients and let it stay that way for 3 hours. Dip the prepared meat in the dough and brown in a big amount of well-heated fat.

The dough

Dilute the flour with warm milk, add the vegetable oil, eggs, and salt, mix well and let it rise for 15—20 minutes.

PORK BAKED IN DOUGH

4 lb (2 kg) pork, 2 oz (50 gm) salt, sweet peppercorns, bay leaves, and 1 root horse-radish

The dough: *1 lb (500 gm) flour and water*

Rub the salt in the pork, edge it with the peppercorns and bay leaves, put in a saucepan and put the lid on. Stand it in a warm place for one day. When the juice comes out, put the dish in a refrigerator for 2—3 days. Turn over the meat from time to time. Wash the pork well and dry with a washcloth. Make thin dough from the flour and water, divide in half and roll it out. Spread one layer on a dripping-pan, lay the meat on top of it, put the other layer on it, join the edges and bake them in an oven. When the meat is done, remove the dough. Cut the meat into large pieces, lay them on a dish, and sprinkle with the grated horse-radish. Serve with boiled potatoes or cooked cabbage.

SUCKLING PIG WITH HORSE-RADISH

Wrap a prepared suckling pig in a sheet of parchment, tie up, wash cold water over it and boil on low heat for about an hour. At last add salt. Cut the cooked pig into portions, lay them as a whole on an oval dish and arrange boiled potatoes around it. Serve the sour cream sauce and horse-radish in separate sauce-boats. Decorate with herbs.

ROAST PIG WITH BOILED BUCKWHEAT

2 lb (1 kg) suckling pig, 4 oz (120 gm) fat, 0.9 oz (25 gm) sour cream, 3 cups boiled buckwheat, 3 onions, 2 eggs, 4 oz (100 gm) brains

Cut the pig's body lengthwise. Slightly notch the backbone, cut the pelvic bones into pieces, clear the abdominal cavity, wash well, and dry. Spread the body, rub salt on the inside, oil the outer surface with the sour cream, and roast in an oven, greasing it with fat in the process.

Cut the roast pig lengthwise, and then crosswise into pieces. Lay them on a dish with the boiled buckwheat and pour meat liquid over them. Mix the boiled buckwheat with the browned onions, minced hard-boiled eggs, bits of cooked brains, and brown slightly.

Dishes with Pork

PORK CHOPS

1 lb (500 gm) pork, 2 tbsp. fat, salt, and ground black pepper

Cut the pork into chops with bones. Remove the film and meat from the bones and sharpen their ends. Pound the chops well, salt, pepper, brown evenly in a heated greased frying-pan until covered with light-brown crust. Serve with lettuce, soaked cowberries, cauliflower, canned plums, cucumbers, tomatoes, olives, slices of lemon, and parsley.

Dishes With Various Kinds of Meat

GRILLED MEAT, AMATEUR STYLE

4 oz (100 gm) beef, 4 oz (100 gm) pork brisket, 4 oz (100 gm) mutton, 1 onion, 0.9 oz (25 gm) melted butter, 5 oz (150 gm) potatoes

Take three pieces of meat (beef, pork brisket, and mutton), pound well, and brown evenly in the butter in a frying-pan until covered in light-brown crust. Separately fry the potatoes and onion. Put the potatoes in the middle of the frying pan, edge them with the pieces of meat, and top with the onion. Set the pan on a burner and pour some meat broth into it. Heat for several minutes and serve in the frying-pan.

RISSOLES

1 lb (500 gm) beef and pork, 3 oz (85 gm) white bread, salt, pepper, 1 onion, 1 raw egg, and 4 oz (100 gm) fat

Mince the onion and brown slightly. Put the meat and soaked dry bread through a meat-grinder. Add the salt, pepper, browned onion, and an egg. Mix well. If the resulting mass is too thick, add 2—3 tbsp. of milk. Shape into rissoles, sprinkle with flour or dried bread-crumbs, and brown on both sides until covered in crust. Serve with potatoes, macaroni, or greens.

MEAT PATTIES WITH BUCKWHEAT STUFFING

10 oz (350 gm) beef, 10 oz (300 gm) pork, 5 oz (150 gm) white bread, 3 tbsp. lard, $1/2$ cup milk, 2 tbsp. butter, 3 tbsp. buckwheat, 1 onion, salt, and pepper

The sauce: *$1/2$ cup sour cream, 1 tbsp. flour, 1.5 cup meat broth, and salt*

The garnish: *2 lb (1 kg) potatoes, 2—3 tbsp. butter, and salt*

Put the beef and pork through a meat-grinder, add the milk-soaked and slightly pressed out white bread, pepper, and salt. Put through the meat-grinder again. Put half the amount of lard and grated onion in the mass and mix well. Divide the mass into portions, make a depression in each of them, put the buckwheat cooked in the remaining lard in them, shape into patties, brown until pink, pour the sauce over them, and cook for 15—20 minutes.

The sauce

Boil wheat flour in a small amount of water, pour part of the broth in it, mix well, and strain. Serve with the fried potatoes topped with the sauce in which the dish was cooked.

Hot Meat Dishes

Dishes With Mutton

ROAST MUTTON JOINT

1 leg of mutton, 5 potatoes, 1 lb (0.5 kg) kidney beans, 10 oz (300 gm) boiled haricots, tomato sauce, 3 tomatoes, and butter

Stuff the mutton leg with garlic, salt, pepper, and roast in an oven pouring it with the meat juice and fat.

Cut off slices of the flesh from the mutton leg and lay them on the middle of a large oval dish. Lay the fried potatoes (in the shape of mounds), boiled kidney beans, boiled haricots (dressed with the tomato paste), and fried tomatoes on the other side of the leg. Before frying, select thick tomatoes, scald them, remove the skin, cut in half, and fry in butter.

MUTTON LEG WITH PRUNES

1 leg of mutton, 1 onion, 1 carrot, 20 prunes, 3 apples, 1 tsp. sugar, a pinch of cinnamon, sodium nitrate (on the point of a knife's blade), herbs, and spices

Separate the haunch from the mutton leg and marinate for 6 hours with the addition of salt and culinary nitrate. Dip the marinated mutton in boiling broth, add the onion, carrot, and 3 or 4 prunes, and cook until done.

Boil the remaining prunes in a little water with sugar. Remove the apples' cores, sprinkle the apples with sugar mixed with cinnamon, and bake in an oven. Lay the cooked mutton on a dish, pour the mutton broth over it, adorn with the prunes, apples, and herbs.

ROAST LAMB STUFFED WITH BOILED BUCKWHEAT

3 lb (1.5 kg) mutton with ribs, 1.5 cup buckwheat, 2 cups water, 4 onions, 5 oz (150 gm) melted butter; salt to taste

Rub the mutton with salt, boil the buckwheat but make sure it is crumbly, add the butter, mix with the minced raw onions, put in a dripping-pan between the lamb's breast and ribs, add a little water, and roast in an oven until done. Keep stirring the buckwheat to brown the onions evenly.

MUTTON WITH ONIONS

2 lb (1 kg) mutton, 1 small garlic, 5 onions, 5 potatoes, 5 oz (150 gm) melted butter or milk butter, and salt

Keep the mutton in salted water for several hours (4 tbsp. of salt per litre of water). Before starting cooking, dry the meat, stuff it with garlic, spread the butter over it, and put in a dripping-pan. Add the sliced potatoes and rings of onions. Put it in a heated oven and roast until done. Don't forget to pour the meat juice over it as often as possible.

Serve with sauerkraut or a vegetable salad.

«USHNOYE» (RUSSIAN STEW)

7 oz (200 gm) mutton, 1 onion, 2 carrots, 1 turnip, 1 swede, 3 tbsp. butter, 2 tbsp. flour, 5 cloves garlic; pepper and salt to taste

It is an old Russian dish which is mostly made with mutton.

Cut the mutton into small pieces, sprinkle with salt and pepper, and roast. Then put the mutton, the sliced carrots, onion, turnip, and swede in a clay pot, salt, put the lid on, and cook until done. At last add the garlic. Pour off part of the broth, dilute the browned flour with it, and pour the sauce in the clay pot.

MUTTON CHOPS

It is desirable to use fat mutton. Cut out the meat between the ribs, remove the vertebraes and tendons. Beat the chops with a pounder, sprinkle with salt and coarsely ground pepper, and brown on high heat in a frying-pan greased with slightly boiled milk butter. Make sure you do not overdo the chops, see that they are juicy enough. Do not sprinkle the chops with dried breadcrumbs.

MUTTON RISSOLES WITH AN ONION SAUCE

1.5 lb (600 gm) mutton with a bone (shoulder-blade), 2.5 oz (70 gm) fat, 2 oz (60 gm) dried white bread, 1 onion, 2 eggs, 3 cloves garlic; salt and pepper to taste

Tne onion sauce: *1 big onion, 2 oz (50 gm) fat, 2 tbsp. flour, 2 tbsp. thin sour cream, vinegar, sugar, and salt*

Soak the white-bread roll in milk and press it out. Remove the meat from the bone, put the meat and roll through a meat-grinder two times, salt, add the raw egg, mix thoroughly until the mass is even and light. Shape the stuffing into rissoles and brown them on the heated fat until covered in pink crust. At last put the rissoles in an oven for 10 minutes.

The sauce

Peel, wash and mince the onion, pour a cup of boiling water over it, boil until done, and grate through a sieve together with the broth. Mix half a cup of cold broth with the flour, add the grated onion, and boil on low heat. Pour in the sour cream, salt, and add the pepper and sugar to taste.

Pour the sauce over the mutton rissoles and serve them with boiled potatoes in a long oval dish.

Dishes With Poultry

CHICKEN WITH TOASTS

1 chicken, 3 cups water, 4 carrots, 2 tomatoes, 1 root celery, 1 bay leaf, salt, ground black pepper, 1 tbsp. flour, 4 tbsp. soft butter

Cut the prepared fat chicken into portions. Pour water in a saucepan, put the carrots (cut into rings), sliced tomatoes, celery, and bay leaf in it, salt and pepper them. Bring the vegetables to a boil, add the portions of chicken, and boil till done. Take out and transfer the cooked portions into a colander. Then brown them until golden.

Cut some stale bread into slices, dip each slice in milk, then in a beaten egg, and brown until golden.

Strain the broth and separately grate the cooked vegetables through a sieve. Brown the flour in a little butter, add the grated vegetables, dilute with the broth until the sauce is relatively thick. Simmer the sauce for 8—10 minutes.

Lay the toasts on a dish, put a portion of chicken meat on top of each one, and pour the sauce over them. Separately serve two kinds of vegetable dressing.

CHICKEN BRAISED WITH MUSHROOMS

1 chicken, 3 carrots, several fresh mushrooms, 5 tbsp. soft butter, 6 cloves garlic; parsley and salt to taste

Cut the prepared chicken into pieces and salt. Wash the mushrooms and peel the carrots. Chop them fine and scald. Put 1 tbsp. of butter, pieces of chicken, mushrooms, and carrots in small clay pots, add 1 more tablespoon to the content of each pot, put the lids on, and stand in an oven. After half an hour add the minced parsley and garlic, mix well, and cook with the lids on until done.

CHICKEN WITH TOMATOES

2 lb (900 gm) chicken, 10 oz (353 gm) mushrooms, 2 onions, 3 tomatoes, 5 cloves garlic, 4 oz (100 gm) butter, 1 cup water or broth; salt to taste

Cut the chicken into pieces, brown in the butter until covered in golden crust, and transfer into another pan. Put the chopped fresh mushrooms, onions, and salt in the remaining butter and brown, stirring, for another twenty minutes. Put the chicken back in the frying-pan, pour in 1 cup of hot water or broth, mix well, and cook until done.

CHICKEN WITH HONEY AND WALNUTS

1 chicken, 2 tbsp. honey, 1.5 tbsp. soft butter, 1 tsp. rose water, 1 tbsp. finely chopped walnuts, and fat

Boil the butter and mix it with the honey. Fill the chicken's breast and legs with the mixture. Dilute the remaining mixture with the rose water and rub the chicken with the liquid. Brown the chicken in the fat until done. Cut in two and lay on a dish the back part up. Sprinkle with the chopped nuts.

STUFFED CHICKEN

1 chicken, 15 oz (400 gm) pork, 4 oz (100 gm) salted pork fat, 3 eggs, 4 oz (100 gm) canned green peas, 1/2 cup milk, 0.04 oz (1 gm) nutmeg, 0.04 oz (1 gm) pepper, and salt

Cut the prepared chicken lengthwise, along the backbone, and cut off the whole of the skin, leaving a layer of the flesh about 1/3 in (1 cm) thick. Put the rest of the chicken flesh and the pork through a meat-grinder two or three times, grate, add the raw eggs and milk, and beat well. Put small cubes of the pork fat, green peas, salt, and nutmeg in the filling. Mix well.

Fill the skin and flesh with the stuffing, sow up the cut, and shape into a whole chicken. Wrap it up in a napkin or oil paper, tie up with a length of twine, and boil in chicken broth for 1—1.5 hours. Chill the cooked chicken in the broth, put it under a light press, and stand in the cold.

CHICKEN, DVINA REGION STYLE

1 lb (500 gm) boiled chicken fillet, 7 boiled potatoes, 2 onions, 5 cloves garlic, 2 oz (50 gm) sour cream, 5 oz (150 gm) mayonaise; herbs, cranberries or cowberries, and salt to taste

Rub the boiled chicken fillet with the garlic and lay on a frying-pan. Cut the boiled potatoes and onions into rings and lay them on top of the fillet. Pour the mayonaise mixed with sour cream over them and bake in an oven until covered in golden crust. Serve with the herbs, cranberries or cowberries.

«POZHARSKIYE» CHOPS À LA NATURELLE

2 pieces of chicken fillet, 2 raw eggs, 2 tbsp. milk, 3 tbsp. finely ground dried bread-crumbs, 4 oz (100 gm) butter; salt and pepper to taste

Take the two pieces of chicken fillet with a bone, pound them slightly, salt, pepper, and soak in the raw eggs beaten with milk, roll in the dried bread-crumbs, and brown on both sides for about 15 minutes until done.

Serve with the rice or vegetables.

«POZHARSKIYE» RISSOLES

1 medium-size chicken, 1 cup milk or cream, 9 oz (250 gm) white bread, 3 tbsp. soft butter, 3 eggs, 5 tbsp. finely ground dried bread-crumbs, 4 oz (100 gm) fat; salt to taste

Singe a not very fat chicken, gut it, wash well, remove the skin, and separate the flesh from the bones. Soak the stale white bread in the milk or cream, put through a meat-grinder together with the chicken meat, salt, add the butter, raw eggs, and mix well. Shape the stuffing into rissoles, roll them in the finely ground bread-crumbs, and brown evenly until done.

CHICKEN HASLETS IN SOUR CREAM

15 oz (400 gm) chicken pluck, 2 onions, 3 tbsp. soft butter, 1/3 cup water, 5 tbsp. sour cream; salt and herbs to taste

Wash the chicken liver, scald, cut into 3—4 pieces, and brown. Clean and wash the stomachs, boil in slightly salted water until semi-done, and chop fine. Cut the chicken hearts in half, wash well, dry, and brown in a frying-pan together with the minced onions; add the stomachs, pour the

Dishes with Poultry 57

water or broth over them, salt, put the lid on, and cook until done. Add the fried liver, top with the sour cream, boil well, strew with the herbs, and serve.

TURKEY BAKED IN SOUR CREAM

15 oz (400 gm) turkey (chicken, duck), 3 marinated apples, butter, 4 oz (120 gm) sour cream, a little cheese, parsley or dill

Boil the turkey, cut the flesh, excepting the loin, into strips, brown in the butter, add part of the sour cream, and heat well. Lay the mass on a medium-size frying-pan, put a small piece of the loin on top of it, decorate with slices of the marinated apples, pour the remaining sour cream over them, sprinkle with the grated cheese, add the boiled butter, and bake in an oven.
Before serving, strew the dish with the minced parsley or dill.

GOOSE WITH APPLES

3 lb (1.5 kg) apples and 2 tbsp. soft butter for 1 goose

Salt and stuff the prepared goose with the sliced apples (with the cores removed). Sow up the hole in the goose's stomach.
Lay the goose on a frying-pan with its back down, add half a cup of water, and stand in an oven.
While frying, pour the goose fat and juice several times over the meat. Keep frying for 1.5—2 hours. Remove the thread, take out the apples with a spoon, and lay them on a dish. Chop the goose into slices and lay on the apples.
Serve with the baked apples, minced boiled cabbage, or boiled potatoes.

GOOSE WITH APPLES AND SAUERKRAUT

1 goose, 1 lb (0.5 kg) apples, 1 lb (500 gm) sauerkraut, 5 onions, 7 oz (200 gm) soft milk butter; salt to taste

Squeeze the sauerkraut sufficiently dry and brown with the minced onions. When the sauerkraut is browned enough, add the peeled sliced apples. Singe, wash, and rub the goose with salt, stuff with the squeezed sauerkraut, and brown in an oven pouring its own juice over it.

GOOSE BAKED WITH APPLES AND POTATOES

1 goose, 1 lb (0.5 kg) apples, 4 cloves garlic, potatoes, and salt

Gut the goose, wash well, and salt.
Peel and quarter the apples, and stuff the goose with them. Sow up the goose's carcass, lay on a dripping-pan, pour half a cup of water into it, and bake in a well-heated oven. As the sauce is boiling away, keep adding water to it.
When the goose is almost done, rub it with the garlic, edge with the potatoes, salt, and bake till done.
Cut the goose into portions, lay on a dish, edge with the baked potatoes and apples.

GOOSE WITH BOILED BUCKWHEAT AND CRACKLINGS

1 goose, 1 cup buckwheat, 7 oz (200 gm) fat for cracklings, 2 onions, and salt

Gut and singe the goose, remove the legs, wash well, and put in an oven. While the goose is roasted, periodically pour its fat over it for the crust to be soft and juicy. When it becomes light-brown it is already done. Take it out of the oven and cut into portions.
Boil the buckwheat until crumbly and stuff with the cracklings and browned onions.

«WEDDING GOOSE», SIBERIAN STYLE

1 goose, 9 oz (250 gm) millet, 4 oz (100 gm) butter; spices and salt to taste

It is an old Russian dish which is made at village weddings.
Rub the surface and inside of the prepared goose carcass with the salt and spices. Boil

the millet until semi-done, transfer into a sieve, add the butter, and stuff the goose with the mass. Sow up the goose's neck and pelvic hole with white twine, lay it on a brazier, put the lid on, and stew in an oven for 3—4 hours until done.

GOOSE OR DUCK WITH POTATO STUFFING

1 goose or duck (with the bones), 5 potatoes, 2 tbsp. melted fat, and cowberries

Prepare the goose's or duck's carcass and brown it. To make the stuffing, peel and fry the potatoes whole or in slices, put inside the carcass, and tie it up or sow up the cut. Stand the stuffed bird in an oven and roast until done pouring the melted fat and juice over it. Before serving cut into portions together with the stuffing. Serve with the soaked cowberries.

ROASTED DUCK WITH APPLES

1 duck, 5 apples, 2 tbsp. sugar, lettuce, $1/2$ loaf white bread

Roast the duck whole in an oven, pouring its melted fat and juice over it. Cut the roasted duck into portions. Put slices of the browned bread in a dish. Lay the slices of roasted duck on them. Cut the apples in two, remove the cores, sprinkle with the sugar, and bake. Place the apple pieces around the duck. Adorn the dish with the lettuce.

DUCK WITH TURNIPS

1 duck, 2 small turnips, 1 tbsp. soft butter, 1 onion, $1/2$ bay leaf, and herbs to taste

Chop the prepared duck into pieces and brown in the butter. Peel the turnips, cut into small cubes, put in a sauce-pan or a clay pot, pour a little broth into it, and bring to a boil. Add the pieces of duck meat, browned minced onion, and wine, salt, pepper, and cook till soft. Serve with boiled buckwheat or fried potatoes.

DUCK STUFFED WITH PICKLED MUSHROOMS

1 duck, 1 lb (500 gm) pickled mushrooms, 3 onions, 3 tbsp. soft butter, $1/2$ cup sour cream, 1 egg; salt and herbs to taste

Rinse the milk mushrooms or some other kind of mushrooms, dry, mince, and brown with the onions in the butter, add the sour cream mixed with the egg, then salt and herbs to taste. Fill the prepared carcass with the stuffing, sow up, put in a sauce-pan or dripping-pan, and roast in an oven pouring the duck-meat juice over it. When the duck is done, remove the cord, cut into portions, and serve with boiled potatoes, parsley or dill.

CHICKEN-MEAT ROLL, MOSCOW STYLE

10 oz (300 gm) boiled chicken flesh, 7 oz (200 gm) boiled duck flesh, 7 oz (200 gm) boiled goose flesh, 4 oz (100 gm) grated cheese, 2 oz (50 gm) cream, 4 eggs, 4 oz (100 gm) canned green peas, 2 oz (50 gm) boiled beef liver, and $1/3$ oz (10 gm) herbs

Put the chicken, duck, and goose flesh and the beef liver two times through a meat-grinder with a fine grating, pound well, add the grated cheese, canned green peas, minced herbs, cream, and beaten egg-whites. Mix the mass well, lay on cellophane shaping into a roll, and put in an oven. Bake until golden crust forms.

Dishes with Poultry

Dishes With Game and the Meat of Wild Animals

WILD DUCKS

4 wild ducks, 4 oz (100 gm) pork fat and 4 oz (100 gm) ham, 4 onions, 2 cups bouillon, 3 tbsp. soft butter, 1 lemon, 1 bay leaf; salt and pepper to taste

Clean the wild ducks, stuff them with the pork fat, and brown in the bouillon's grease until golden crust forms on both sides.

Add several small pieces of the pork fat and ham, salt, pepper, 4 minced onions, one bay leaf, 2 cups of bouillon, dress with flour and butter, and cook in a sauce-pan with the lid on. At last squeeze the lemon's juice into the pan, boil well again, take out the pork fat and melted fat, lay the ducks on a dish and pour the sauce over them.

BAKED WILD DUCKS (TEALS)

3 teals, 7 oz (200 gm) pork fat, 2 oz (50 gm) fat, salt, and herbs

Wash and rub the prepared wild ducks' carcasses with salt. Chop part of the frozen pork fat fine and stuff the teals' legs with it. Cut the remaining fat into large flat slices, place them around the teals' carcasses and tie up with twine. Heat the fat in a dripping-pan, put the teals in it, and bake in a heated oven, pouring the forming sauce over them. Remove the twine and cut each teal in half.

Put the halves together in a dish, pour the sauce over them, and adorn with parsley. Serve with soaked cowberries.

ROASTED SMALL GAME BIRDS

2 carcasses of small wild birds, 2/3 oz (20 gm) salted pork fat, 1/2 oz (15 gm) butter, white bread, jam or cowberries, and cranberries

Pluck, clean, wash, dry, and remove the eyes from woodcocks, great snipes, snipes, or quails. Chop off the talons, make three or four incisions in the legs and interweave them. Place thin slices of the pork fat around a carcass and tie it up with a length of thread. Fry the game in frying-pans, turn the carcasses over their backs down and continue cooking in an oven until done. Before serving remove the thread. Brown slices of the white bread in the butter and lay the roasted game on them. You can serve the dish with the soaked cowberries or cranberry jam.

BOILED BUCKWHEAT WITH HAZEL-GROUSE

Boil several hazel-grouse until done with the addition of one onion, salt, and pepper. Rub the hazel-grouse through a colander, strain the broth, and boil buckwheat in it. Serve the boiled buckwheat with the hazel-grouse meat.

FRIED HAZEL-GROUSE

5 hazel-grouse, 4 oz (120 gm) salted pork fat, 9 oz (250 gm) butter, 4 tbsp. meat broth, 4 tbsp. sour cream, dill, and finely ground dried bread-crumbs

Clear the hazel-grouse, salt well, and lard with the pork fat. Fry the hazel-grouse in the sizzling butter in an open deep frying-pan on a high heat. When the hazel-grouse are browned enough, take them out and cut each one in two. Pour the broth and sour cream into the used butter and bring to a boil. Roll the hazel-grouse in the finely ground dried bread-crumbs and pour the sauce over them. Stand in an oven for 10—15 minutes. Before serving strew with the finely cut dill.

Hot Meat Dishes

HAZEL-GROUSE RISSOLES

4 hazel-grouse, 2 eggs, finely ground dried breadcrumbs, 3 tbsp. butter, salt, pepper, and herbs

Clear the hazel-grouse, cut each one in two, and remove the bones. Remove the skin, pound them a little, spread the beaten eggs over the meat, salt, pepper, and fry in the butter on both sides.

ROASTED PARTRIDGES

Clean, pluck, and wash several partridges well. Roast them a little over burning coals greasing them with melted pork fat. Stuff the carcasses with salted pork fat sprinkled with salt and spices, spit them, and roast until done greasing with butter all the while.

PARTRIDGE BRAISED IN RED CABBAGE

2 partridges, 4 oz (100 gm) fat, 1 big onion, 2 lb (1 kg) red cabbages, 2 tbsp. flour, condiment; salt, vinegar, juniper to taste

Wash the prepared carcasses of the partridges, rub with the salt mixed with the mashed juniper. Melt some of the fat in a sauce-pan and brown the partridges evenly, cut them in two or, depending on the size, four parts, add water and cook on low heat with the lid on. Chop the cabbages, cut the onion into rings, put in the pan, and add half a cup of water. Make a dressing from the remaining fat and flour in a stew-pan, pour it over the cabbage, add some salt, sugar, and vinegar.

ROAST BLACK GROUSE

1 black grouse, 2 oz (50 gm) fat, 1 tbsp. vinegar and wine, 2 tbsp. sour cream, and salt

Pluck and clean a black grouse, hang it up outdoors and keep there for several days. Then soak it in vinegar or in vinegar and wine, for 6 days. Let the vinegar flow down, rub the black grouse with salt, stuff with pork fat, and roast in a frying-pan in an oven continually pouring the meat juice over it. Add some sour cream to the gravy.

RISSOLES FROM WILD-BOAR MEAT

Put the rissole part of the wild-boar meat with the bones in a marinade for 4 hours. Then put it in a sauce-pan with the addition of culinary roots and condiment. Pour in 1 cup of meat broth and 1 cup of dry red wine, set on a burner and cook until soft. Cut the meat into helpings in the shape of rissoles with bones, strew with cinnamon, pour the wine over them, and put in a heated oven for about 20 minutes, pouring the meat juice over them.

BLACK GROUSE STEWED IN SOUR CREAM

2 black grouses, 2 oz (50 gm) fat, 2 tbsp. flour, 1.5 cup thin sour cream, ground sweet red pepper, 2 tbsp. minced parsley, and salt

Rub the prepared carcasses with the salt and spices, brown evenly in the scorching fat, quarter each carcass, put in a sauce-pan or grazier, add very little water, and cook on low heat with the lid on until done. At last add the sour cream mixed with the browned flour, cook several minutes more, and salt to taste.

Strew the black grouses with the minced parsley, dress with pickled podded haricots, pickled plums, and cranberries, and serve.

HARE IN SOUR CREAM, À LA RUSSE

1 hare's kidney and ham, 4 oz (100 gm) pork fat, 2.5 oz (70 gm) fat, 2 tbsp. flour, 1 cup thin sour cream, and salt

The pickle for the hare's hind part. Boil water with minced onions and spices, chill, and add vinegar. Lay the kidney part in an enameled bowl, pour the cold pickle over it and stand in a cold place for 3—4 days, turning over every day. Take out the meat, rinse, remove the film, stuff with the pork fat, and rub the surface with the salt. Heat the fat in a dripping-pan, add the meat, pour the melted fat over it, add some water,

Dishes with Game and the Meat of Wild Animals

and stand in an oven. Cook for about 2 hours until done, all the while pouring the sauce over it. As the sauce is evapourating, add water not to let the hare be too dry. At last take out the meat, cut into portions, and lay on a heated oval metal dish.

Add the rest of the flour to the remaining sauce, salt and pepper to taste, and pour it over the hare.

Serve with soaked cowberries, grated horse-radish in vinegar or a red cabbage salad.

ROAST RABBIT (HARE)

1 rabbit (hare), 2 oz (60 gm) pork fat, 3 tbsp. soft butter, 2 cups thin sour cream, $1/2$ cup vinegar, salt, and parsley

Pickle the rabbit's carcass for 5—6 hours. Remove the film, rub with the salt, stuff the hind legs and kidneys with the pork fat, and brown in a greased dripping-pan in an oven for 25—30 minutes, periodically pouring the rabbit's juice and fat over the meat. Pour the sour cream over the browned carcass, boil properly, and add the well-boiled vinegar to taste. Cut the carcass into portions, pour the sauce over it, strew with the minced parsley, and dress with a boiled beetroot. Wash a beetroot well, boil until semi-done, peel, cut into strips, slightly, brown in the butter with the addition of flour, sugar, vinegar, and salt, and cook until done.

STUFFED HARE

1 hare, $1/4$ pork fat, $1/2$ loaf white bread, 7 oz (200 gm) milk, clove, pepper, and salt

Cut off all meat from the bones in the kidney part of the hare. Do not break or cut the bones. Chop the meat fine, add the pork fat, white bread soaked in milk, pepper, and clove. Mix well and lay the stuffing around the bones of the hind kidney part of the hare. Boil some milk butter in a small amount of water in a frying-pan, put the hare in it, and roast in an oven pouring soft butter over it. Sprinkle with minced lemon rinds and serve.

BAKED VENISON

10 oz (300 gm) venison, 3 onions, 0.01 oz (0.3 gm) citric acid, 4 potatoes, 1 hard-boiled egg, 4 oz (100 gm) sour cream, $1/5$ oz (6 gm) grated cheese, 0.9 oz (25 gm) butter, $1 1/4$ oz (7 gm) parsley and dill, 2 fresh tomatoes; salt and spices to taste

Pickle the venison with the onions and citric acid or, better still, with lemon juice. Brown the meat in butter in a frying-pan until golden crust forms, put it in a saucepan, and cook in a small amount of broth. Add the spices. Cut the cooked meat into several pieces, put in the middle of the frying-pan, edge with the sliced potatoes, pour some sour-cream sauce over it, sprinkle with the grated cheese, and spurt the slightly heated butter into it.

Stand in an oven and bake.

Adorn the dish with rings of the fresh tomatoes, eggs, parsley, and dill.

HOT FISH DISHES

In Russian cuisine fish dishes are some of the most favourite ones. The rivers, lakes, and seas by which Russian people settled always gave them this tasty and accessible food.

Apart from fresh-water fish our ancestors also ate sea fish, i.e., cod, navaga, etc. However, especially valued were sturgeon, salmon, and other fishes of this kind. Most often fish dishes are served with potatoes and boiled buckwheat.

FISH IN BROTH

Make a broth from the heads, fins, and bones of several fishes. Let it draw. Strain the broth. Boil the filletted fish with the root of parsley, onion, cucumber pickle, pepper, and bay leaf. Boil the fish in a little water in a pan with the lid on until done, removing the scum.

Take out the fillet. Strain the broth. Heat some flour in a frying-pan, dilute it with the fish broth, add cubes of peeled pickled cucumbers (with the seeds removed). Pour this sauce over the pieces of the filletted fish.

BOILED LARGE RUFFS

2—3 ruffs, 1/2 lemon, 1 carrot, 2 boiled potatoes, 5 tbsp. soft butter, 1 bay leaf, salt and pepper to taste

Gut, scale, and wash the ruffs, lay on the grill of a fish-pot, pour broth over them, add some onions, carrot, pepper, culinary roots, bay leaf and boil. Carefully remove the boiled ruffs' skin, pour the hot broth over them, lay on a dish, put slices of the lemon (without the dried peel and seeds) on each ruff, and pour a small amount of the strained broth with the addition of the boiled minced roots over the whole of it.

BOILED PIKE WITH A LEMON AND RAISINS

1/2 cup white wine per 2 lb (1 kg) pikes, vinegar to taste, 1 carrot, 1 sprig parsley, 1 sprig celery, 1 onion, 1/2 cup raisins, 1/2 lemon, 2 bay leaves

The sauce: 2 tbsp. soft butter, 1.5 tbsp. flour, sugar to taste, and 3 cups strained broth

Scale and gut the fish, cut into helpings, salt, and stand in a refrigerator for one hour. Pour the wine and vinegar over the chilled fish, add the onion, washed raisins, lemon rings (without the seeds), and bay leaves. Pour in some water so that it will cover the helpings. Boil on sufficiently high heat.

The Sauce

Rub the butter thoroughly with the flour and sugar, add the fish broth, set on a burner, and boil until the sauce gets thick. Transfer the hot pike together with the raisins and lemon into a dish and pour the sauce over it. Serve with hot boiled potatoes. You can make the same kind of dish with a sheat-fish, cod, hake or the fillet of these fishes. Olive oil can be used instead of butter.

PIKE WITH MINCED GARLIC

7 oz (200 gm) boiled pike, 3 boiled potatoes, 3 cloves garlic

Lay portions of the boiled pike on a dish, pour the fish broth with the minced garlic over them, and serve with the boiled potatoes.

BOILED PIKE IN MUSTARD SAUCE

2 lb (1 kg) pikes, 1 sprig parsley, 1 sprig celery, 1 onion, 2 bay leaves, 4 sweet peppercorns, 1 cup thinned vinegar.

The sauce: 1 tbsp. mustard paste, 1/2 tbsp. flour,

1 tbsp. soft butter, 3 egg-yolks; lemon juice, salt, and sugar to taste

Scale, gut, wash, and cut the fish into portions. Put the heads, fins, and tails in a sauce-pan. Add the onion, spices, and salt, pour in 4 cups of cold water. Set on a burner and boil for 1 hour. Salt the portions, lay them in clay pots, and pour the hot thinned vinegar over them. Strain the fish broth, add the helpings to it, and boil on high heat until done (for about 20 minutes). Make the sauce. Mix the mustard paste, flour, and butter thoroughly, dilute with the hot strained broth, add the lemon juice, sugar, and salt and boil well. Beat the raw egg-yolks gradually adding the hot sauce to them. Keep stirring to make sure the egg-yolks do not coagulate. Lay the portions on a dish and pour the sauce over them. Serve with hot boiled potatoes.

BOILED CHUB WITH APPLES AND GRATED HORSE-RADISH

1.5 lb (600 gm) chub, 1 sprig parsley, 1 carrot, 1 sprig celery, 2 onions, 3 bay leaves, 5 black peppercorns; salt to taste

The sauce: *$1/3$ oz (10 gm) horse-radish, 3 apples; thinned vinegar and sugar to taste*

Scale and gut the fish, cut into portions, salt, pepper, pour the thinned vinegar over them, and put in a fridge for an hour.
Make a broth from the parsley, celery, carrot, spices, and onions. Transfer the chub into a sauce-pan, pour the strained broth over it, and cook on high heat. Grate the apples and horse-radish fine and immediately add the sugar, vinegar, and several table-spoons of the fish broth to it. Lay the portions on a dish and pour the sauce over them.

BOILED SHEAT-FISH IN TOMATO SAUCE

1.5 lb (700 gm) sheat-fish, 1 carrot, 1 sprig parsley, 1 onion, 2 bay leaves, 5 sweet peppercorns, and salt to taste

Cut the prepared fish into portions preliminarily removing the bones. Pour 3 cups of cold water in a sauce-pan, set on a burner, bring to a boil, and add the chopped carrot, minced parsley, salt and spices. Forty minutes thereafter add the fish and boil until done. Transfer the fish into a different dish together with the vegetables and stand in a warm place so that the ingredients will not chill. Strain the broth and make a tomato sauce in it. Lay the fish and vegetables on a dish and pour the sauce over it. Serve with boiled potatoes.

BOILED DRIED VOBLA (CASPIAN ROACH)

1 lb (500 gm) vobla, 1 carrot, 1 sprig parsley, 2 onions, 1 bay leaf, 1 bunch herbs, 1 tbsp. melted butter

Soak the vobla in water for 6 hours.
Pour cold water over the soaked vobla, add the onions, carrot, herbs, and the bay leaf. Set on a burner and boil for 20 minutes. Lay the fish on a dish. Pour the melted butter over it and strew with the minced parsley. Edge with hot boiled potatoes and serve.

PIKE-PERCH À LA RUSSE

1.5 lb (600 gm) pike-perch, 8 fresh mushrooms, 2 bay leaves; salt to taste

The sauce: *1 carrot, 1 root parsley, 3 pickled cucumbers, 2—3 tbsp. tomato sauce, 1 cup fish broth; salt and sugar to taste; $1/4$ lemon, 2.5 oz (75—100 gm) olives*

Scale, gut, and cut the fish into portions. Salt and pour hot water over them, add the mushrooms, salt, and bay leaves. Boil until done. Separately boil the root of parsley and carrot in a little water. Peel the pickled cucumbers and remove the seeds, cut into thin slices, and boil until done. Take the mushrooms out of the fish broth and cut into thin slices. Mix the vegetables with the mushrooms, add the tomato sauce and a little strained fish broth. Add some salt and sugar to taste. Heat it. Transfer the fish into a dish and pour the sauce over it. Decorate with the sliced lemon, sprigs of parsley, and olives.

STEWED STURGEON, SEVRUGA OR BELUGA

2 lb (1 kg) fish, 12 boletusses, 6 tbsp. white wine, 2 tbsp. butter, 3 tbsp. flour, $1/2$ lemon; salt and ground pepper to taste

Scale, gut, and wash the fish. Cut into large slices, salt, pepper, and put in a stew-pan or deep sauce-pan. Clean and wash the mushrooms thoroughly. Cut into slices and put on top the fish in a layer. Pour in 3 cups of the hot fish broth or boiling water and add the dry white wine. Boil on low heat with the lid on. When the fish is done, pour out the broth carefully, leaving a small amount of it in the pan to heat the fish in.

The sauce

Mix the flour with the butter, dilute with the broth, and boil on low heat for 10 minutes stirring. Strain and add small bits of butter and salt. Transfer the fish and mushrooms into a dish, pour the sauce over them, and decorate with rings of the lemon (without the seeds).

Serve with hot boiled potatoes or fresh cucumbers.

BOILED STURGEON, SALMON OR SEVRUGA WITH POTATOES

1.5 lb (600 gm) fish, 1 lb (500 gm) potatoes, $1/2$ carrot, $1/2$ sprig parsley, 1 onion, 1 tbsp. melted butter; salt to taste

Scale, gut, and wash the fish. Peel and chop the onion, mince the parsley and carrot. Put the ingredients in a sauce-pan, pour cold water over them, add some salt, and boil until done.

Peel the potatoes and boil them in a separate pan.

Take the cooked fish out of the broth and cut into thick slices. Lay in a dish and pour the melted butter over it. Edge with the hot boiled potatoes strewn with the minced parsley. Separately serve pickled or fresh cucumbers and tomatoes and grated horseradish and vinegar in a sauce-boat.

BOILED SEVRUGA WITH GARLIC AND SAUCE

2 lb (1 kg) sevruga, 5 tbsp, 6% vinegar, parsley and dill

Make a lengthwise cut in the prepared sevruga and spread it out, lay on a grill in a sauce-pan, pour some water in it, set on a burner and boil on low heat. Bring to a boil, put in some salt, herbs, and vinegar essence and boil for another 40 minutes. Transfer the boiled fish onto a tray, put a heavy press on top of it and chill for 5 hours. Cut the fish into portions. Make a thin white sauce with the addition of garlic, dry wine, and herbs. Pour the sauce over the fish and serve.

STURGEON, SEVRUGA, BELUGA, OR STERLET IN PICKLE

2 lb (1 kg) fish, 10 boletusses, 2 pickled cucumbers, 2 tbsp. butter, 1 tbsp. flour; salt and pepper to taste

Cut the prepared fish into portions, salt, and pepper. Remove the skin and seeds from the pickled cucumbers and cut into slices. Wash the fresh mushrooms thoroughly, clear away the earth, and cut into slices.

Lay the fish on the bottom of a stew-pan and top it with the cucumbers and mushrooms. Pour 1—1.5 cups of water over them and add 2 table-spoons of the strained cucumber pickle. Put the lid on and boil the fish until done (for about 15—20 minutes). Pour out the broth leaving a little liquid to heat the fish in.

Mix the flour and butter thoroughly, add a little broth, and add the resulting sauce to the remaining broth. Set on a burner and boil, stirring, for 7—10 minutes. Strain the broth, add some salt and several bits of butter and mix well. Lay the fish, mushrooms and cucumbers on a dish, pour the sauce over them, and strew with minced parsley. Serve with boiled potatoes. Fresh mushrooms can be substituted for pickled ones washed with cold water.

PIKE-PERCH, HOME STYLE

1 pike-perch, 3 tbsp. vegetable oil, 1 bay leaf, 1 onion, 3 potatoes; salt and pepper to taste

Scale and gut the fish. Cut off the

Hot Fish Dishes

head, fins, and tail. Wash the fish with cold water, chop into pieces, and soak in cold salted water for 10 minutes. Take the pieces out with a colander, roll them in flour, and brown in vegetable oil until semi-done. Add some salt, pepper, and bay leaf. Cut some potatoes into cubes, chop an onion into strips, and lay them on the fish. Pour boiled water over the ingredients so that it will cover them. Put the lid on tight. Cook for 15 minutes. Serve hot.

PIKE-PERCH STEWED IN SAUCE

2 lb (800 gm) pike-perch, 4 potatoes, 3 tbsp. cream, 2 egg-yolks, 4 oz (100 gm) butter, 3 oz (80 gm) grated cheese, 1 tbsp. flour; salt and ground pepper to taste

Cut the fish into portions, salt, pepper, pour hot water over them, add some salt and spices. Boil for 15 minutes. Transfer the portions into a stew-pan and edge them with slices of boiled potatoes.

The sauce

Mix the cream, raw egg-yolks, soft butter, grated cheese, flour, salt, and ground pepper, dilute with the strained fish broth until sufficiently thick (like sour cream). Pour this sauce over the fish, stand in a heated oven for 15 minutes. Serve with lettuce.

CRUCIAN COOKED IN SOUR CREAM

2 lb (1 kg) crucians, 2 oz (50 gm) fat, 1 tbsp. flour, 1 cup sour cream, 2 tbsp. minced dill; spices and salt to taste

Scale, gut, and wash the crucians. Cut off the heads and tails, salt, sprinkle with the flour, and brown both sides in the scorching butter. Pour a little water in a sauce-pan, put in 1—2 pieces of clove, a pinch of ground nutmegs, 2 sweet peppercorns and cook on very low heat for about 20 minutes. At last add the sour cream and a little salt, and heat. Before serving strew with the minced dill and pour the resulting sauce over the ingredients.

FRESH-WATER FISHES BOILED WITH WALNUTS

7 oz (200 gm) fish, 3 tbsp. butter, 5 walnuts, 2 eggs, 1 tbsp. mustard, 1 oz (30 gm) 3% vinegar, 1 oz (30 gm) vegetable oil, a little fish broth, dried bread-crumbs, 1 onion, and 1 piece parsley

You can make the dish with a pike-perch, pike, carp, etc. Boil the fish in a little amount of water. Shell the walnuts, crush them in a mortar, add the egg-yolks and mustard, and mix well. Gradually add the vegetable oil. Dilute the sauce with the vinegar, add the dried bread-crumbs, and pour it over the fish.

FRESH-WATER FISHES WITH SOUR CREAM AND PICKLED CUCUMBERS

7 oz (200 gm) fresh-water fish, 1 onion, 3 sprigs parsley, $1/3$ cup sour cream, 1 cup chopped pickled mushrooms, and 2 boiled potatoes

This dish is made with a cod, hake, pike, burbot, etc. Boil the fish in a little amount of water. Add the sour cream to the fish broth and cook until semi-done. Chop the pickled mushrooms fine, scald, squeeze dry, and put in the mixture of the sour cream and fish broth. Pour the sour cream and mushrooms over the dish and serve with the boiled potatoes.

STEWED FISH

7 oz (200 gm) fish, 1 onion, 1 sprig parsley, $1/3$ oz (10 gm) dry wine, 1 oz (30 gm) boletusses, 4 boiled potatoes, 3 tbsp. soft butter, and $1/2$ lemon

This is the way the dishes with pike-perch-

Hot Fish Dishes

es, sturgeons, salmons, flounders, and other kind of fishes are made. Grease the bottom of a sauce-pan with butter, put the fish in it, add some broth, parsley, onion, salt, citric acid or dry white wine. You can also add boletusses' liquid to it. Put the sauce-pan's lid on tight and cook until done, at first on high and then on low heat. Make the sauce on the basis of the sour cream.

Cut white bread into slices, brown, top with the fish, pour the sauce over them, and lay the slightly boiled boletusses, sliced lemon (with the seeds removed), and dried lemon peel on top. Edge with the boiled potatoes, pour the soft butter over the ingredients, and strew with the minced parsley.

SEVRUGA GOULASH

10 oz (300 gm) filleted sevruga, 1 onion, 2 tbsp. flour; tomato paste, pepper, and salt to taste

Scale the sevruga and remove the gristles. Cut into cubes $1/3$ oz (10—15 gm) each. Soak in thick pickle for about 15 minutes, roll in the flour, brown in vegetable oil in a pig-iron or electric frying-pan, add the shredded onion, tomato paste, salt, and ground pepper and cook until semi-done. Put the fish and ingredients in an aluminum sauce-pan, add the fish broth, and cook for 20 minutes.

Serve with a combination of rice, boiled cabbage, boiled potatoes, and canned green peas. Pour melted butter over it and serve.

BAKED FISH, RUSSIAN STYLE

7 oz (200 gm) fish, 2 tbsp. grated cheese, 1 tbsp. fish broth

Grease a frying-pan with fat, lay rings of boiled potatoes along the edges, place the raw fish in the middle, pour the thick fish broth over it, bring to a boil, strew with the grated cheese, and bake in an oven. This way you can bake a pike-perch, pike, sheat-fish, carp, cod, etc.

BAKED FISH, MOSCOW STYLE

1.5 lb (600 gm) filleted fish, a little flour, 10 oz (300 gm) potatoes,
1 hard-boiled egg, 1 onion, $2/3$ cup boiled mushrooms, 2 oz (50 gm) grated cheese, and $1/2$ cup thin sour cream; salt and pepper to taste

Cut any kind of filleted fish into pieces, salt, pepper, roll in a little flour, and brown in vegetable oil. Cut the potatoes into rings and fry in vegetable oil.

Grease a small frying-pan with butter, put the browned fish in the middle, and edge with the fried potatoes. Top with the browned onion, slices of the hard-boiled egg, and sliced boiled mushrooms. Pour the sour cream over the whole of it, sprinkle with the grated cheese, and bake in an oven until light-brown crust forms.

FISH BAKED WITH AN EGG

7 oz (200 gm) fish, 2—3 potatoes, 1 onion, 2 tbsp. milk, 1 egg, and 1 oz (30 gm) vegetable oil

Brown the fish, lay it on a frying-pan together with the boiled or fried potatoes and browned onion.

Mix the egg with the milk, add some salt, pour the mixture over the fish and potatoes, and bake in an oven.

FISH, MONASTERY STYLE

15 oz (400 gm) fish, 2 onions, fried potatoes, 1 egg, 1 cup boiled mushrooms, 3 tbsp. grated cheese; salt and peper to taste

Roll some fish (better fresh-water ones) in flour, edge with fried potatoes, slightly browned onions, sliced hard-cooked egg, and browned or boiled mushrooms. Add some mushroom liquid and pepper, top with sour cream, strew with the grated cheese, and bake for 30—50 minutes.

FISH BAKED IN A CLAY POT

7 oz (200 gm) filleted cod, $2/3$ oz (20 gm) butter, 1 egg, 2 oz (50 gm) milk, 1.5 oz (40 gm) grated Dutch cheese, 2—3 sprig herb

Boil the fish in a sauce-pan, mix the milk with egg, and mince the herb. Now that everything is ready, grease the pot with the butter, put the fish in it, sprinkle with the grated cheese, and pour

the mixture of milk and egg over the ingredients. Strew with the minced herb and stand in an oven. Serve the dish in the clay pot.

BAKED PIKE-PERCH

1 pike-perch, 5 tbsp. vegetable oil, a little grated cheese, 2—3 potatoes

Scale, gut and wash the fish. Remove the gills and eyes. Cut into portions. Soak in pickle for 15 minutes, transfer into a frying-pan with the fish in the middle and thick rings of potatoes around it. Pour the vegetable oil over it, sprinkle with the grated cheese, and stand in an oven. Bake for 30 minutes.

FISH BAKED IN SAUCE WITH HORSE-RADISH

3 lb (1.5 kg) fish, 4 oz (100 gm) margarine, 1 lemon, and salt

The sauce: *1 root grated horse-radish, 2 oz (60 gm) margarine, 2.5 oz (70 gm) flour, 1 cup fish or vegetable broth, 4 tbsp. sour cream, 2 raw egg-yolks, half a lemon's juice, sugar, and salt*

Scale, gut, and wash the big fish. Cut off the gills, salt, and let them stay that way for the night. On the following day wash them in cold water, wrap each fish in oil paper greased with the margarine, lay them very close on a dripping-pan, put in a heated oven, and bake for about an hour.

The sauce

Brown the flour in margarine until golden-brown, add the grated horse-radish, pour the fish or vegetable broth over it and bring to a boil, stirring all the while. If the sauce is too thick, dilute it with the broth. Stop boiling the sauce, pour in the sour cream and lemon juice, put in the beaten egg-yolks, salt, and add the sugar to taste.

When the fish is baked, remove the paper, lay the helpings on oval dish, decorate with rings of the lemon, and pour part of the sauce over them. Serve the remaining sauce in a sauce-boat.

You can serve the dish hot or cold.

FISH, OSTANKINO STYLE

4 oz (100 gm) filleted sturgeon or sevruga, 1 oz (30 gm) tomato paste or sauce, grated cheese, olives, $1/4$ medium-size onion, $1/6$ oz (5 gm) butter, and herbs

Cut the fish into small cubes. Brown the onion in the butter until golden-brown. Remove the stones from the olives, chop fine, and boil in a little water until soft. Put the ingredients in a small stew-pan, at first the fish, then the onion and olives. Pour the tomato paste or tomato sauce over them, sprinkle with the grated cheese, and spurt the hot butter into them. Heat it all on low heat, stand in an oven, and bake. You can decorate the dish with parsley or dill.

FISH IN BOILED MANNA-CROUP

2—3 medium-size fishes, 2 tbsp. manna-croup, 4 potatoes, 1 onion, salt, pepper, and herbs

Cut the fresh-water or sea fishes into pieces, roll in the manna-croup mixed with a small amount of salt and pepper. Brown on high heat for 3—5 minutes. Put the sliced boiled potatoes (and slightly browned onion) in a sauce-pan, lay the fishes on top, add some boiling water, and stand in an oven for 5—6 minutes.

Strew with the fresh herbs and serve.

FISH À LA SUZDAL WITH BOILED BUCKWHEAT

1.5 lb (700 gm) fish, $1/2$ cup buckwheat, 7 oz (200 gm) fresh mushrooms, 3 hard-boiled eggs, 2 onions, 4 tbsp. sour cream, 5 tbsp. soft butter, 1 oz (30 gm) grated cheese, 2 tbsp. dried and finely ground bread-crumbs; salt to taste

Soak, boil, and mince the mushrooms. Cut the fish into pieces, salt, and brown in the butter. Separately brown the onions with mushrooms. Boil the buckwheat until crumbly, add the chopped eggs, and mix up. Grease clay-pots with the butter, sprinkle with the dried and finely ground bread-crumbs, put in the boiled buckwheat and eggs, onions with mushrooms, and fish and pour the sour cream over the ingredients. Strew with the grated cheese and bake in an oven.

BREAM WITH BOILED BUCKWHEAT

2 lb (1 kg) breams, 6 dried mushrooms, 3 tbsp. flour, 7 oz (200 gm) buckwheat, 2 onions, 7 oz (200 gm) vegetable oil; salt and pepper to taste

Boil the buckwheat until thick. Make 1 cup of mushroom liquid. Scale, gut, wash, salt, and pepper the fish. Mince the onions, brown them in the vegetable oil, and mix with the boiled buckwheat. Add, stirring, the mushroom liquid. Stuff the breams with the filling, sow them up, roll in the flour, put in a frying-pan with the heated vegetable oil in it, and stand in a heated oven. Bake adding the butter. When the breams are done, transfer into a dish, remove the thread, and pour the butter in which they were baked over them.

BAKED FISH PUDDING WITH RICE

2 lb (900 gm) fish, 6 oz (170 gm) rice, 1.5 tbsp. flour, 1.5 tbsp. soft butter, 2 hard-boiled eggs, 1 tbsp. butter for the rice; salt to taste

Boil the fish and have it chilled. Strain the fish broth. Slightly brown the flour in the butter, dilute with the hot broth (2 cups), salt, and boil thoroughly. Shell the hard-boiled eggs and cut them into rings. Boil the rice until crumbly and add the butter and salt. Cut the chilled fish into small bits. Grease a stew-pot well and put a layer of the rice in it, top it with the fish and cover with the eggs' rings. Pour the sauce over the ingredients. Bake in an oven. The fish pudding can be made from any kind of fleshy fish.

FISH *SOLYANKA* (MEDLEY) IN A FRYING-PAN

1.5 lb (600 gm) sturgeon, 2 lb (1 kg) cabbage, 3 tbsp. soft butter, 3 tbsp. dried bread-crumbs, 3 pickled cucumbers, 2 tbsp. grated cheese, $1/4$ lemon

The cooked cabbage: 5 tbsp. tomato paste, 2 onions, 2—3 tbsp. melted butter or melted fat, and 1 tbsp. flour and sugar

Chop the cabbage into strips, put in a sauce-pan, add some water and spices, and cook with the lid on. When the cabbage is heated properly, lower the heat. Slightly brown the minced onions. At last add the tomato paste, salt, and sugar and sprinkle with the flour. Mix with the cabbage and cook until soft.

Scald the prepared fish, wash with cold water, and cut into small cubes 1 oz (30—40 gm) each without removing the skin. Scald again, wash, and put in a greased stew-pan together with the chopped pickled cucumbers (with the skin and seeds removed). Add hot water so that it will cover half the ingredients. Put the lid on and set on a burner. When the cooking is done put half the cabbage in a well-greased frying-pan, top with the fish and sauce with cucumbers, and cover with another layer of cabbage. Smooth out the surface, sprinkle with the grated cheese and dried bread-crumbs, and pour the butter over it. Put it in an oven. Decorate the dish with the sliced lemon. *Solyanka* in a frying-pan is one of the best Russian dishes.

STURGEON FRIED IN PORTIONS

1.5 lb (750 gm) sturgeon, 2 tbsp. flour, 3 tbsp. butter, $1/3$ lemon; salt and pepper to taste

Cut the prepared fish into portions (helpings), scald, wash well, dry, then salt, pepper, and roll in the flour. Heat the butter properly in a frying-pan and brown both sides of the fish until golden crust forms. Lay on a dish, pour the butter from the frying-pan over it, decorate with slices of the lemon and sprigs of parsley. Serve with fried potatoes.

SEVRUGA FRIED IN MARINADE

1 lb (500 gm) sevruga, 3 onions, 3 carrots, $1/2$ garlic, $1/2$ tbsp. vegetable oil, $1/2$ tbsp. broth; pepper and salt to taste

Cook the marinade. Peel and cut the carrots into strips and brown in the vegetable oil.

Hot Fish Dishes

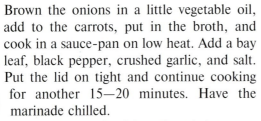

Brown the onions in a little vegetable oil, add to the carrots, put in the broth, and cook in a sauce-pan on low heat. Add a bay leaf, black pepper, crushed garlic, and salt. Put the lid on tight and continue cooking for another 15—20 minutes. Have the marinade chilled.

Prepare the fish and cut it into portions. Keep in a salt solution for 10—15 minutes, then roll in flour and brown in the vegetable oil until golden crust forms.

Before serving pour the chilled marinade over the fish.

ROAST SEVRUGA

10 oz (300 gm) sevruga, 2 lb (800 gm) potatoes, 1 tbsp. tomato paste, 2 tbsp. melted butter, 3—4 bay leaves

Scale, gut, and wash the fish. Remove the gristles, cut into cubes, wash in cold water, and brown slightly in the butter in an iron frying-pan. Lay the fish in a stew-pot. Cut the potatoes into cubes $1/8$ oz (15—20 gm) each and fry in a separate frying-pan until semi-done. Put the fried potatoes in the stew-pot, lay the fish on them (in a layer), and top it all with the slightly boiled tomato paste and browned onions. Make a thick broth from the gristles. Pour the broth into the stew-pot for it to cover the bottom layer of the dish. Add some salt, pepper, and bay leaves. Cook on low heat for 30 minutes. Serve the dish hot.

FRIED HAKES OR CRUCIANS

Scale and gut small crucians or hakes. Remove the eyes and gills, wash well, salt, roll in flour, and fry in vegetable oil. Put the fish in an oven and roast until done. Mix boiled crumbly buckwheat with chopped hard-cooked eggs and browned onions, and put the mixture in a dish in the shape of a mound. Pour melted butter over it. Edge the boiled buckwheat with the crucians or hakes and lay rings of the browned onions on them.

FISH IN DOUGH

4 lb (2 kg) lean fish, 6 eggs, 4 oz (100 gm) butter, 7 oz (200 gm) vegetable oil, 7 oz (200 gm) flour, 1 tbsp. minced parsley; salt and pepper to taste

Remove the flesh of the prepared fish from the bones and skin, cut into slices, dry with a wash-cloth, salt, pepper, dip each slice in the dough, and put in a frying-pan with the heated vegetable oil in it. Brown the slices of the fish on both sides, keep in a dripping-pan for several minutes, and put in a heated oven. Serve with a sliced lemon and strew with the minced parsley.

The dough

Grind the butter until as thick as sour cream, rub the egg-yolks (one by one) in it, sprinkle with the flour, and add the beaten egg-whites. Salt and mix carefully. Keep the sauce-pan with the dough in it in cold water.

STUFFED CARP IN DOUGH

7 oz (200 gm) carp, 4 tbsp. vegetable oil, 2 onions, parsley, 2 tbsp. flour, 4 oz (100 gm) walnuts, black pepper, and salt

Cut the prepared carp lengthwise, along the spine. Remove the vertabrae and fill with stuffing. Make the stuffing from the slightly browned onions, minced milt and roe, parsley, and crushed walnuts. Add the black pepper and salt. Sow up the stuffed fish and wrap it in a sheet of thick dough made from the flour, vegetable oil, salt, and water. Bake in an oven.

PIKE-PERCH IN DOUGH

2 lb (1 kg) filleted fish, $2/3$ oz (20 gm) salt, 2 oz (50 gm) flour, 7 oz (200 gm) fat

The dough: *7 oz (200 gm) flour, 3 eggs, 7 oz (200 gm) beer, 2 oz (50 gm) vegetable oil, and $1/6$ oz (5 gm) salt*

To make the dough, mix the egg-yolks with the beer and salt, add the flour, and nead properly. Add the well-beaten egg-whites and mix carefully from top to bottom. Salt the sliced fish, roll it in the flour, dip in the dough, and brown in a considerable amount of oil.

PIKE-PERCH ROLL

4 oz (100 gm) filleted pike-perch, 4 oz (100 gm) field mushrooms, 1 onion, 2 tbsp. melted butter, 1/4 egg, finely ground dried bread-crumbs, olive or vegetable oil

Scale and gut the fish, remove the skin and bones, and pound the fillet with a chopper. Cut the mushrooms into slices, brown together with the chopped onion in the oil, and have them chilled. Put the mushrooms in the middle of the filleted pike-perch, fold the fillet giving it an oblong shape, soak in the egg, roll in the dried bread-crumbs, put in the sizzling vegetable oil in a frying-pan, and fry until golden brown on both sides. Serve with marinated fruit and mayonnaise.

SMALL FISH ROLLS

7 lb (3 kg) carps or pikes, 2 eggs, 1/3 cup milk, 1 cup dried bread-crumbs, 4 oz (100 gm) butter, 1 cup vegetable oil, flour, grated horse-radish, parsley, and salt

The filling: 2 cups rice, 4 hard-boiled eggs, 4 oz (100 gm) margarine, pepper, and salt

Scale, gut, and wash the fish. Cut them lengthwise along the spine. Remove the fillets from the bones, salt, and keep in the cold for 1—2 hours. In the meantime make the filling. Wash the rice well and boil in a large amount of water until semi-done. Pour out the water, add the margarine to the rice, put the lid on, and stand in a heated oven for 10—15 minutes. Chill the rice, lay it in a tureen, salt, pepper, and mix with the hard-boiled eggs. Lay the filling on the fillets, fold in the shape of rolls, tie up with thread, roll in the flour, soak in a raw egg mixed with milk, and cover with the finely ground dried bread-crumbs. Brown in a considerable amount of butter. Remove the thread and lay the rolls in a stew-pot. Pour the melted butter over them, and stand in an oven without the lid on. Before serving, lay it in an oval dish, sprinkle with the grated horse-radish, and adorn with parsley. Garnish the fish with a salad of carrots and apples.

COOKED MINCED FISH MEAT

4 oz (100 gm) fish flesh, 2/3 oz (20 gm) bread, 2/3 oz (20 gm) milk, 2—3 cloves of garlic, 1 egg, and butter

Clear, wash, and fillet the fish (pike-perch, pike, cod, salmon, or burbot). Put the flesh through a meat-grinder together with the garlic, add some bread soaked in milk, salt, pepper, one egg, and softened butter and knead well. Shape the mass into a long «loaf» 2.5 in (6 cm) thick, wrap it up in a napkin, tie up with a cord, lay on a grating in a sauce-pan, pour some broth over it, and boil for 30—40 minutes. Chill in the broth, unwrap, cut into slices, heat in the broth again, and serve as a separate dish or garnish.

FISH, SURSKY STYLE

10 oz (300 gm) fish fillet, 4 oz (100 gm) white bread, 10 oz (300 gm) mashed potatoes, 1 egg, 1/3 cup milk, 1/2 cup soft butter, and dried bread-crumbs

Put the filleted fish and milk-soaked white bread through a meat-grinder. Make a potato puree. Mix the mashed potatoes and fish filling thoroughly, spread the egg and milk mixture over them, roll in the finely ground bread-crumbs, and brown in a great amount of butter. Serve 2—3 pieces per portion.

PIKE-PERCH ZRAZY (CHOPS)

15 oz (400 gm) filleted fish, 2 onions, 2 oz (50 gm) dried bread-crumbs, 3 hard-boiled eggs, 1 oz (30 gm) boiled rice, 2 oz (50 gm) butter, 2 oz (50 gm) vegetable oil; pepper and salt to taste

Remove the skin and bones from the fillets of the pike-perches. Pound them slightly. Make a filling from the rice, chopped eggs, and browned onions. Add the pepper and salt.
Wrap the filling in the pounded fillets, roll them in the bread-crumbs, and brown in the vegetable oil.
Pour the melted butter over the zrazy and serve with the boiled potatoes.

Hot Fish Dishes

ZRAZY, À LA DON

10 oz (300 gm) pike-perch, 2 onions, 1.5 oz (40 gm) margarine, 2 hard-boiled eggs, parsley; salt and pepper to taste

Remove the skin and bones from the fillets. Pound with a wooden pounder.

The filling

Shred and brown the onions slightly. Add the chopped hard-boiled onions, parsley, salt, and pepper. Wrap up the filling and the pounded fillets. Shape them into sausages, roll in flour, and brown in the margarine. Serve with tomato sauce or mayonnaise.

PIKE-PERCH RISSOLES

15 oz (400 gm) pike-perch, 2 oz (50 gm) white bread-crumbs, $1/3$ cup milk, 1 onion; salt and pepper to taste

Soak the fillet of the pike-perch (without the bones and skin) in the milk for one hour, whereupon put it together with the bread and onion through a meat-grinder two times, add the salt and pepper.

Divide the filling into two portions 1 oz (30—50 gm) each, shape into medium-size round cakes, roll in the white bread-crumbs or flour, and brown in a small amount of butter. Serve with the potatoes or vegetable salad.

PICKLED HERRING CAKES

15 oz (400 gm) herring, $1/3$ white bread loaf, 2 eggs, 3 onions, 2 tbsp. milk butter, 2 tbsp. thin sour cream, 1.5 tbsp. finely ground bread-crumbs; ground pepper to taste

Soak the herring in cold water or milk. Mince the onions and slightly brown in the butter. Soak the white bread-crumbs in cold milk. Put the filleted herring, onions, and pressed-out white bread through a meat-grinder. Add the raw eggs, sour cream, and pepper to the filling. Shape the minced filling into cakes, soak them in the eggs, roll in the bread-crumbs, and brown on both sides. Put a bit of butter in a dish and on top of each fish cake. Serve with mashed potatoes. You can make the dish using vegetable oil. It is possible to use boiled potatoes instead of the white bread.

BAKED PIKE-PERCH OR PIKE CAKES

1.5 lb (700 gm) fish, 3 tbsp. butter, 2 tbsp. flour, $1/4$ loaf white bread, $1/2$ cup milk, 1 onion, 1 raw egg, 1 sprig parsley, $1/2$ lemon; salt and pepper to taste

Soak the bread in the milk, mince and slightly brown the onion in the butter. Put the fish's flesh, soaked bread, and onion two times through a meat-grinder. Add the soft butter, salt, pepper and egg to the filling. Mix well, shape into cakes, and roll in the flour. Grease a stew-pot with the butter, put the fish cakes in it, strew with the minced parsley, and top with slices of the lemon (with the seeds removed).

Put the lid on and stand in an oven for about 10—12 minutes. Serve with canned green peas dressed with oil.

BURBOT *TEFTELI* (FISH-BALLS) IN TOMATO SAUCE

1.5 lb (600 gm) fish, 2 oz (50 gm) white bread, 1 onion, 1 cup milk, 3 tbsp. vegetable oil, 3 tbsp. tomato, 1.5 tbsp. flour; salt and ground pepper to taste

Cut the fish's fillet into slices and soak the bread in the milk. Put the sliced fillet, soaked white bread, and onion twice through a meat-grinder. Salt and pepper the filling. Add the soft butter. Mix well and shape into small balls (two balls per portion). Roll in the flour and put in a stew-pot. Heat a frying-pan with vegetable oil in it and slightly brown the tomato paste. After

Hot Fish Dishes

five minutes, sprinkle with flour and brown for another 3—5 minutes. Remove from the burner and dilute with hot water ($1/2$ cup). Pour the sauce over the fish-balls and bake in an oven.

Transfer into a dish together with the sauce and strew with minced parsley. Serve with mashed potatoes. You can also dress it with parsley.

CAKES FROM BOILED FISH

1 lb (500 gm) boiled fish, $1/2$ white bread loaf, 2 eggs, 4 tbsp. grated cheese, 3 tbsp. finely ground dried bread-crumbs, 3 tbsp. butter; salt and pepper to taste

Soak the bread in cold milk. Put the fish's flesh and soaked bread through a meat-grinder. Add the raw eggs, grated cheese, salt, and pepper. Mix thoroughly, shape into round cakes, and roll in the bread crumbs. Grease a frying-pan, heat well, and brown the fish cakes on both sides. Serve with mashed potatoes or boiled cauliflower.

FISH AND MUSHROOM ZRAZY WITH A SAUCE

2 lb (1 kg) fish, 7 oz (200 gm) field mushrooms, 2 onions, 5 oz (150 gm) vegetable oil, 1 tbsp finely chopped parsley; salt and pepper to taste

The sauce: 2 tbsp. butter, 1 tbsp flour, 0.5 cup fish broth, 0.25 cup white wine, 0.5 cup cream, 3 egg-yolks; lemon juice to taste

Remove the bones from the fish and cut across the fibres into oblong pieces. Slightly pound each piece with a chopper on a moist board. Make sure the fibres are not damaged. Trim the pieces' edges, sprinkle with salt and pepper, and put some mushroom filling in the middle of each piece of fish. Fold the edges of every piece. Put the *zrazy's* pieces in a deep frying-pan the folded side down. Make a little fish broth from the fish's head and bones, pour it into a frying-pan, put the lid on and cook on a low heat until done. Put the *zrazy* in a porcelain tureen, pour the sauce over them, and serve.

The mushroom filling

Chop the mushrooms fine, brown in the vegetable oil together with the finely chopped parsley and onions. Add some salt, pepper and 2 or 3 table-spoons of water. Stir well.

The sauce

Salt and mix 1 table-spoon of butter and 1 table-spoon of flour in a deep frying-pan. Gradually pour some fish broth over the mixture and bring to a boil. Add the white wine and cream, steam well until a little thick. Knead 1 table-spoon of butter in a separate pan, mix 3 egg-yolks (one by one) into it, gradually add the sauce to it, and steam well until as thick as sour cream. Add the lemon juice to taste.

FISH CAKES

5 oz (150 gm) filleted fish, 1 onion, 1 tbsp. wheat flour, 1 egg, finely ground dried bread-crumbs, 1 slice lemon, parsley, butter or melted butter

Cut the filleted pike-perch, hake, or mackerel into fine strips. Add the browned onion, wheat flour, a little lemon juice, raw egg, and minced parsley to them. Mix well, shape the filling into small balls, dip in the raw egg, and roll in the white bread crumbs. Brown the fish balls in sizzling butter in a frying-pan. Serve with boiled or fried potatoes.

STUFFED CABBAGE-ROLLS, FISHERMEN'S STYLE

7 oz (200 gm) cabbage, 15 oz (400 gm) cod or hake, 1 onion, 2 oz (50 gm) carrots, 2 oz (50 gm)

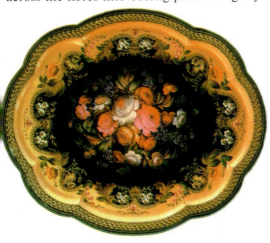

soft or boiled butter, 2.5 oz (75 gm) tomato sauce; salt and pepper to taste

Cut the filleted fish into small pieces. Mince the carrots and onion. Melt the butter in a frying-pan. When it sizzles, put in the fish, carrots, onion, and pepper. Salt and brown slightly. Remove the top leaves from the cabbage, wash in running water, and boil a little in salted water. Take the cabbage head out of the sauce-pan, disjoin the leaves, and pound the thick ones. Put the filling in each leaf and fold it like an envelope.

Grease a dripping-pan with the butter, put the cabbage-rolls in it, and stand in an oven. Bake until golden crust has formed on both sides. Take out the dripping-pan, pour the tomato sauce over the cabbage-rolls and bake in the oven until done.

BOILED LOBSTERS (CRAYFISH)

Variant one

Wash live lobsters, lower in boiling salted water, put the lid on, and keep boiling for 10—15 minutes. Take the boiled lobsters out with a colander, let the water flow out, and lay on a napkin-covered dish in the shape of a mound.

Variant two

Put some salt, onions, roots or sprigs of parsley, dill, peppercorns, and bay leaf in a pot. Add some red table wine, put in live lobsters, and boil for 10—15 minutes. Lay the boiled lobsters on a dish and decorate with parsley. Serve hot in a tureen with the broth in it.

CRAWFISHES BOILED IN BEER OR KVASS

10—12 crawfishes, 1 lb (500 gm) water, 7 oz (200 gm) wine, 15 oz (400 gm) beer or kvass, 1 bay leaf, herbs, $1/2$ oz (12 gm) salt, and 3—4 black peppercorns

Dilute 15 oz (400 gm) of beer or kvass in water and pour into a pot. Add the salt, condiment, wine, bring to a boil, put the crawfishes in the pot, and boil for 10 or 15 minutes. Serve hot together with the liquid.

HOT VEGETABLE AND MUSHROOM DISHES

It is impossible to imagine Russian cuisine without vegetables and mushrooms. The once used swade and turnip are now a little forgotten, while cabbage in Russia has always been and is one of the favourite food ingredients today. Ever since the 10th century, Russian people have come to know the beetroot, and from the time of Peter the Great, the potatoes. Now these vegetables are regular Russian fare.

Mushrooms, too, have always been very popular with our people. It is also worth mentioning that vegetables and mushrooms are essential during the Orthodox fast.

FRIED POTATOES

10 oz (300 gm) potatoes, 7 oz (200 gm) fat, $2/3$ oz (20 gm) soft butter, 2 onions, and 5 oz (150 gm) fresh mushrooms

Peel the potatoes, slice them into bars, rings, slices, or small cubes and brown in the fat, turning them to be browned evenly whereupon salting them. Pour the soft butter over them and add the browned onions and mushrooms. Shred and brown the onions. Mix them with the potatoes and top with the finely cut browned mushrooms.

BAKED POTATOES

Salt some peeled potatoes, put them in a dripping-pan, let them gradually bake and crust in an oven. Serve with butter.

POTATOES BAKED WITH ONIONS AND MUSHROOMS

10 oz (300 gm) potatoes, 2 oz (50 gm) fresh mushrooms, 2 onions, $2/3$ oz (20 gm) grated cheese, $1/2$ cup sour cream, dried bread-crumbs

Peel, boil, dry and slice the potatoes into rings. Grease a frying-pan with fat, put a layer of the sliced potatoes, a layer of the browned onions, a layer of the mushrooms, and another layer of the sliced potatoes. Pour the sour cream over them, strew with the bread-crumbs or grated cheese and bake.

BOILED POTATOES À LA TSARSKOYE SELO (TSAR'S VILLAGE)

1 lb (0.5 kg) potatoes, 7 oz (200 gm) butter, dill, parsley, and 3 hard-boiled eggs

Peel, slice, steam or boil the potatoes in salted water, and strain the broth. Strew with the minced dill and parsley. Heat 7 oz (200 gm) butter, mix with the hard-boiled eggs, heat well without bringing to a boil. Serve with the potatoes.

BOILED POTATOES IN HORSE-RADISH SAUCE

Potatoes and horse-radish sauce

Peel the potatoes, boil in salted water, strain the broth, and cut the boiled potatoes into slices. Put in a deep dish and pour the hot horse-radish sauce over them.

BOILED POTATOES WITH BOLETUSSES IN RED SAUCE

2 oz (50 gm) boletusses, potatoes, 4 tsp. flour, $1/4$ cup syrup from slightly browned sugar, lemon juice (1 lemon), granulated sugar, $1/2$ cup thin sour cream, 1 tbsp. soft butter

Boil 2 oz (50 gm) dried boletusses in salted water, strain the liquid, and mince the mushrooms. Cut the potatoes into cubes, boil, salt and strain the liquid. Bring one cup of mushroom liquid to a boil and trickle, stirring, some cold mushroom liquid

Hot Vegetable and Mushroom Dishes

mixed with 4 tea-spoons of flour into it. Bring to a boil. When the broth gets thick, add $1/4$ cup of sugar syrup, the juice from one lemon, sugar, $1/2$ cup of sour cream, and one table-spoon of butter. Heat without bringing to a boil. Pour the sauce over the hot potatoes with mushrooms, mix well, and heat without bringing to a boil.

The syrup

Sprinkle 7 oz (200 gm) granulated sugar in a frying-pan. Set on a burner and brown, stirring. Carefully pour 1.5 cups of boiling water into it and boil, stirring, until done.

POTATOES À LA PRINCE

15 oz (400 gm) potatoes, 10 oz (300 gm) cottage cheese, 4 oz (100 gm) butter, 3 egg-yolks, and 4 oz (100 gm) milk

Boil the potatoes, peel and cut them into slices, and salt. Put half the sliced potatoes in a sauce-pan. Grease the sauce-pan's inside with the butter. Mix the cottage cheese and butter until as thick as sour cream and put in the sauce-pan. Put the remaining potatoes in the sauce-pan. Shake up the egg-yolks in the milk. Pour the mixture over the potatoes and stand the sauce-pan in an oven for about one hour whereupon the dish is ready to be served.

POTATOES WITH MUSHROOM FILLING

18 potatoes, 2 oz (50 gm) dried boletusses, 1 onion, butter, flour, and 4 oz (100 gm) cream

Bake the potatoes. Peel, cut off the tops, and hollow out to make enough space to hold the stuffing. Boil the dried boletusses, strain the liquid, and chop the mushrooms fine. Shred and slightly brown the onion in the butter. Bring $1/2$ cup of the mushroom liquid to a boil, trickle, stirring, $1/2$ cup of cold mushroom liquid mixed with one tea-spoon of the flour into it. Bring to a boil. After it gets thick, add one table-spoon of butter, sour cream, mushrooms, onion, and salt. Mix well. Stuff the potatoes, lay them in a deep dish greased with the butter and sprinkled with the flour. Cover with the cut-off potato tops and sprinkle with melted butter. Gradually heat and brown in an oven. Serve the butter.

POTATO CAKES

5-6 peeled boiled potatoes, 1 egg, 1—1.5 tbsp. potato starch, salt to taste, milk, butter or sour cream

Boil the peeled potatoes until done, pour out the water, and mash until the mass is even. Add one raw egg, salt, starch, and a little milk until as thick as thick sour cream. Pour (with a spoon) into a greased (with salted pork fat) frying-pan and brown on both sides. Dip the cakes in the melted butter or sour cream, lay in a clay pot, put the lid on, and stand in a heated oven.

Serve hot with milk or clotted sour milk.

CAKES FROM RAW POTATOES

10 oz (300 gm) potatoes, $1/3$ oz (10 gm) flour, 0.04 oz (1 gm) cooking soda, $1/3$ oz (10 gm) melted butter, 1 oz (30 gm) sour cream or soft butter

Peel, grate, and press out the potatoes. Add the flour, cooking soda, and salt. Mix well, shape into cakes, and bake. Serve with butter or sour cream.

FRIED POTATO *ZRAZY* (STUFFED PIES)

Potatoes, 1 onion, $1/3$ oz (10 gm) melted butter, dried bread-crumbs, 1.5 cups cream or milk, 6 eggs, and flour

Boil and grate the potatoes. Shred and brown the onion in the butter. Pour the hot cream or milk over the bread-crumbs, have them chilled, and rub through a sieve. Gradually add the melted butter, eggs, and flour. Mix well. Add to the potatoes, mix thoroughly, shape into *zrazys*, roll in the flour, and brown in butter.

POTATO CAKES IN THE MANNER OF CHEESE CAKES

3 big potatoes, 3 egg-yolks, and 1 tbsp. soft butter

The filling: 1 lb (500 gm) cottage cheese, two eggs, sugar, and salt to taste

Boil the potatoes in slightly salted

Hot Vegetable and Mushroom Dishes

water, dry, and rub through a sieve. Mix the hot potatoes with the egg-yolks and butter. Salt to taste. Mix thoroughly. Rub the cottage cheese through a sieve and add the eggs, sugar, and salt. Shape the potato mass into cakes and stuff them with the filling. Spread the beaten egg-yolks over them and put in a dripping-pan oiled with vegetable oil.

POTATOES WITH PRUNES

15 oz (400 gm) potatoes, 2 oz (50 gm) butter, 4 eggs, $1/2$ cup cream or milk, salt, sugar, and prunes

Steam and grate the potatoes, mix the butter and eggs thoroughly and add to the potatoes. Add the cream or milk, salt, sugar to taste, and some flour to make moderately thick pastry. Roll the pastry out, cut into round flat cakes with a cup, and lay the steamed prunes (without the stones) on each of them. Fold the flat cakes up, spread the egg-whites over them, and brown in a frying-pan. Sprinkle with sugar and serve.

SHEPHERD'S PIE

10 oz (300 gm) potatoes, 2 oz (50 gm) milk, 1 egg, 1 oz (35 gm) sour cream, $2/3$ oz (20 gm) butter

Put the prepared potato puree in a frying-pan greased with the butter. Make a pattern with a spoon or knife on the surface of it. Spread the mixture of egg and sour cream over it and bake.

SHEPHERD'S PIE WITH SORREL

Potatoes, 3 eggs, 15 oz (400 gm) sorrel, butter, 1.5 cup milk, and 3 tbsp. flour

Peel and boil the potatoes in salted water. Strain the liquid, grate the potatoes, and add, stirring, the beaten egg-yolks and egg-whites. Mix well. Lay (in layers) in a deep dish greased with the butter, sprinkle with dried bread-crumbs, and add the sorrel leaves. Sprinkle with dried bread-crumbs, add some butter, and let it brown in an oven.

BOILED CABBAGE WITH MUSHROOMS

4 oz (100 gm) dried boletusses, cabbage, 4 tsp. flour, and butter

Boil the boletusses, strain the liquid, and mince. Chop the fresh cabbage into small bits, boil in the mushroom liquid, and strain. Lay in the middle of a deep dish in the shape of a mound and edge with the mushrooms. Bring three cups of the cabbage broth to a boil, sprinkle with the browned flour, salt, add one table-spoon of butter, and heat. Pour the resulting sauce over the cabbage.

FRIED CABBAGE IN THE SAUCE BECHAMEL

1 cabbage head, 1 cup milk, 3 oz (80 gm) vegetable oil, 3 eggs, 7 oz (200 gm) sour cream, 1 tbsp. flour, 2 oz (60 gm) pungent grated cheese, finely ground bread-crumbs; salt to taste

The sauce: *3 tbsp. vegetable oil, 2 tbsp. flour, 15 oz (400 gm) sour cream, 1 egg-yolk, 1 tbsp. lemon juice, and salt*

Cut the cabbage head in two, pour the hot salted milk over it, and boil until soft. Transfer the boiled cabbage into a colander, cut in long slices, roll in the flour, and brown in a frying-pan. Put in layers in a deep frying-pan greased with the oil and sprinkled with the bread-crumbs. Top each layer with the hot sauce covering the top layer with a thick layer of the sauce, sprinkle with the bread-crumbs and grated cheese, and brown in in oven.

The sauce

Mix the oil with the flour, brown a little, dilute with water, add the lemon juice and salt to taste, mix with the egg-yolk and sour cream. Heat without bringing to a boil.

CABBAGE STUFFED WITH RICE AND EGGS

1 medium-size cabbage, $2/3$ cup rice, 4 eggs, 4 oz (100 gm) vegetable oil, 2 oz (50 gm) margarine, 1 tbsp. finely ground dried bread-crumbs, 1 tbsp. minced parsley, 1 tbsp. minced dill, and salt to taste

The sauce: *1 cup milk, 2 tsp. flour, $1/2$ cup sour*

Hot Vegetable and Mushroom Dishes

cream, 1/2 cup tomato paste, 2 oz (50 gm) vegetable oil, and salt to taste

Cut the cabbage cross-wise, pour salted boiling water over it, lay on a piece of cheese-cloth the cross-section down. Separate the cabbage leaves from one another and put the filling between them. Wrap the leaves with the filling in the cheese-cloth tying its ends with a length of twine, and boil in vegetable oil in a sauce-pan with the lid on. When the cabbage is done, lay it out in a deep frying-pan, sprinkle with the bread-crumbs, pour the vegetable oil over it, brown in an oven, and pour the sauce over it. Shape the remaining filling into small balls, roll in the flour, brown in the vegetable oil, and lay around the cabbage.

The filling
Boil the rice in a small amount of water, add the heated margarine, salt, dill, and parsley, mix well and mix the raw eggs into it.

The sauce
Bring 1/2 cup of milk to a boil, pour, stirring, 1/2 cup of cold milk and flour in it. Let it set. Add the sour cream, tomato paste, margarine, and salt and heat without bringing to a boil.

CABBAGE-ROLLS STUFFED WITH BOILED BUCKWHEAT AND ONIONS

Boiled buckwheat, 1 cabbage, 1 onion, butter, eggs, 7 oz (200 gm) sour cream, dill, and parsley

Make 1/2 portion of crumbly boiled buckwheat. Shred the onion, brown in the butter, add to the boiled buckwheat, pour 1 table-spoon of butter into it, and mix well. Remove the top cabbage leaves, skald, and transfer into a colander. Lay the filling on the top cabbage leaves, fold in the shape of *zrazy*, bending the leaves' edges inside to prevent the buckwheat filling from falling out. Tie up the cabbage-rolls with a length of twine, roll in flour or (dipping in the eggs) bread-crumbs, and brown in the butter. Lay in a deep dish greased with the butter and sprinkled with the flour, sprinkle with the bread-crumbs, add some soft butter, and let it gradually brown in an oven. Pour the sour cream over it and heat well without bringing to a boil. Strew with the minced dill and parsley.

FRESH CABBAGE CAKES

1 cabbage, 200 gm finely ground dried white bread-crumbs, 2 cups milk, 3 eggs, 4 tbsp. butter; salt to taste

Chop the cabbages fine, boil in the boiling milk until done, and pour 1 table-spoon of melted butter into it. Pour the hot milk over the bread-crumbs and have them chilled. Add 1 raw and 2 hard-boiled eggs to the cabbages and salt. Shape into cakes and brown in the butter on both sides.

CABBAGE-ROLLS IN MUSHROOM SAUCE

1 cabbage head, 2 oz (60 gm) dried mushrooms, 1 cup rice, 4 oz (100 gm) butter, 4 oz (100 gm) margarine, 2—3 onions, pepper, and salt

The sauce: *2 cups mushroom liquid, 2/3 cup sour cream, 2 tsp. flour, and salt*

Wash the mushrooms in cold water and boil in three cups of water. Mince the onions and brown in fat. Add the chopped mushrooms and steamed rice. Salt and pepper. Cut out the cabbage's stump without letting the leaves come apart. Put the cabbage in a sauce-pan and boil on low heat until semi-done. Separate the leaves. Cut off the ribs. Lay the filling on each leaf and fold them in rolls. Put the rolls in a stew-pot with its bottom laid out with cabbage leaves. Salt, pour the liquid into it (up to 3/4 of the stew-pot's capacity), and simmer for two hours (preferably in an oven). It would be best to add half a cup of sour cream to the dish shortly before done. Serve with the sauce.

VEGETABLE *SOLYANKA*

1 lb (0.5 kg) sauerkraut, 1 onion, 2 pickled cucumbers, 1/2 cup pickled mushrooms, butter, cheese, dried bread-crumbs, herbs, soaked red bilberries and cranberries

Boil the sauerkraut. Mince and brown the onion, chop the pickled cucumbers (peeled and with the seeds removed), and pressed out pickled mushrooms. Grease a frying-pan with the butter, sprinkle with the grated cheese, lay the boiled cabbage into it, sprinkle with the finely ground bread-crumbs, and bake. Decorate with the herbs, soaked red bilberries, cranberries, and pickled cucumbers.

BAKED CARROT PUDDING

Carrot, 2 oz (50 gm) butter, dried bread-crumbs, 1.5 cup cream or milk, 6 tsp. flour, and 4 eggs

Chop and boil the carrot in butter. Pour the hot cream or milk over the bread-crumbs. Have them chilled. Mix 2 oz (50 gm) of melted butter with 3 egg-yolks and 6 teaspoons of flour. Add the ground bread-crumbs, carrot, and salt and mix well. Add three beaten egg-whites, mix well, and transfer into a deep dish greased with the butter and sprinkled with the bread-crumbs. Spread the raw eggs over it, sprinkle with the butter, and let it gradually brown in an oven. Serve the butter.

CARROT CAKES

15 medium-size carrots, 2.5 tbsp. manna-croup, $1/2$ cup milk, 4 tbsp. butter, 1 egg, 5 tbsp. finely ground bread-crumbs, and 1 cup sour cream or milk sauce

Boil the carrots and put them through a meat-grinder. Add the milk and butter and bring to a boil. Add the manna-croup, mix well, and boil, stirring, for about 15 minutes. Put in the egg and salt, mix thoroughly, chill, shape into cakes, roll in the finely ground bread-crumbs, and brown in the butter. Serve with the sour cream or milk sauce.

BOILED CUCUMBERS

4—5 cucumbers, 2 tbsp. flour, 3 tbsp. melted butter, 3 tbsp. tomato paste, $1/2$ cup sour cream, and herbs

Remove the skin from the cucumbers, cut into rings about $1/3$ in (1 cm) thick each, salt, roll in the flour, and brown in the boiled butter. Lay in a deep frying-pan or stew-pan. Add a little water, sour cream, and tomato paste and boil until done. Put the cucumbers and sauce in a dish and edge with toasts.

BROWNED VEGETABLE MARROWS

15 oz (400 gm) vegetable marrows, 2 tbsp. flour, 3 tbsp. butter; salt to taste

Skin the vegetable marrows, cut into rings about 1 in (3 cm) thick each, salt to taste, dip in the flour or thin dough, and brown in the hot butter. Serve hot.

VEGETABLE MARROW CAKES

5 small vegetable marrows, 2 eggs, 4 tbsp. flour, 2 tbsp. piquant grated cheese, 1 tsp. minced herbs, 4 oz (100 gm) vegetable oil; salt to taste

Peel the vegetable marrows, cut into cubes, lay into a colander, and put in boiling salted water for five minutes. Transfer into the colander, mash, and mix with the flour, egg, cheese, and herbs and salt to taste. Bake thick cakes from the resulting mass in the sizzling oil in a frying-pan.

VEGETABLE MARROWS WITH MUSHROOMS

2 lb (800 gm) vegetable marrows, 7 oz (200 gm) mushrooms, 2 onions, 3 tomatoes, 5 tbsp. vegetable oil, 2 tbsp. flour, $1/2$ cup mushroom liquid, 4 tbsp. sour cream, and salt

Peel and cut the vegetable marrows into rings $1/5$ in (0.5 cm) thick each, roll in the flour, and brown on both sides until golden brown. Wash the mushrooms thoroughly, boil, and chop fine. Brown the onions in a little oil, fry the mushrooms, add some mushroom liquid, sour cream, sliced tomatoes (with the skin removed), salt, and boil the mixture. Pour the sauce over the vegetable marrows, heat well, and serve with boiled potatoes.

CAULIFLOWER WITH BROWNED ONIONS

15 oz (400 gm) cauliflowers, 1 onion, 1—2 tbsp. vegetable oil; salt and black pepper to taste

Boil the cauliflower. Then cook it for another 5 minutes in the heated oil with

Hot Vegetable and Mushroom Dishes

the pan's lid on. Separately brown the onion in the vegetable oil. Sprinkle the cauliflower with the black pepper and pour the mixture of vegetable oil and browned onion over it.

BAKED CAULIFLOWER

15 oz (400 gm) cauliflowers, 3 tbsp. soft butter, 1.5 oz (40 gm) grated cheese, 1 tsp. finely ground dried bread-crumbs; salt to taste

Boil the cauliflowers in salted water, put in a frying-pan, sprinkle with the grated cheese and dried bread-crumbs, add some butter, and bake in an oven. Pour the butter over them and serve.

CHOPPED BEETROOT WITH SOUR CREAM

1 beetroot, 1 onion, butter, 1 cup sour cream, dill, and parsley

Boil the red beetroot in slightly salted water, strain, and chop. Mince and brown the onion in the butter. Add the onion, sour cream, and salt. Heat without bringing to a boil. Strew with the minced dill and parsley.

BEETROOT BAKED IN SOUR CREAM

1 beetroot, flour, butter, 7 oz (200 gm) sour cream, 2 eggs dill, and parsley

Bake or boil the beetroot, cut crosswise into slices, roll in the flour, and brown in the butter. Grease a deep dish with the butter, sprinkle with dried bread-crumbs, put the hot beetroot slices in layers in it, cover each layer with sour cream mixed with raw eggs (200 gm sour cream and two eggs), chopped dill, and parsley. Let it gradually heat in an oven without bringing to a boil.

BEETROOT COOKED WITH SAUERKRAUT

15 oz (400 gm) shredded sauerkraut, 800 beetroots, 2 oz (50 gm) butter, 1 cup sour cream, beetroot juice, dill, and parsley

Cook the sauerkraut and minced beetroots in the butter (with the lid on). Add the sour cream, beetroot juice, and salt. Heat without bringing to a boil. Strew with the minced dill and parsley and serve.

GREEN PEA OR HARICOT PUREE

1 cup green peas or haricots, $1/2$ cup milk, 4 tbsp. soft butter, and 1 onion

Boil the green peas or haricots, pour out the liquid, and grate immediately. Add the hot milk or butter and mix well. You can also add the browned onion to the puree.

BAKED TURNIPS

1 turnip, butter or butter with browned onions, or a ragout with fresh mushrooms

Lay the turnip on a dripping-pan and let it gradually brown in an oven. Serve the butter or butter with browned onions, or fresh mushrooms in sour cream.

TURNIP CAKES

7 oz (200 gm) finely ground white bread-crumbs, 4 small turnips, 2 cups milk, 4 tbsp. butter, 3 eggs, 2 medium-size onions, 5 tsp. flour; salt to taste

Cut the turnips into slices, scald, brown in the butter, and cook, adding boiling water, until done. Grate the cooked turnips. Pour the hot milk over the white bread-crumbs, have them chilled, and add to the turnips. Add, stirring, some boiled butter, eggs, sliced browned onions, and bread-crumbs. Shape the mass into cakes, roll them in the flour, and brown in butter.

TURNIPS STUFFED WITH SEMOLINA

Turnips, milk cream or milk, 3 tsp. manna-croup, butter, 2 eggs, 2 tsp. flour, 1 lemon, 4 oz (100 gm) sour cream, $1/2$ cup syrup from browned sugar, grated cheese, and 1.5 cup milk

Peel the turnips, make cuts on their tops, put in a dripping-pan, pour salted boiling water over them, and stand in an oven. When the turnips begin to get soft, take them out, hollow each one out so that the walls and bottom could hold the filling. Make semolina from 1.5 cups of milk and three tea-spoons of manna-croup, add one table-spoon of butter, mix well, and chill. Mix two eggs into it and salt. Stuff the turnips, lay in a deep dish greased with the butter and sprinkled with dried breadcrumbs. Rub the turnips' pulp through a sieve, add one table-spoon of butter browned with the two tea-spoons of flour, 1/2 cup of turnip broth, and bring to a boil. Pour the juice of one lemon in it, add the sour cream (100 gm), 1/2 cup of sugar syrup, and the sufficient amount of turnip broth and cream (milk) to make three cups of sauce. Mix well and heat without boiling. Top the turnips with the sauce, sprinkle with the grated cheese, add some butter, and let them gradually brown in an oven. Serve the rest of the sauce separately.

ROAST SWEDES

2—3 swedes, 3 tbsp. flour, 4 tbsp. vegetable oil, 1/2 cup sour cream, and herbs

Peel the swedes, boil until semi-done, cut into rings about 1/3 in (1 cm) each, salt, pepper, roll in the flour, brown on both sides in the vegetable oil, and roast in an oven until done. Lay the roasted swedes in a frying-pan, pour the sour cream over them, heat, and strew with the herbs.

HOT RUSSIAN SALAD (VINAIGRETTE)

Vegetables, 3 pickled cucumbers, 10 oz (300 gm) pickled mushrooms, and sauce

Cut potatoes fine and boil them in salted water. Separately boil turnips, carrots, celery, onion, cauliflower, swedes, canned green peas, and leek. Strain each broth and mix them together. Add the pickled cucumbers (chopped) and pickled mushrooms to the boiled vegetables. Make a lemon sauce, pour part of it over the vinaigrette, and heat without boiling. Serve the remaining sauce separately.

FRIED MUSHROOMS

3 lb (1.5 kg) fresh or 2 lb (800 gm) pickled milk-agarics or saffron milk caps, 1 cup sour cream, and butter

Roll the mushrooms in flour and brown a little in the sizzling butter. Add the sour cream and heat in an oven without boiling. Serve boiled potatoes.

FRESH MUSHROOMS WITH SOUR CREAM

Mushrooms, 1 onion, butter, flour, and 7 oz (200 gm) sour cream

Shred the onion, brown a little in the butter. Chop and roll the mushrooms in the flour, add them to the shredded onion, salt, add some butter, and brown in a frying-pan until done. Pour the sour cream in it, mix well, heat without bringing to a boil, and serve.

DRIED AND FRESH MUSHROOMS IN SOUR CREAM

7 oz (200 gm) fresh mushrooms, 1.5 oz (40 gm) dried mushrooms, 7 oz (200 gm) pickled mushrooms, 1/3 oz (10 gm) melted butter, and 1/2 cup sour cream

Wash and cut boletusses or other kind of mushrooms. Grease a frying-pan with fat and heat it. Shred some onions, brown, add the mushrooms (chopped), and fry until most of the liquid is evaporated. Add the sour cream and cook. Press out the pickled mushrooms liquid, wash with warm water, brown and cook with the sour cream.

BOLETUSSES WITH POTATOES

2 oz (50 gm) dried boletusses, potatoes, and sour-cream sauce

Keep the boletusses in salted water for about six hours. Boil them in the same water, strain, and chop fine. Use the mushroom liquid to make the sauce. Peel the potatoes, cut them into slices, boil in salted boiling water, and strain. Make the sauce. Heat the mushrooms and potatoes in it without boiling.

MUSHROOMS, TAMBOV STYLE

1.5 lb (700 gm) fresh mushrooms, 8 potatoes, 2 onions, 2 oz (50 gm) butter, 1/2 cup sour cream, 1.5 oz (40 gm) grated cheese; salt to taste

Boil, shred, and brown the mushrooms with the onions. Peel the potatoes, cut into cubes, salt, brown a little, mix with the mushrooms and onions, pour the sour cream over them, sprinkle with the grated cheese, and bake in a frying-pan in an oven.

Hot Vegetable and Mushroom Dishes

PICKLED MILK-AGARICS OR SAFFRON MILK CAPS IN SOUR CREAM

1.5 lb (600 gm) pickled mushrooms, 1/2 cup sour cream, butter, and potato puree

Brown the mushrooms in the sizzling butter, pour the sour cream over them, heat in an oven without bringing to a boil. Serve the potato puree.

ROAST MUSHROOMS

15 oz (400 gm) fresh mushrooms, 5 oz (130 gm) butter, 3—4 tbsp. wheat flour, 1 onion, clove, parsley; salt, pepper, sugar, and lemon juice to taste

Put the mushrooms in the boiling butter, add salt, pepper, sugar, and lemon juice to taste. Let them boil for about five minutes, trickle the flour, add 1/2 cup of the mushroom liquid, a pinch of minced parsley and the onion stuffed with clove. Keep on browning on low heat for another thirty minutes. Take out the onion and splash the lemon juice on the roast mushrooms.

MUSHROOM PUDDING

10 oz (300 gm) mushrooms, 2 raw eggs, 4 oz (100 gm) flour, 2 oz (50 gm) grated cheese, 1/2 cup milk, and dried bread-crumbs

Boil the mushrooms in salted water, transfer into a colander, have them dried, and chop fine. Pour boiling milk over the bread-crumbs and have them chilled. Shake well, add the butter mixed with two egg-yolks, mushrooms, salt, pepper, flour, and grated cheese. Make sure the mixture is sour-cream thick. Mix the egg-whites into the mass and nead the resulting pastry carefully. Bake in a greased mould. Pour melted butter over it and serve.

MUSHROOM AND RICE PUDDING

15 dried mushrooms, 1 cup rice, 3 onions, 3 raw eggs, 5 tbsp. butter, 3 tbsp. dried bread-crumbs, ground pepper, and salt

Boil the mushrooms until done, strain, and chop fine. Put the salt, butter, and rice in the mushroom liquid, mix well, and simmer. When the rice is sufficiently saturated with the liquid, mix thoroughly, put the lid on, and cook on low heat in an oven until done. Add the rice and beaten egg-yolks to the chopped mushrooms and mix well. Add the beaten egg-whites and mix thoroughly again. Lay the filling in a greased mould or frying-pan sprinkled with the finely ground dried bread-crumbs, put the lid on, and bake for 50—60 minutes. Take the pudding out of the oven, 5—10 minutes later lay it out in a dish, and pour the melted butter over it.

MUSHROOM PIE

10 oz (300 gm) white bread, 2 oz (50 gm) dried boletusses, 2 tbsp. melted butter, 2 tbsp. finely ground dried bread-crumbs, 1/2 cup sour cream, 1 tbsp. grated cheese, and 1 egg

Wash the mushrooms several times in running water, put in a sauce-pan, pour four cups of water over them. Boil in the same water until soft. Take the mushrooms out and cut into noodles. Sprinkle the liquid with the finely ground dried bread-crumbs, add the minced mushrooms and sour cream, and steam well without bringing to a boil. Cut the bread into thin slices and brown in the butter on one side. Lay out the mushroom mass in a deep frying-pan and top with the bread the browned side down. Spread the egg over it, sprinkle with the grated cheese, and bake.

MUSHROOM QUENELLES

2 oz (50 gm) dried mushrooms, 1 onion, 1 egg, 4 oz (100 gm) sour cream, 3 tbsp. ground dried bread-crumbs, and 4 oz (100 gm) butter

Soak dried mushrooms in cold water for 2—4 hours. Boil in the same water, transfer into a colander, and wash well. Chop the mushrooms fine and add to minced browned onions. Mix dried bread-crumbs into eggs and sour cream, salt, mix well, shape into balls the size of nutmegs, and put in boiling water.

CEREALS, ROUND LOAVES, *KRUPENIKS*, AND PUDDINGS

This part deals with the most popular Russian food, i.e. cereals. Actually, it is quite understandable, since the tiller people mostly ate cereals.

One could make not only gruel but also round loaves, *krupeniks*, and different kinds of puddings from grain. The above are very useful and nourishing dishes.

SEMOLINA IN MILK

1 cup manna-croup, 4 cups milk, 2 tbsp. sugar, 1/2 tsp. salt; butter to taste

Boil the milk, then trickle, stirring, the manna-croup, add the salt and sugar, and boil for about ten minutes until thick.

SEMOLINA WITH CREAM

2/3 cup manna-croup, 1.5 cups cream, 4 tbsp. sugar, and 4 oz (100 gm) butter

Pour the cream into a not too deep large sauce-pan, set on a burner, remove the forming scum, and keep it aside. When you have half the cream left, trickle, stirring, the manna-croup, add the sugar, butter, and scum. Mix well, boil thoroughly, and stand in an oven to have the gruel sufficiently browned.

MILK SEMOLINA WITH FRUIT

6 cups milk, 24 tsp. manna-croup, 3 tbsp. butter, 6 eggs, sugar, fresh or 15 oz (400 gm) dried fruit, and 1 cup sugar

Cook semolina in milk, add the butter, mix well, and have it chilled. Mix the egg-yolks into 1/2 cup of sugar, mix with the semolina, add the beaten egg-whites, and mix thoroughly. Put the semolina, then peeled sliced pears or apricots, plums or apples sprinkled with sugar, in a deep dish greased with the butter and sprinkled with finely ground dried bread-crumbs. Cover the top layer with three beaten egg-whites mixed with three tea-spoons of sugar. Brown in an oven. Serve the cream or milk.

MILK SEMOLINA WITH PRUNES

15 oz (400 gm) manna-croup, 3 tbsp. butter, 2 cups sugar, milk, 10 oz (300 gm) prunes (without the stones), 5 eggs, prune broth, 3 tsp. corn flour or potatoe-starch

Pour the manna-croup into half a sauce-pan, add salt, sugar (1/2 cup), and the butter. Pour the hot milk over it and mix well. Stand in an oven, in a frying-pan with boiling water, adding more boiling water as it boils away. Put four egg-yolks mixed with 1/2 cup of sugar in the chilled semolina, add four beaten egg-whites, and mix well. Boil the prunes (without the bones) with one cup of sugar, and strain the liquid. Grease a deep frying-pan with butter and sprinkle with dried bread-crumbs. Put the semolina and prunes in the frying-pan, spread the raw eggs over it, and brown gradually in an oven. Serve cream (milk) or the prune sauce.

The prune sauce

Add to the prune broth the amount of water to make three cups of sauce. Have it chilled, mix 1/2 cup of the broth with three tea-spoons of corn flour or potatoe-starch. Trickle, stirring, into the remaining boiled broth and bring to a boil until thick.

GRUEL *GURYEVSKAYA*

24 tsp. manna-croup, 9 cups milk (7 cups milk and 2 cups cream), 4 oz (100 gm) candied nutmegs, 4 oz (100 gm) almonds, 7 oz (200 gm) candied fruit, 3 egg-yolks, 1/2 cup sugar, 2 oz (50 gm) butter, and sugar syrup

Make semolina from the manna-croup and

6 cups of milk, add 1/2 cup of sugar, and 2 oz (50 gm) of butter. Pour two cups of cream and one cup of milk into a flat clay tureen, and stand in an oven. Bring to a boil. When brown scum forms, lower it to the bottom with a spoon. Do it again three times. Sprinkle the gruel with 4 oz (100 gm) of crushed candied nutmegs and almonds, add 7 oz (200 gm) of sliced candied fruit, and mix thoroughly. Take the browned scum out of the milk. Mix three egg-yolks into the milk, add to the gruel, and mix well. Grease a deep dish with some butter, sprinkle with finely ground dried bread-crumbs, lay the gruel on it interspersing it with the browned scum. Sprinkle it with sugar, add some butter, and let it brown in an oven. Pour the sugar syrup and cream (milk) over it and serve.

BOILED BUCKWHEAT

4 oz (100 gm) buckwheat, 5 oz (150 gm) water, 10 mg melted butter

According to Russian tradition, boiled buckwheat is made in clay pots. Put buckwheat in them (3/4 of its capacity), add salt and boiled milk, and pour boiling water over it as high as the pot's top, mix well, and stand in an oven for about three or four hours. One hour before the end of boiling the pot is covered with a frying-pan and turned upside down. Half an hour before serving, it is covered with moist fabric for the porridge to come apart from the pot. Serve with cold boiled milk.

PUFFED BOILED BUCKWHEAT

2.5 cups buckwheat, 5 cups milk, 4 oz (100 gm) butter; salt to taste

Sort out the buckwheat, wash well, put in a dripping-pan and dry in an oven. Transfer into a claypot or sauce-pan, add the milk and butter, salt, mix well, and stand in an oven. Have it chilled, rub through a colander or sieve, lay in a dish, and serve cold. Separately serve milk and sugar.

THIN BOILED BUCKWHEAT

15 oz (400 gm) crushed buckwheat, 9 cups water, butter, milk, and salt

In popular cuisine thin boiled buckwheat is only cooked from crushed buckwheat while normal buckwheat is used to make crumbly boiled buckwheat.
Sort out the crushed buckwheat, wash well, pour boiling water over it, and boil until the buckwheat is saturated with the water. Add the salt, butter, and hot milk and cook until done.

GRECHNEVIK (BUCKWHEAT PIES)

1/3 oz (10 gm) buckwheat, 1 egg, vegetable oil; salt to taste

Make boiled glutinous buckwheat, chill to about 60°C, add the beaten raw egg, mix well, transfer into sauce-pans or dripping-pans greased with butter. When the boiled buckwheat sets, cut it into pieces 1.5 in (4×4 cm) each and brown on both sides in the vegetable oil.

KRUPENIKS

2 cups boiled buckwheat, 1 cup cottage cheese, 2 tbsp. sugar, 2 eggs, butter, and sour cream

Add the cottage cheese (rubbed through a sieve), salt, sugar, butter, and raw eggs to the chilled glutinous gruel and mix well. Lay the mass in dripping-pans greased with the butter and sprinkled with finely ground dried bread-crumbs in a layer 1 in (2.5—3 cm) thick. Spread the sour cream and eggs over the surface of the dripping-pans and bake.

Cereals, Round Loaves, *Krupeniks*, and Puddings

SALNIK (A DISH WITH VEAL FAT OR SALTED PORK FAT)

2 cups boiled buckwheat, 2 eggs, 2—3 tbsp. butter, some veal fat or salted pork fat

Put the butter in the viscid boiled buckwheat and add two chopped hard-boiled eggs. Cover the bottom and walls of a clay pot with the veal fat. Fill the pot with the boiled buckwheat, top it with bits of the veal fat, and bake for about 1 hour in a hot oven. Instead of the veal fat you can use sliced pounded salted pork fat. You can bake the dish in a frying-pan.

BOILED BUCKWHEAT WITH MUSHROOMS

15 oz (400 gm) buckwheat, 10 oz (300 gm) fresh mushrooms, 1 onion, 1.5 oz (40 gm) melted butter, and salt

Sort out, wash, and mince the mushrooms. Boil in salted water. When the mushrooms are done, sprinkle the buckwheat in the boiling mushroom liquid and boil on low heat. Serve with the finely chopped and browned onion.

CRUMBLY MILLET PORRIDGE

10 oz (300-400 gm) millet, 2 oz (50 gm) butter, and salt

Boil millet porridge in water with the addition of the fat. Serve with butter, cottage or sheep's milk cheese, or with minced dill in tomato sauce.

MILLET GRUEL WITH A PUMPKIN

2/3 cup millet, 7 oz (200 gm) pumpkin, 3 cups water or milk, salt and sugar

Remove the skin and seeds from the pumpkin, cut into small cubes, put in the boiling milk or water, add the salt and sugar, and bring to a boil. Add the washed millet and boil until done.

RICE GRUEL WITH MILK

6 cups milk, 10 oz (300 gm) rice, 1 tbsp. butter, 3/4 cup sugar, and 4 oz (100 gm) raisins

Make a gruel from the rice and milk, add the butter, salt, and sugar and mix well. Add the raisins and heat without bringing to a boil.

CRUMBLY PEARL-BARLEY PORRIDGE

1 cup pearl-barley, 3 cups water, 2 oz (50 gm) butter or pork fat, and salt

Sort out the pearl-barley. Wash and pour hot water over it. Bring to a boil.

Pour out the water and again pour slightly salted hot water over it. Add the fat, mix well, put the lid on, and boil in an oven until the pearl-barley is well saturated with the water. Mix well. The resulting mass becomes crumbly and does not get dry.

Serve with milk or cracklings and browned onions.

BOILED PEARL-BARLEY WITH ONIONS

4 oz (100 gm) pearl-barley, pork fat, 1 onion

Pour warm water over the pearl-barley, pour it out, and wash the pearl-barley with hot water.

Bring the water to a boil, add salt and the pearl-barley, and make crumbly pearl-barley porridge. Shred the onions, brown slightly in the fat, and add to the mass.

CRUMBLY FINE-GROUND BARLEY PORRIDGE

10 oz (300 gm) fine-ground barley, 1.5 oz (40 gm) fat, and salt

Cook fine-ground barley porridge the way pearl-barley porridge is made. Serve with onions browned in the fat and some kind of sauce usually served with stewed meat.

OATMEAL PORRIDGE

1.5 cup oatmeal flakes, 3.5 cups milk; butter, sugar, and salt to taste

Put the flakes in the hot milk, add some sugar, salt, and butter and boil, stirring, for 10 minutes.

MESHANKA (MISHMASH)

To cook *meshanka* a mixture of different groats is used, one of them being whole and

the rest crushed. Grate not less than two kinds of vegetables on a coarse grater (one cup of vegetables per cup of mixed groats). Lay one third of the vegetables on the bottom of a pan. Put a layer of the mixed groats on the vegetables, then again the vegetables until you have three layers (with the vegetables on top). Pour hot salted water over it covering the top layer. Stand in an oven for 6—8 minutes. Serve with sour cream.

CRUMBLY BOILED GERMAN WHEAT

15 oz (400 gm) German wheat, butter, cream or milk

It is cooked like crumbly pearl-barley porridge. Serve the butter, cream or milk.

GERMAN WHEAT BOILED IN MILK

15 oz (400 gm) German wheat, butter, cream or milk

Cook it the way described above but pour hot milk instead of water over it. Serve the butter and cream or milk.

KARAVAI WITH MUSHROOMS

4 oz (100 gm) fine-ground barley, 7 oz (200 gm) water, 1 oz (30 gm) dried mushrooms, 1.5 oz (40 gm) onions, 1 raw egg, $2/3$ oz (20 gm) dried bread-crumbs, 2 oz (50—60 gm) sour cream

In Russia *karavai* is any kind of round loaf or cake made from cereals.
Make a glutious gruel with the mushrooms and browned onions, add one egg-yolk and salt. Mix well. Add the beaten egg-white and bake a *karavai*. Serve with the sour cream.

BUCKWHEAT *KRUPENIK* WITH SOUR CLOTTED MILK

2 oz (50 gm) butter, 4 eggs, 6 cups sour clotted milk and sour cream, 10 oz (300 gm) buckweat, and 1 tsp. sugar

Rub the butter through a sieve, mix with three eggs, gradually add, stirring, the sour clotted milk and sour cream. Add the buckwheat, sugar, and salt. Mix well. Lay the mixture in a deep frying-pan greased with butter and sprinkled with flour. Spread one raw egg over it, sprinkle with butter, and let it brown in an oven. Serve butter and cream or milk.

BOILED BUCKWHEAT *KRUPENIK* WITH BROWNED ONIONS

Boiled buckwheat, 2 onions, 7 oz (200 gm) sour cream, 4 eggs, cheese, and butter

Make half a portion of crumbly boiled buckwheat. Mince 2 onions, brown in the butter, and add to the boiled buckwheat. Add 7 oz (200 gm) sour cream, 1 tablespoon of butter, 3 beaten eggs, and salt. Mix well. Lay in a deep frying-pan greased with butter and sprinkled with dried breadcrumbs. Spread one egg over it, sprinkle with grated cheese and butter, and let it brown in an oven. Serve the butter.

BUCKWHEAT *KRUPENIK* WITH EGGS AND CHEESE

Buckwheat, milk, 5 tbsp. grated cheese, 3 eggs, and butter

Boil buckwheat in the milk, add 2 tablespoons of the butter and 3 table-spoons of the grated cheese. Mix well. Add 3 chopped hard-boiled eggs and mix thoroughly. Put in a deep frying-pan greased with butter and sprinkled with finely ground dried breadcrumbs. Sprinkle with the butter and grated cheese and let it brown in an oven. Serve the butter or cream (milk).

RICE PUDDING WITH RAISINS

$1/2$ cup rice, 1 cup milk, about 1 cup water, 1 egg, salt, sugar, raisins, and a spot of vanilline

Put the rice, raisins, salt, and sugar (to taste) in the boiling water and boil, stirring, for 10—15 minutes. Pour the hot milk into it and stir again. Grease a frying-pan with butter, sprinkle the bottom and brims with dried bread-crumbs, lay the boiled rice in the pan, spread 1 egg and sour cream over the mass, add the vanilline, and bake on low heat in an oven. Serve cold, with jam, raisins, butter or sour cream.

FRITTERS FROM SEMOLINA

7 oz (200 gm) manna-croup, 5 cups milk, butter, 2 eggs, and flour

Boil a thick semolina with 5 cups of milk. Add 1 table-spoon of the butter and salt. Mix well and chill. Cut into cubes, roll in the flour, and brown in the butter.

FRITTERS FROM BOILED BUCKWHEAT

7 oz (200 gm) buckwheat, flour, and butter

Boil the buckwheat and have it chilled. Cut into thin slices, roll in the flour, and brown in the butter.

RICE OR PEARL-BARLEY CAKES

10 oz (300 gm) rice or pearl-barley, butter, dried bread-crumbs, 1 cup cream or milk, eggs, flour, dill and parsley

Boil the rice (pearl-barley), pour 2 oz (50 gm) butter into it, and mix well. Pour one cup of hot cream or milk over the bread-crumbs, chill, and rub through a sieve. Add three eggs, bread-crumbs (in cream or milk), salt, flour, dill, and parsley. Mix well and shape into small cakes. Roll in the flour (or finely ground bread-crumbs, dipping them in an egg), and brown in the butter.

CAKES FROM BOILED BUCKWHEAT WITH SOUR CREAM

Onions, 10 oz (300 gm) buckwheat, butter, dried bread-crumbs, 1 cup cream or milk, eggs, and flour

Boil the buckwheat until crumbly. Make cakes from it (the way rice cakes are made), using shredded browned onions instead of dill and parsley.

OATMEAL PANCAKES

4 oz (100 gm) groats, 10 oz (300 gm) milk, $^2/_3$ oz (20 gm) sugar, 1 egg, and melted butter

Cook thin porridge, rob it through a sieve, add one egg, and bake pancakes. Eat them with sour milk, sour cream, cowberries, and sugar. Oatmeal pancakes are served in addition to soups and fish-soups.

SEMOLINA PUDDING WITH CHERRIES

10 oz (300 gm) white bread, 1 cup manna-croup, 1 lb (500 gm) cherries, 2 pints (1 litre) milk, $^1/_2$ cup granulated sugar, 2 tsp. grated almonds or nuts, 3 tbsp. margarine, 3 eggs; salt to taste

Bring the milk to a boil, add the salt, grated almonds or nuts, sugar, and margarine. Sprinkle the manna-croup into it and boil, stirring, until thick. Chill slightly, add the eggs and the grated crumbs of white bread. Mix the cherries (with the stones removed) with the mass and lay in a greased frying-pan. Bake in an oven.

PUDDING WITH APPLES AND SYRUP

7 oz (200 gm) white bread, 1 cup milk, 6 medium-size apples, 2 eggs, 2 tbsp. sugar, 1 tbsp. soft butter, 1 tbsp. finely ground dried bread-crumbs, $^3/_4$ cup flavoured syrup

The syrup: *3 tbsp. sugar and 1 tbsp. sweet wine per $^3/_4$ cup water*

Slice the white bread into rectangular pieces. Cut the left-overs into small cubes and dry them a little. Peel the apples, cut them into small cubes, and mix with the dried cubes of bread. Grease a frying-pan with the butter and sprinkle with the finely ground dried bread-crumbs. Lay the rectangular pieces of bread on the bottom and along the walls of the pan, preliminarily soaking them in a mixture of the eggs, milk, and sugar. Mix the apple cubes with the dried bread-crumbs and put them in the middle of the frying-pan. Pour the rest of the mixture (eggs, milk, and sugar) over them. Top them with the slices of bread and spread raw eggs over them. Bake in an oven. Keep the pudding in the frying-pan for 7—10 minutes, lay out in a dish, and soak in the flavoured syrup.

To make the syrup dilute the sugar in water, bring to a boil, chill, and pour one tablespoon of sweet wine into it.

APPLE PUDDING

12 apples, 9 eggs, 1 cup sugar, 1 cup sour cream, 12 finely ground sweet bread-crumbs

Bake the apples. Beat 8 egg-yolks with the sugar. Add the sour cream and finely ground sweet bread-crumbs. Mix well. Add eight beaten egg-whites and mix well. Put half the mass in a deep dish greased with butter and sprinkled with the bread-crumbs. Cover with the apple puree and top it with the rest of the mass. Spread one raw egg over it and brown in an oven. Serve some cream (milk) or fruit syrup.

PUDDING FROM FRESH APPLES AND RAISINS

12 fresh apples, 1 lemon, 4 oz (100 gm) dried sugary bread-crumbs, 8 eggs, 1 cup sugar, 4 oz (100 gm) butter, and 7 oz (200 gm) raisins

Peel the apples, remove the core, cut into slices, and sprinkle with the juice of one lemon. Mix 7 beaten egg-whites thoroughly with a cupful of sugar and add the grated butter. Mix well. Add the mixture to the sliced apples, finely ground dried bread-crumbs, and raisins. Mix again. Add 7 beaten egg-whites and mix well. Transfer into a deep tin container greased with some butter and sprinkled with bread-crumbs. Spread the egg-yolk over it, sprinkle with sugar, and let it gradually brown in an oven. Serve with cream.

THE MONKS' CAKE

7 oz (200 gm) rye bread, 0.5 cup sugar, 2 tbsp. butter, 2 cups nuts, a little finely cut lemon peel, 5 oz (150 gm) prunes, and 2 eggs

Soak the bread in water, pound it into a gruelly mass, and squeeze the water out of it. Add the beaten egg-yolks preliminarily mixing them with the sugar. Add the butter, finely cut lemon peel, crushed nuts, and thoroughly beaten egg-whites. Mix carefully and transfer into a greased tin form. Top it with the prunes and bake in a heated oven.

RYE BREAD-CRUMBS PUDDING WITH NUTS

4 oz (100 gm) finely ground rye bread-crumbs, 1 cup milk, 4 oz (100 gm) ground nuts, 3 tbsp. butter, 9 eggs, and 1 cup sugar

Pour the milk over the finely ground rye bread-crumbs. Stir well and mix with the ground nuts and warm butter. Gradually add, stirring, eight egg-yolks mixed with some sugar. Add eight beaten egg-whites and mix well. Lay it out in a deep dish greased with some butter and sprinkled with the bread-crumbs. Spread one egg over the mass, sprinkle with the remaining sugar, and brown in an oven. Serve cream or milk.

DISHES FROM EGGS, COTTAGE CHEESE, AND MILK

In Russian cuisine widely used are fried, baked, boiled, and raw eggs. Most popular are different kinds of omelettes and fried eggs, i.e., the sources of biologically active substances.

Cottage cheese has also been quite popular in Russia. In olden times it was called cheese. Cottage cheese was used not only for making sweet dishes, pies, and curd dumplings but also made the base of hot second courses.

Milk dishes had a place of their own in Russian cuisine.

BOILED EGGS

Wash the eggs well, lower in boiling water, and boil for 3—4 minutes. You will have soft-boiled eggs.

If you boil an egg for 5—6 minutes, you will have a scrambled egg and if for 8—10 minutes, it will be a hard-boiled egg.

BAKED EGGS

Pierce an egg on both sides, put in a dripping pan, and bake in a hot oven for about 10 minutes. Turn the egg over 2—3 times.

FRIED EGGS

4 eggs and butter

Let the butter sizzle in a large frying-pan, put the eggs in it and salt. Serve the eggs once they are done.

BAKED EGG PASTE

7 eggs, butter, green onions, dill, and parsley

Put the butter in a large frying-pan, let it sizzle, and remove from the oven. Carefully put the eggs in it, salt, and sprinkle with some butter. Gradually bake it in an oven. Serve with the addition of the minced green onions, dill, and parsley.

EGGS WITH FRESH MUSHROOMS

10 oz (300 gm) mushrooms, butter, 5 oz (150 gm) sour cream, 9 eggs, 15 tbsp milk, and parsley

Mince the mushrooms, salt, brown in the butter, pour in the sour cream, and mix well. Transfer into a deep dish greased with some butter and sprinkled with finely ground dried bread-crumbs. Heat in an oven without bringing to a boil. Mix the fresh eggs with 15 table-spoons of milk, salt, pour the mixture over the mushrooms, and brown in the oven. Serve immediately with butter, minced dill, and parsley.

EGGS WITH NETTLE

5 oz (150 gm) nettle, 1 oz (30 gm) minced onions, herbs, eggs, and butter

Boil the nettle in salted boiling water and transfer into a sieve. Heat the minced onions in butter in a frying-pan, put the cut nettle in it, add the minced herbs (garden-cress or celery), salt, mix well, and boil thoroughly. Spread the eggs over the mass, brown slightly in the frying-pan, and heat in an oven until done.

THE «BABUSHKA» (GRANDMOTHER) EGGS

10 eggs, 7 oz (200 gm) sour cream, and butter

Beat the egg-yolks with the sour cream, add the beaten egg-whites, salt, and mix well. Put the mixture in the sizzling butter in a large frying-pan. Keep stirring until done.

OMELETTE WITH DILL AND PARSLEY

12 eggs, 24 tbsp. milk, dill, parsley, and butter

Beat the egg-yolks, dilute with the milk, add the minced herbs, salt, and beaten egg-whites. Mix well. Put in the sizzling butter in a frying-pan. Let it rise and brown in an oven and serve.

DOUBLE OMELETTE WITH VEGETABLES

Vegetables, 7 oz (200 gm) canned green peas, 8 eggs, 16 tbsp. milk, butter, 16 tsp. flour, and sauce

Cut and cook asparagus, turnip, potatoes, carrots, and cauliflower in salted boiling water. Strain, add the canned green peas. Shake 4 eggs with 8 tea-spoons of milk and 8 tea-spoons of flour, salt, pour out into a large frying-pan with sizzling butter in it, and let it gradually brown in an oven. Make the same kind of omelette. Make a sauce with dill and parsley. Grease a deep dish with butter, put one hot omelette in it, cover it with the vegetables, sauce, put the other hot omelette on top, sprinkle with butter, and gradually heat in an oven. Serve the remaining sauce separately.

OMELETTE WITH MINCED APPLES

9 apples, 6 eggs, 3 egg-whites, 5 oz (150 gm) sugar, and butter

Peel and mince the apples. Mix the egg-yolks with the sugar, add the minced apples, and mix well. Add the beaten egg-whites and mix thoroughly. Put in a frying-pan with the sizzling butter in it and gradually brown in an oven.

MUSHROOM OMELETTE

9 oz (250 gm) mushrooms, 3 eggs, 4 tbsp. flour, mineral soda water, parsley, and spice

Cut the mushrooms into small slices, cook in butter together with the parsley and spice for 5—10 minutes. Separately beat the egg-whites. Make a dough (as thick as sour cream) from the egg-yolks, flour, and mineral soda water. Mix it all with the mushrooms and bake in a frying-pan like a normal omelette. Serve hot with a vegetable salad.

BOILED COTTAGE-CHEESE PANCAKES

2 lb (800 gm) cottage cheese, 4 oz (100 gm) sour cream, 3 eggs, flour, 1 tbsp. butter

Squeeze and rub the cottage cheese through a sieve. Add, stirring, one table-spoon of the soft butter, sour cream, eggs, salt, and a little flour.

Roll out and slice into thin strips two fingers wide and cut in the shape of diamonds two fingers long. Cook in salted boiling water and strain. Serve the sour cream and hot butter.

COTTAGE-CHEESE *BABKI* (CAKES)

5 oz (150 gm) cottage cheese, 2 tbsp. flour, 1 egg, sour cream

Make a cottage-cheese paste (a little thinner than the one for cottage-cheese pancakes), shape it into dumplings with a spoon, and put in boiling water. When the *babki* have surfaced, take them out, lay into portion frying-pans, cover with the sour cream, and bake in an oven.

COTTAGE-CHEESE PUDDING

1 lb (500 gm) cottage cheese, 5 eggs, 1 cup sugar, vanilline, dried lemon peel, butter to taste, and 1/2 cup jam

Rub the cottage cheese through a sieve, add the egg-yolks, sugar, vanilline, dried lemon peel, and butter. Mix thoroughly. If the cottage-cheese paste is thick, you can add some jam to it. Put the paste in a sauce-pan greased with butter and sprinkled with finely ground dried bread-crumbs and bake in an oven for 30—40 minutes.

Before serving, sprinkle the *babki* with finely ground dried bread-crumbs and vanilla and adorn with jam.

Dishes from Eggs, Cottage Cheese, and Milk

FRIED COTTAGE-CHEESE PANCAKES

7 oz (200 gm) cottage cheese, 1/3 cup flour, 1 egg, sour cream, and butter

They are made like cottage-cheese *babki*, but fried in sizzling butter. Serve pouring the sour cream upon them.

COTTAGE-CHEESE BALLS WITH APPLES

Apples, 2 eggs, 1 tbsp. sugar, 9 oz (250 gm) cottage cheese, 1 tsp. cooking soda, 2—3 tbsp. flour, and salt

Mix the eggs with sugar and salt, add the cottage cheese and cooking soda with vinegar, sprinkle with the flour and make a dough. Peel the apples, remove the core, and grate them. Add the sugar.

Cut the dough into small pieces, roll out, and put the apple mass in the middle of each piece. Shape them into small balls. Fry them like doughnuts in vegetable oil (butter or boiled butter). Sprinkle with castor sugar and serve.

COTTAGE-CHEESE PUDDING WITH RAISINS

2 lb (800 gm) cottage cheese, 6 eggs, 1/2 cup sugar, 4 oz (100 gm) butter, and 7 oz (200 gm) raisins

Put a weight on the cottage cheese. Put it through a sieve. Rub the egg-yolks through a sieve, mix with the butter and cottage cheese, add the raisins and beaten egg-whites, and mix well. Put it all out in a deep dish greased with the butter and sprinkled with finely ground bread-crumbs. Let it gradually brown in an oven. Serve sour cream or milk cream.

COTTAGE-CHEESE AND HONEY PUDDING

15 oz (400 gm) cottage cheese, 0.5 cup honey, 2 eggs, 2 tbsp. manna-croup, 4 tbsp. sugar, 3 tbsp. butter, lemon peel (0.5 lemon), a little vanilline, and 1.35 cups milk

Make semolina in milk, salt, add the sugar and vanilline. When the semolina is a little chilled, put in the eggs, minced lemon peel, kneaded cottage cheese, and honey. Mix everything well and transfer into a greased tin form. Bake in an oven.

TYANUSHKI (RUBBERY CAKES)

2 cups cream, 2 cups sugar, vanilla or 2 oz (50 gm) chocolate or 2 oz (50 gm) nuts, or 2 oz (50 gm) sweet almonds

Mix the cream with 2 cups of sugar, heat on a gas-stove, stirring, until darkening (without bringing to a boil). Add the vanilla or grated chocolate, or fruit syrup, or crushed nuts, or sweet almonds (with the addititon of bitter almonds). Mix well, trickle into a dripping-pan greased with olive oil. Dry a little in an oven (on a low heat). Cut into pieces when it gets cold.

«QUICKY» COTTAGE-CHEESE PUDDING

2 lb (800 gm) cottage cheese, 1/2 cup cream, 15 oz (400 gm) sour cream, 4 oz (100 gm) butter, 4 eggs, salt, and caraway-seeds

Rub the cottage cheese through a sieve, gradually add, stirring, 1/2 cup of thick cream, sour cream, 4 beaten eggs, grated butter, salt, and caraway-seeds. Put in a form with moistened cheese-cloth inside, and have it chilled in the cold.

FRESH-SALTED COTTAGE-CHEESE CAKE

1.5 lb (600 gm) cottage cheese, 2 oz (50 gm) cheese, 2 oz (50 gm) butter, 2 eggs, 4 oz (100 gm) sour cream, 1 tsp. sugar, salt, and caraway-seeds

Press out and rub the cottage cheese through a sieve. Gradually add, stirring, the grated cheese, grated butter, beaten eggs, sour cream, sugar, salt, and caraway-seeds at your wish. Lay in a moistened form, put a weight on it, and stand in the cold.

NOODLES AND COTTAGE-CHEESE PUDDING

10 oz (300 gm) noodles, 15 oz (450 gm) cottage cheese, 1—2 eggs, 4 tsp. sugar, 2 oz (50 gm) butter, 4 tbsp. sour cream; finely ground bread-crumbs and salt to taste

Boil the noodles (macaroni, vermicelli) and transfer into a colander. Add the eggs, sugar, and salt to the cottage cheese. Mix thoroughly, add to the boiled noodles and lay into a frying-pan greased with the butter and sprinkled with the bread-crumbs. Spread the sour cream over the surface of the pudding and bake in an oven.

PUDDING FROM COTTAGE CHEESE AND VERMICELLI WITH NUTS

6 oz (180 gm) vermicelli, 1 lb (500 gm) cottage cheese, 4 tbsp. butter, 0.5 cup sugar, 4 eggs, 1.5 cups shelled walnuts, 0.5 cup raisins, and salt

Boil and transfer the vermicelli into a colander. Mix well the cottage cheese, egg-yolks, melted butter, and sugar. Add the boiled vermicelli, washed raisins, and crushed walnuts to the mixture and carefully put the beaten egg-whites in it. Transfer the mass into a greased tin form and bake in an oven.

VARENETS

3 jars with milk and 1 tbsp. sour cream

Put the jars with milk in a large and not too deep clay basin. Stand it in an oven. After light brown skin has formed in the jars, put it down to the bottom with a spoon. Do it again four times. Then pour off one cup of milk, have it chilled, mix with one tablespoon of sour cream, and mix with the rest of the milk. Pour the milk out into cups with the equal amount of the milk skin in each of them and stand in a warm place. When the milk turns sour place the cups in the cold. Serve the sugar and rye bread-crumbs.

PROSTOKVASHA (SOUR CLOTTED MILK)

9 cups milk, 1 tbsp. sour cream, finely ground rye bread-crumbs, and sugar

Shake one table-spoon of sour cream with a cupful of milk, mix with eight cups of milk, put the lid on, and stand in a warm place. When the mixture turns sour and gets thick take it out to the cold. Serve the sugar and rye bread-crumbs.

Dishes from Eggs, Cottage Cheese, and Milk

KISSEL AND BEVERAGES

In this section you will find the recipes of berry, fruit, oatmeal, and flaky *kissel*.

Most often, the jelly-forming component for all kinds of *kissel* is potato starch. It should be mentioned here that in Russia potato starch began to be used in the 19th century, whereas before only fermented cereals were used in cooking.

In this book you will also read about some national Russian beverages, such as *mors* (fruit water), various kinds of herbaceous tea, etc.

RHUBARB *KISSEL*

15 oz (400 gm) rhubarb stalks, 4 tbsp. starch

The syrup: *3 cups water, 6 tbsp. sugar*

Cut the stalks into small pieces, pour cold water over them, and keep that way for 15 minutes. Make the syrup (3 cups of water and 6 table-spoons of sugar) and boil the rhubarb in it for 10—12 minutes. Rub the boiled rhubarb stalks and syrup through a sieve, bring to a boil adding the starch. Chill the *kissel*.

BILBERRY *KISSEL*

2 lb (800 gm) bilberries, 1 cup sugar, $3/4$ cup potato flour, cream or milk, and whipped cream

Make bilberry juice. Bring 6.5 cups of the juice with 1 cup of sugar to a boil and trickle, stirring, 1 cup of the cold juice mixed with the potato flour into it. When it starts boiling and bubbling, serve or pour it into a tin container and stand in the cold. Sprinkle with castor sugar and serve with the cream or milk. You can also make 0.5 portion of whipped cream, fold a piece of thick white paper into a cone, glue its edges together with some egg-white, and cut off the tip. Fill half of it with the whipped cream and squeeze it out on the *kissel* to decorate it with various fanciful patterns.

RASPBERRY *KISSEL*

7.5 cups raspberry juice, sugar, $3/4$ cup potato flour, cream or milk

Raspberry *kissel* is made in the same way as one from bilberries. Serve the cream or milk.

RED-CURRANT *KISSEL*

2 lb (800 gm) red currants, sugar, and $3/4$ cup potato flour

It is made in the same way as bilberry *kissel*. Serve cream or milk.

BLACK-CURRANT *KISSEL*

7.5 cups black-currant juice, $3/4$ cup potato flour, and $3/4$ cup sugar

Bring 6.5 cups of the black-currant juice with $3/4$ cup of sugar to a boil and trickle, stirring, 1 cup of the cold juice shaken with

Kissel and Beverages

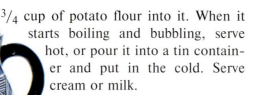

3/4 cup of potato flour into it. When it starts boiling and bubbling, serve hot, or pour it into a tin container and put in the cold. Serve cream or milk.

SORREL KISSEL

5 lb (2.4 kg) sorrel leaves, 15 pints (6 litres) water, 2 cups sugar, 5 oz (150 gm) starch; salt to taste

Wash the sorrel leaves thoroughly, mince them and cook in a small amount of water. Rub through a sieve, add the remaining water and sugar, and boil for 3 minutes. Dilute the starch in cold water and bring to a boil again.

HONEY KISSEL

1.5 cups honey, 6 cups water, and 3/4 cup potato flour

Dilute the honey with 5 cups of water and bring to a boil. Trickle, stirring, 3/4 cup of potato flour shaken with 1 cup of water. When the *kissel* starts boiling and bubbling, serve it hot or pour into a pot, chill, and serve with cream or milk.

HONEY-SYRUP KISSEL

15 oz (400 gm) syrup, 3/4 cup potato flour, and 9 cups water

Dilute 15 oz (400 gm) of syrup in 8 cups of water and bring to a boil. Trickle, stirring, 1 cup of cold water shaken with the potato flour into it. When the *kissel* begins to bubble and thicken, serve it hot (or cold) with cream or milk.

MILK KISSEL

4 cups milk, 1/3 cup starch, 2 oz (50 gm) vanilla sugar, and 1 cup sugar

Add the sugar and vanilla sugar in the boiling milk. Dilute the starch with cold milk and pour it, stirring, into it to prevent from forming clots. Boil the mass to a boil, lay out into a dish, smooth out with a spoon, and put in a cold place. Serve with jam.

FLAKY KISSEL

The milk *kissel*: *2 pints ($1/2$ litres) milk, 1 tbsp. potato starch, and 2 tbsp. sugar*

The cranberry *kissel*: *2 oz (60 gm) cranberries, 1 tbsp. potato starch, 3 tbsp. sugar, and 2 pints ($1/2$ litres) water*

Moisten a tin container with water and sprinkle it with sugar. Pour some milk *kissel* into it and chill well. Pour the chilled but not quite thickened cranberry *kissel* onto the thickened layer of milk *kissel* and have it chilled again. If you wish you can increase the number of the *kissel's* layers. The flaky *kissel* can be made in special vessels according to the desirable number of portions.

RYE-BREAD KISSEL

15 oz (400 gm) rye bread, 2 pints (1 litre) water, 1/3 cup sugar, 3 tbsp. starch, 4 tbsp. cherry-jam syrup, 1 tsp. diluted citric acid

Pour boiling water over the rye bread's slices to make the bread swell. Rub the bread mass through a sieve and put it in an enameled sauce-pan. Bring to a boil, add the sugar, citric acid, and syrup. Boil for some time and trickle the starch diluted with warm water into it. When the *kissel* thickens sufficiently, have it chilled and serve.

COLD KISSEL FROM HOME-MADE KVASS

7.5 cups kvass, 1 cup potato flour, and 1 cup sugar

Bring 6.5 cups of home-made bread kvass with 1 cup of sugar to a boil. Trickle, stirring, 1 cup of the kvass shaken with 1 cup of the potato flour. When it begins to thicken

and bubble, pour it into a pot and stand in the cold. Serve with cream milk.

PUMPKIN KISSEL

1 pumpkin, 2 tbsp. starch, and 3 cups milk

Peel and grate the pumpkin fine. Dilute the starch with 1 cup of milk. Separately boil 2 cups of milk with salt to taste. Trickle the diluted starch into the boiling milk, bring to a boil, remove from the heat, mix with the pumpkin, and heat well without boiling. Serve cold.

You can make this *kissel* sweet, adding some sugar and vanilline to taste.

OATMEAL KISSEL

Pour warm boiled water over oatmeal and keep it that way for 24 hours. Strain the liquid and press out the mass. Boil with salt to taste until thickened. Pour into small vessels and stand in the cold. Cut the thickened *kissel* into portions and pour onion sauce over them (brown minced onions in vegetable oil and have them chilled).

MILK AND OATMEAL KISSEL

4 oz (100 gm) oatmeal flakes, 2 cups milk, 1 tbsp. starch, salt, and 2 tbsp. sugar

Dilute the oatmeal flakes with 2 cups of milk. The moment the flakes swell, strain the milk through a sieve, add starch and salt to taste, and cook the *kissel* without bringing it to a boil and stirring it constantly.

While cooking the sweet *kissel*, add 2 tablespoons of sugar to the sifted milk.

COLD HONEY DRINK

3 eggs, 6 tbsp. honey, 1 pints (0.5 litres) tea, 2 lemons, and 8 tbsp. sugar

Pound the egg-yolks with the honey and dilute with strong hot tea. Put a pan on heat, beat the mixture, and add the juice from 2 lemons. Have the drink chilled, pour it into tall glasses, and put in an ice box.

Pour the egg-whites into a deep pan, add ground lemon peel, sugar and lemon juice, and beat until the mass is light and thick and the sugar is completely diluted. Before serving, put a spoonful of beaten egg-whites in each glass.

ROWAN WATER

2 pints (1 litre) water, 7 oz (200 gm) rowans, and 4 tbsp. honey

Wash the rowan berries, nead them with a wooden pestle, pour water over them, bring to a boil, and strain. Dissolve the honey in the resulting liquid and put in a cold place for 1—5 days.

CARROT AND CRANBERRY DRINK

2 lb (1 kg) carrots, 1 lb (0.5 kg) cranberries, 1.5 cups water, sugar, and ice

Wash, peel, and grate the carrots or put them through a juicer. Sort out, wash, and put the cranberries through a sieve. Join the carrot juice with the cranberry one. Sweeten the mixture, dilute it with the boiled water, and serve in cups putting a piece of ice in each of them.

SLOE DRINK

2 pints (1 litre) water, 9 oz (250 gm) sloe, 1 cup sugar

Sort out and wash the sloe, pour some water over it, and boil for 8—10 minutes. Strain the liquid, add 1 cup of sugar, boil and chill.

CRANBERRY MORS (FRUIT DRINK) WITH HONEY

Crush and boil 1 cup of sorted out, cleared and blanched (which means dipping fresh berries in boiling water for 2—3 minutes) cranberries for 2—3 minutes, crush them and boil for 5—10 minutes. Strain the juice, add 2 table-spoons of honey, and keep for 1—2 hours. Serve cold.

Kissel and Beverages

RASPBERRY MORS

5 oz (150 gm) raspberries, 2 pints (1 litre) water, and 0.5 cup sugar

Crush the raspberries, press out the juice through a piece of cheese-cloth, pour hot water over the dregs, boil for 5—7 minutes, and strain the liquid. Add the sugar and pressed-out raspberry juice.

GUELDER-ROSE AND HONEY MORS

0.5 cup guelder-rose juice, 4 oz (100 gm) honey, and 2 pints (1 litre) water

Sort out, wash, and press out the guelder-rose berries. Pour water over the resulting juice, boil for 5—10 minutes, and strain the liquid. Join the liquid with the pressed-out juice, add some sugar, mix well, and chill.

STRAWBERRY MORS

7 oz (200 gm) strawberries, 2 pints (1 litre) water, and 0.5 cup sugar

Sort out and wash the strawberries, crush, and press them out through a piece of cheese-cloth. Pour hot water over the dregs, boil them for 5—7 minutes, strain the liquid, add the sugar and the pressed-out juice.

BEET MORS

7 oz (200 gm) beet-roots, 2 pints (1 litre) water, 0.5 cup sugar, and 1 lemon

Wash, peel, and grate the beet-roots fine. Press out the juice. Pour hot water over the dregs and keep boiling for 15—20 minutes. Add the sugar, citric acid, and the pressed-out juice of the beet-roots. Bring to a boil and strain.
Serve cold with ice cubes.

BLACK-CURRANTS WATER

1 cup black currants, 2 cups sugar, and 2 pints (1 litre) water

Sort out the black currants. Wash and squeeze out the juice. Pour it out into a clean jar. Pour hot water over the squeezed-out berries, bring to a boil and strain. Mix the liquid with the juice, add the sugar, and stir well.

RASPBERRY TEA

1 tbsp. dried raspberries; sugar and honey to taste

Pour 2 cups of boiling water over the dried raspberries and draw the liquid for about 15 minutes. Strain the tea and add sugar or honey to taste.

APPLE-SKIN TEA

$1/3$ oz (10 gm) dried apple skin, 9 oz (250 gm) water, $2/3$ oz (20 gm) sugar or honey

Put the dried apple skin in cold water, bring to a boil, draw for about 15 minutes, and strain. Add sugar or honey.

BLACK DRINK WITH APPLES

3 lb (1.5 kg) apples, 2 lemons, 5 pints (2.5 litres) strong cold tea, and 1.5 cups sugar

Peel the apples, cut them into several slices, remove the core from each one, and put in a large sauce-pan. Add the juice from the lemons and grated lemon peel, pour the very strong cold tea over the mixture, and add the sugar. Keep the drink in the cold for 6 hours. Pour the drink into a hock-cup vessel and serve.

BOILED FRUIT LIQUID

1.5 lb (600 gm) dried fruit, 2 pints (1 litre) water, 4 tbsp. sugar, and 3 tbsp. starch

Wash and pour cold water over a mixture of dried apples, prunes, apricots, raisins, and cherries. Add the sugar and simmer until soft. Dilute the starch with 2 pints (1 litre) of cold water, pour the hot liquid into it, bring to a boil, and chill.

COMPOT (STEWED FRUIT) FROM FRESH APPLES OR PEARS

10 oz (300 gm) apples or pears, 5 oz (150 gm) sugar, 1 tbsp. wine, 0.04 oz (1 gm) citric acid,

$1/6$ oz (5 gm) cinnamon or lemon peel, and 6 pints ($3/4$ litre) water

Sort out the apples or pears, wash and peel them, cut into slices, remove the cores and stones, and put the fruit in water with the addition of the citric acid. Boil the skin and cores separately for 10—12 minutes, whereupon strain the liquid and add the sugar to it. Put the apple or pear slices in the syrup and simmer for 6—8 minutes. To make it fragrant, put in the lemon or orange peel, or some cinnamon. To make the taste better, chill the *compot* and pour the wine into it.

CHERRY *COMPOT*

10 oz (300 gm) cherries, 5 oz (150 gm) sugar, 1 tbsp. wine, 0.04 oz (1 gm) citric acid, and 6 pints ($3/4$ litre) water

Boil syrup from the sugar with the addition of the citric acid. Sort out and wash the berries. Put them in the boiling syrup. Stop heating them and let them stay that way until fully chilled. Add the wine.

WILD STRAWBERRY *COMPOT*

2 lb (800 gm) wild strawberries, 7 oz (200 gm) sugar, and 3 cups water

Bring the water and sugar to a boil, have it chilled, pour it over the wild strawberries, and take out into the cold.

STRAWBERRY HOCK-CUP

1 lb (0.5 kg) strawberries, 2 tbsp. sugar, $3/4$ strawberry mors, and 1 bottle fruit water

Sort out and wash the strawberries. Add the sugar, pour in $1/5$ part of the strawberry *mors*, and keep it that way for 3 hours. Pour in the remaining chilled *mors* and chilled fruit water, and mix thoroughly. Put some strawberries in each glass.

APPLE *COMPOT* BASED ON WINE

2 lb (1 kg) apples, 10 oz (300 gm) sugar, 4 pints (2 litres) water, 1 cup white table wine, 1 lemon's peel, 2—3 pieces of clove, and boiled berries

Boil syrup from the sugar and wine. Put sliced apples, lemon peel, and clove in it. Keep on low heat until the apples get soft. Serve the chilled *compot* in a glass pot. Put some kind of boiled berries in glasses.

WINTER HOCK-CUP

2 pints (1 litre) canned cherries, 4 oz (100 gm) sugar, 1 bottle red table wine, and 1 bottle of champagne

Remove the stones from the cherries, sprinkle them with the sugar, pour 1 cup of the red wine over them, and put in a fridge for 1 hour. Join the cherries and wine with the chilled canned cherries' liquid and the rest of the wine.

Serve the drink in large wine-glasses with the addition of the champagne.

HUSSAR PUNCH

1 bottle red table wine, 3 lemons, 9 oz (250 gm) lump-sugar, 1 cup rum or cognac, and 2 cups strong tea

Pour the strong tea, heated wine (up to 70°C.), the strained juice from 2 lemons, and rum into a fire-proof basin. Add the lemon peel and sugar. Stir the drink well. Add the lemons' rings and put one rum-soaked lump of the sugar on each of them. Put out the light and burn the sugar. When the fire goes out, pour the punch into ceramic cups.

TEA FROM HONEY AND MINT

3 cups water, 3 cups mint liquid, and 2 oz (50 gm) honey

Dilute the juice of the honey and boiled mint with 3 cups of boiled water. Mix well and keep in the cold for 2 hours. Serve cold. You can bring the tea to a boil but not boil it and drink it hot.

TEA FROM ST. JOHN'S WORT

4 oz (100 gm) dried St. John's wort, sugar, and 4 pints (2 litres) water

Boil the dried St. John's wort in 4 pints (2 litres) of water for 10 minutes. Strain the liquid, add 4 oz (100 gm) of sugar, and bring to a boil.
You can drink it both hot and chilled.

CURRANT AND HIP TEA

Boil 2 table-spoons of currants and hips (1:1) in 2 cups of boiling water. Keep the boiled mixture in a stopped-up vessel. Strain through a piece of cheese-cloth.

CURRANT LEAVES AND HIP TEA

Pour 2 cups of boiling water over the currant leaves and hip (1:1), keep simmering for 10 minutes. Have the cooled for 2—3 hours and strain.

NETTLE AND RED-ROWAN TEA

3 tbsp. chopped nettle sprigs, 1 tbsp. rowans

Pour 2 cups of boiling water over the chopped nettle sprigs and rowans. Chill it for a while and strain.

MEAT DUMPLINGS, *KLOTSKAS* AND NOODLES

Meat dumplings, curd or fruit dumplings, and noodles or *klotskas* have to do with dishes made from unleavened dough. However, there is a special point about it. Strong unleavened dough is assimilated rather poorly, therefore it has to be rolled out longer and until it is quite thin.

Meat dumplings are very popular with the Russians, especially in Siberia. They are mostly stuffed with meat and vegetables. Curd and fruit dumplings are more popular in the southern regions of Russia. Large curd and fruit dumplings are called «*kolduns*» (witches).

Klotskas are also one of the favourite dishes in Russia. They testify to the fine taste of the hostess and her ambition to diversify her fare.

Now for the noodles. Although the dish is of Turkic origin, the home-made noodles and all other dishes with it have long become national Russian dishes.

KLOTSKAS WITH A MUSHROOM SAUCE

The klotskas: *1 cup flour, 1 cup water, 3 eggs, 3 tbsp vegetable oil, and salt*

The sauce: *1 cup dried mushrooms, 0.33 tbsp. cup sour cream, 2 tbsp. flour, and salt*

Salt 1 cup of water, add the vegetable oil and flour. Mix well and set on a burner. Steam the dough thoroughly. Chill it a little and gradually mix the eggs into it, neading it in the process. Pour some water into a sauce-pan, salt, bring to a boil, and cook the *klotskas* in it. To this end scoop the dough out with a spoon, preliminarily dipping it in the boiling water to prevent the *klotskas* from sticking to the spoon. When the *klotskas* surface, boil them for 5 minutes and transfer into a colander. Put the *klotskas* in a deep plate and pour the hot mushroom sauce over them.

The sauce

Soak the mushrooms in cold water, wash well, and boil. Chill the mushroom liquid. Mix the flour with the cold liquid, add the finely cut mushrooms, salt, and bring to a boil. You can also add some sour cream.

SIBERIAN MEAT DUMPLINGS

2 lb (1 kg) meat (3 parts beef, 2 parts pork, 1 part mutton), 2 large onions, 2.5 cups flour, 2 eggs, $2/3$ cup milk; salt and pepper to taste

The dough for any kind of dumplings is mostly the same. Screen the flour and make a mound of it on the table. Make a hollow, add some slightly heated water, eggs, and salt. Mix the dough well until even and thick. Let it «rest» for about forty minutes, roll out into cilinders about one finger-thick, and cut into small pieces. Then roll the pieces out into thin rings.

In the meantime, make the meat stuffing. Put the meat's bits through a meat-grinder together with the onions. Then add the salt, sugar, ground black peppers, and a little boiled milk. Mix well.

Then shape the mixture into small balls and put them in the centre of flat round pieces of dough (*sochni*) (3—4 cm from the edge), fold the *sochni* in the shape of half-moons.

Cook the dumplings in slightly salted simmering water for 10—12 minutes until they have surfaced. Serve immediately. You can use melted butter, six-percent vinegar, and fresh sour cream as a dressing.

HOME DUMPLINGS

To make 2 lb (1 kg) meat dumplings (4 portions) use 15 oz (450 gm) ground beef, salt, pepper, 3 oz (90 gm) water, and 1 onion

Remove the film and tendons from the beef and put it through a grinder together with the onion. Mix well, add the salt, pepper, and cold water and mix thoroughly again. Make dumplings (see above) and cook in boiling water.

DUMPLINGS STUFFED WITH CABBAGE

To make 2 lb (1 kg) dumplings use 10 oz (350 gm) minced pork, 1 onion, $1/2$ head of cabbage, salt, and pepper

Remove the film from the pork flesh, put it through a grinder together with the onion, add the salt, pepper, water, and minced cabbage. Mix well. Make dumplings shaping them into half-moons or «knots».

FRIED MEAT DUMPLINGS

10 dumplings, $1/2$ oz (15 gm) butter, $2/3$ oz (20 gm) sour cream

Fry the frozen dumplings in red-hot frying-pans greased with the butter. Brown them first on one side and then on the other. Serve in the same pans pouring the sour cream over the dumplings.

BAKED MEAT DUMPLINGS

10 dumplings, 1 oz (30 gm) sour cream, 2 tbsp. grated cheese, and butter

Put the boiled or fried meat dumplings in frying-pans (in portions), pour the sour cream over them, sprinkle with the grated cheese and melted butter, and bake.

DUMPLINGS STUFFED WITH CHICKEN MEAT

1 chicken, 1 cup milk; salt and spice to taste

Remove the meat from the bones, put the chicken meat twice through a meat-grinder, salt, mix with the milk or sour cream. The filling should not be too thin. Then continue cooking according to the above recipe. Serve the chicken meat dumplings with butter.

MEAT DUMPLINGS, FAR-EASTERN STYLE

10 oz (300 gm) minced filleted fish, 9 oz (250 gm) pork, 2 onions, 2 eggs, salt, and pepper

Put 10 oz (300 gm) of filleted humpbacked salmon, Siberian salmon, or other fish together with the pork and onions twice through a meat-grinder. Add the eggs, salt, pepper, and water. Mix well. Make dumplings, boil and fry them in butter.

DUMPLINGS WITH PIKE-PERCH FILLING IN BROTH

7 oz (200 gm) filleted pike-perch, 2 oz (60 gm) boiled milk, 1 onion; salt and pepper to taste

Put the filleted fish through a meat-grinder with a coarse grate. Add the finely cut onion, black pepper, and salt. Pound the mass thoroughly. Add the milk for juicyness. Make dough the way you do it for meat dumplings.

Boil the dumplings in the broth made from the head, fins, and bones of the pike-perch. When making the broth put some herbs and fried onion in it to lend it a light-coloured hue. Serve the dumplings either in the broth or with butter or sour cream.

MUSHROOM DUMPLINGS

Pour 2 cups of flour on a kitchen board, make a hollow, pour out the content of one egg into it, add salt, some water and nead thick dough. Cover the dough and let it stay that way for 20—30 minutes. Roll out and shape it into a cylinder. Cut the cylinder crosswise into rings and put the stuffing in the centre of each of them. Fold the rings in the shape of dumplings. Lay the dumplings on a dripping-pan sprinkled with flour, spread egg-whites over them and stand in the cold.

The filling

Soak a cupful of dried mushrooms in cold

water (3—4 hours). Boil them in the same water. Chill the boiled mushrooms and put them through a meat-grinder. Heat some vegetable oil until it has no smell, fry the mushrooms in it with the addition of a teaspoon of flour, salt, pepper, and finely chopped slightly browned onion.

Put the prepared dumplings in boiling water and boil until they have surfaced. You can also steam them for 10—15 minutes. Dress them to taste with vegetable oil, mustard, vinegar, sugar, salt, and pepper.

DUMPLINGS STUFFED WITH A GRATED RADISH

15 oz (400 gm) peeled radish, 1 onion, 1.5 cup sour cream, salt, and spice

Grate the peeled and washed radish on a coarse grater, add the onion, sour cream, salt, and spice. Mix well. To make the radish tastier, keep it in slightly salted water before grating. Pour a little vinegar into it. Better serve the dumplings with vegetable oil.

NETTLE DUMPLINGS

10 oz (300 gm) stinging-nettle leaves, 2 oz (50 gm) chopped onions, 2 tbsp. soft butter

Nead dough for dumplings. Let it stay for 30—40 minutes, roll out into a layer 1.5—2 mm thick. Mix the finely cut nettle leaves and chopped onions and brown in the butter. Make dumplings and cook them in boiling salted water. Serve with butter or sour cream.

USHKI (EARS)

Ushki is the same as dumplings shaped as triangles, half-moons, or «ears». Join the ends of half-moons to make them round. The *ushki* are cooked in water or broth and then served. You can also brown them in boiling butter and then serve separately to the broth.

USHKI WITH MEAT FILLING

The dough: 2 cups flour, 2 eggs
The filling: 15 oz (400 gm) beef, 4 oz (100 gm) near-kidney fat

Make a hollow in a mound of flour. Pour the content of the eggs into it. Mix well until uniform. Let the dough «rest» for 15—20 minutes covering it with a napkin so that the dough would not have a «weathered» look. Roll out into a thin sheet, cut into squares, lay the filling on each square, fold in the shape of triangles, half-moons or «ears». Put the *ushki* in boiling water. When they surface they are ready to be served.

SAUERKRAUT-AND-FISH FILLING FOR *USHKI*

7 oz (200-300 gm) cooked or fried (in vegetable oil) fish, 7 oz (200 gm) sauerkraut, 3 onions; salt, sugar, and pepper to taste

Cut the cooked or fried fish fine, add the finely chopped and browned sauerkraut and onions, salt and sprinkle with a little sugar and ground pepper. Mix well.

FILLING FROM CEREALS

One cup of any kind of cereals — rice, buckwheat, pearl-barley, barley, etc.

Cook some cereals until thick and crumbly. Brown in vegetable oil to with finely chopped onions.

If necessary, add some broth to make the filling more gluey. Salt and pepper to taste.

POTATO DUMPLINGS

The dough: 15 oz (400 gm) flour, 2 eggs, 1.5 cup water

The filling: 2 lb (1 kg) potatoes, 4 tbsp. sunflower oil, 4 oz (100 gm) onions, 1 tsp. finely chopped dill; pepper and salt to taste

The dough

Make, the dough. Roll it into a thin sheet, cut out small rings, lay one tea-spoon of chilled filling on each ring, fold the dough rings in the shape of dumplings. Make sure the filling does not fall out of them.

Dip the dumplings in slightly salted boiling water in small portions so that they could float freely in it. When the dumplings surface, keep them in simmering water for about 5—7 minutes. Take them out of the water with a skimmer and transfer into a colander. Pour hot water over them, wait till the water has flowed down, and put in a basin. Serve the dumplings with slightly salted sour clotted milk.

The filling

Peel the potatoes, salt them, pour water over them, boil until done and put them through a meat-grinder without chilling. Chop the onions fine, salt and fry in the whole amount of oil until golden brown. Pepper and mix thoroughly with the potato paste with the addition of the dills.

DUMPLINGS STUFFED WITH BOLETUSSES AND ONIONS

The dough: *2 eggs, 8 tbsp. water, 1 tsp. salt, 2 cups flour*

The filling: *2 oz (50 gm) dried boletusses, onions, and butter*

Make $2/3$ portion of dough for the dumplings. Cook 2 oz (50 gm) of dried boletusses in slightly salted boiling water. Strain, chop fine (using the mushroom liquid for a soup or sauce). Brown the minced onions in vegetable oil and mix with the mushrooms. Roll the dough thin, cut out rings, lay the filling on them, and fold in the shape of dumplings. Boil in slightly salted boiling water.

DUMPLINGS WITH CABBAGE AND MUSHROOM FILLING

The dough: *2 eggs, 8 tbsp. water, 1 tsp. salt, 2 cups flour*

The filling: *1 cabbage, onions, butter, 2 tbsp. boiled and finely chopped dried boletusses*

Chop the cabbage fine, brown in butter, add the finely chopped browned onions and salt. Mix well. Make $2/3$ portion of dough for dumplings. Roll thin, cut out rings. Lay the filling on each of them and fold in the shape of dumplings. Cook the dumplings in slightly salted boiling water. Separately serve the mushroom sauce with sour cream.

COTTAGE-CHEESE DUMPLINGS

The dough: *2 eggs, 2 cups flour, 9 tbsp. water, and salt*

The filling: *15 oz (400 gm) cottage cheese, 2 eggs, 4 oz (100 gm) sour cream, salt, and sugar*

Make $2/3$ portion of dough. Put it under weight, rub the cottage cheese through a sieve, add 2 eggs, 4 oz (100 gm) sour cream, salt, and sugar. Mix well. Roll the dough thin, cut out rings, put a tea-spoon of cottage-cheese paste on each of them and fold into dumplings. Boil in slightly salted water, transfer onto a colander, and let the water flow away. Serve immediately with sour cream and hot butter.

«LAZY» DUMPLINGS

1 lb (500 gm) cottage cheese, 7 oz (200 gm) boiled potatoes, 4 eggs, 2 tbsp. flour, $1/3$ cup sour cream, 2 oz (50 gm) starch, 1 tbsp. butter, and salt

Put the boiled potatoes and well-pressed-out cottage cheese through a meat-grinder. Mix the butter with the egg-yolks, add to the potato-cum-cottage-cheese paste, and then the starch and beaten egg-yolks. Lay the resulting dough on a board sprinkled with flour. Roll the dough into a cylinder 1 in (3 cm) in diameter, flatten it a little and cut into diamond-shaped pieces $3/4$ in (2—3 cm) wide. Put the «lazy» dumplings in salted boiling water, stir well, and cook in a sauce-pan with the lid on. When the dumplings surface, lay them out on a dish, and pour the sour cream over them.

BILBERRY DUMPLINGS

15 oz (400 gm) bilberries, 4 oz (100 gm) sugar, 10 oz (350 gm) flour, 1 egg, $2/3$ oz (20 gm) margarine or butter, 2 pints ($1/4$ litre) sour cream

Make dough from 10 oz (350 gm) of flour, add one egg, salt, and lukewarm water. Roll out the dough and cut out rings from it. Put a tea-spoon of frozen bilberries on each ring and sprinkle with sugar. Shape the rings into dumplings. Boil about 6 pints (3 litres) of slightly salted water in a large pan. Put the dumplings (one portion at a time) in the boiling water. When they surface, take them out with a skimmer, transfer onto a colander, and pour cold water over them. Have them chilled, mix the sour cream with sugar, pour it over the dumplings, and serve.

«WITCHES» (KIND OF DUMPLINGS)

The filling: *5 oz (150 gm) beef, 1 onion, 2 oz (50 gm) pork (beef) fat, salt, and pepper*

The dough: *10 oz (300 gm) flour, 4 oz (120 gm) milk, 2 eggs, butter, and salt*

Chop the meat fine, add the pork or beef fat, and 1 onion. Cut it all fine or put through a meat-grinder. Add some water or finely ground ice, pepper, and salt. Mix well. Make big-size dumplings («witches») with this filling and cook them in slightly salted water.

«WITCHES» STUFFED WITH BOILED BUCKWHEAT AND EGGS

5 oz (150 gm) buckwheat, 2 eggs, dough for noodles, and 1 tbsp. butter

Cook 1/2 portion crumbly buckwheat. Pour 1 table-spoon of butter into it. Mix well, add 2 chopped hard-boiled eggs and salt. Mix well. Make 1/2 portion of dough for noodles (see further), roll thin, cut out rings, put some filling on each of them, and fold into the shape of dumplings. Cook in slightly salted boiling water and strain. Serve butter.

«WITCHES» WITH SAUERKRAUT AND MUSHROOMS

The dough: *2 cups flour, 2 eggs, 8 tbsp. water, 1 tsp. salt*

The filling: *7 oz (200 gm) finely chopped sauerkraut, 2 oz (50 gm) dried boletusses, and butter*

Cook the chopped sauerkraut with butter. Boil the boletusses, strain the liquid, chop, mix with the sauerkraut, and salt. Make 2/3 portion of dough for noodles (see further). Roll thin, cut out rings, put some filling on each of them, and shape into dumplings. Cook in slightly salted boiling water. Serve the mushroom liquid with sour cream without putting the chopped mushrooms in it (see «*Klotskas* with a Mushroom Sauce»).

«WITCHES» WITH RICE AND EGGS

The filling: *4 oz (100 gm) rice, 1 tbsp. butter, 2 eggs, dill, parsley*

The dough: *2 eggs, 2 cups flour, 8 tbsp. water, 1 tsp. salt*

Boil the rice until crumbly, pour 1 tablespoon of butter into it, stir well, add 2 chopped hard-boiled eggs, dill, parsley, and salt. Mix well. Make the dough for noodles. Roll the dough thin, cut out rings, put some filling on each of them, and shape into dumplings. Cook in slightly salted boiling water. Serve with butter.

SEMOLINA *KLOTSKAS*

4 cups milk, 16 tsp. manna-croup, 1 tbsp. butter, 2 eggs, and flour

Boil 4 cups of milk and pour the manna-croup into it. When it is done, add 1 tablespoon of butter, mix well, chill, and rub through a sieve. Add the eggs, mix well, salt, and add some flour. Take tea-spoonfuls of the mass and dip (one by one) in boiling broth or water.

KLOTSKAS, ST.PETERSBURG STYLE

2 tbsp. butter, 8 eggs, 6 tbsp. sour cream, 1 nutmeg, and flour

Beat the butter until it turns into spume, add the eggs, sour cream, a little finely grated nutmeg, and a sufficient amount of flour for the *klotskas* not to fall apart. Beat the mass thoroughly.

FRIED *KLOTSKAS* STUFFED WITH RAISINS

7 oz (200 gm) butter, 15 oz (400 gm) flour, 12 eggs, 2 cups raisins, 1.5 cups sour cream, and sugar

Boil 1 cup of water with the butter. Pour the flour into it and mix well. Mix the eggs into it, add the sugar and salt. Nead the dough well. Add 2 cups of raisins and mix well. Dip small klotskas (one at a time) in boiling butter until browned. Serve the sour cream mixed with sugar powder and vanilla.

KLOTSKAS FROM POTATO PASTE WITH A VINEGAR SAUCE

The dough: 2 lb (1 kg) potatoes, 10 oz (300 gm) flour, 2 eggs, 2 oz (50 gm) onions, 2 tbsp. vegetable oil; salt to taste

The sauce: 4 oz (100 gm) onions, 2 tbsp. vegetable oil, 1.5 cups broth or water, 1 tsp. flour, 1 tsp. mustard, 1 tsp. granulated sugar, 1 bay leaf, $1/4$ cup white wine; salt and pepper to taste

Wash the potatoes well, boil them in slightly salted water until done, peel and put through a meat-grinder. Add the flour, eggs, salt, and browned onions. Nead dough. Heat, stirring, until thick. Have it chilled slightly. Roll out and shape the dough into cylinders 1 in (3 cm) thick. Cut the cylinders into pieces and roll them in flour, pressing them slightly with fingers. Dip small portions of the pieces in boiling water. When the *klotskas* are done, lay them on a colander with a skimmer, pour hot water over them, transfer into a salad bowl, and serve immediately. Serve a sauce separately.

APPLE *KLOTSKAS*

Peel the apples, chop them fine, and brown in pork fat. Add half the amount of ground bread-crumbs, ground sugar, and cinnamon and make a paste with the addition of two egg-yolks. Shape it into *klotskas*, roll them in flour, and brown in fresh fat. Serve them dry or with any kind of sweet sauce.

HOME-MADE NOODLES

3 eggs, 3 cups flour, 12 tbsp. water, 2 tsp. salt

Make thick dough from 3 eggs, 12 tablespoons of water, 2 tea-spoons of salt, and 3 cups of flour. Roll the dough thin and let it get dry. Cut the dough into strips, lay one strip on another, and chop fine.

HOME-MADE BOILED NOODLES

3 eggs, 12 tbsp. water, 1.5 tsp. salt, 3 cups flour, and butter

Make the home-made noodles, cook them in and strain. Serve the butter hot.

NOODLES WITH MUSHROOMS

4 oz (100 gm) noodles, 1 oz (30 gm) dried mushrooms, $1/2$ onion, and melted butter

Boil the mushrooms, chop them fine, add the browned onion, and fry all of them together. Mix the browned mushrooms with the boiled noodles.

PASTRY

In Russian cooking bread and pastry have always been especially important. Guests were met with bread and salt. Of no lesser importance were pies — a symbol of wealth and well-being.

Russian women were famous for their skills in making different sorts of cookies: *blini* (pancakes), *kulebyakas, rasstegais,* cheese cakes, spice-cakes, etc. However, especially popular were patties made from sourdough.

Pancakes and Pancake-like Pies

WHEAT PANCAKES

1.5 cup wheat flour, 1/3 oz (10 gm) sugar, 1/3 oz (10 gm) vegetable oil, 2 eggs, yeast, salt, 2 cups water or milk

Butter or some kind of fat for baking

Heat about 3/4 of the milk up to 30—35°C, dissolve the yeast, add the sugar, salt, egg, and melted butter. Mix well with a dough-spaddle. Pour the sifted wheat flour into the mixture and stir promptly. Cover the container with the dough in it with a piece of cloth and stand in a warm place. When the dough has risen, nead it and add the remaining milk. 1 hour later bake pancakes.

BUCKWHEAT PANCAKES

3 cups buckwheat flour, 4 cups milk, 1 oz (35 gm) yeast, salt

Pour 1 cup of warm milk over the buckwheat flour, add the yeast diluted with a small amount of warm water and stand in a warm place for a couple of hours. After that pour 2 cups of hot milk into it, add the salt, stir well, and let it stay in the warm place until done. Then carefully, without stirring, bake pancakes in greased frying-pans.

«PRECOCIOUS» GURYEVO PANCAKES

2 lb (1 kg) wheat flour, 10 eggs, 7 oz (200 gm) butter, sour milk

Put the wheat flour, egg-yolks, and butter in a sauce-pan and mix well with a dough-spaddle. Dilute with the sour milk until sufficiently thick. Chill and beat the egg-whites until spumy, put in the dough, mix with the dough-spaddle, and bake pancakes.

APPLE PANCAKES

2 lb (1 kg) flour, 7 sour apples, 5 eggs, 3 oz (80 gm) yeast, 2 cups milk, and cream

Make sourdough in milk. To this end dilute the yeast with a small amount of warm milk, pour half the flour into it and stand in a warm place to let the dough rise. Bake the apples in an oven, rub through a sieve to make apple paste. Mix the apple paste with the sourdough, add the remaining flour and egg-yolks. Mix well and dilute with the cream until as thick as sour cream. Let the dough rise again and bake pancakes.

PANCAKES WITH MEAT FILLING

The dough: *2 cups flour, 3 cups milk or water, 1/2 tbsp. sugar, 3 eggs, 3 tbsp. butter*

The filling: *1 lb (500 gm) meat flesh, 1 onion, 2 tbsp. butter, salt, and pepper*

Boil the meat, cut into bits, mix with the slightly browned chopped onion, put through a meat-grinder, salt, pepper, mix

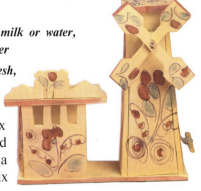

thoroughly, and heat well. Put some filling in the middle of each baked pancake, fold in the shape of an envelope, and brown on both sides. Pour some melted butter over each pancake and serve.

THICK PANCAKES MADE FROM LEAVENED DOUGH

2 cups milk or water, yeast, 1 tsp. salt, 2 tbsp. sugar, 3 cups flour, and butter

Shake 2 cups of warm milk with the yeast, salt, and sugar. Gradually pour, stirring, 3 cups of flour into it. Make pancakes, brown them in the sizzling butter in a frying-pan. Serve jam or honey.

THICK PANCAKES WITH APPLE FILLING

10 oz (300 gm) flour, 1.3 cup milk, 1 egg, 1 tbsp. sugar, 0.9 oz (25 gm) yeast, 5 apples, $1/2$ cup vegetable oil, 1 tbsp. butter; salt to taste

Peel the apples and remove the core, cut into rings. Dip each ring in the thick leavened dough and brown on low heat in the heated vegetable oil until brown on both sides. It is desirable to sprinkle the ready pancakes with icing and vanilla.

FAST THICK PANCAKES

The dough: 1 cup flour, 1 pints (0.5 litres) kefir, 1 tbsp. sugar, 0.5 tsp. salt

Pour 1 cup of flour, salt, sugar, and kefir into a basin. Mix well. The resulting dough will be light and cream-like, close to thick sour cream in its consistence. Pour the dough with a table-spoon into a greased red-hot frying-pan.

PANCAKE-LIKE PATTIES WITH MUSHROOM AND BOILED-BUCKWHEAT FILLING

Boiled buckwheat, 2 oz (50 gm) dried boletusses, 1 onion, pancakes butter, eggs, and parsley

Cook thick boiled buckwheat, pour 1 table-spoon of butter into it, and mix well. Cook the dried boletusses in slightly salted boiling water, strain the liquid, and chop the mushrooms. Brown the minced onion in the butter, mix with the mushrooms and boiled buckwheat. Bake pancakes from wheat flour browning them on one side. Cover the browned side of each pancake with filling, fold the edges into a tube and tie up with thread. Roll in flour or dried bread-crumbs (dipping in the eggs), and brown in the butter. Decorate with the fresh or browned parsley.

BLINNITSA

5—8 pancakes, 1 egg

Lay 5—8 wheat or buckwheat pancakes in a fryng-pan in a multi-layered tower-like mound, spreading the fresh egg over each pancake, and bake the mound. Before serving cut into several parts.

PANCAKE-LIKE PIE WITH PLUM-PASTE FILLING

2 lb (800 gm) fresh plums without the stones or 15 oz (400 gm) prunes, pancakes, sugar, 4 egg-whites, candied fruit or peel, fruit jelly

Rub the stoneless plums through a sieve, mix with 4 oz (100 gm) sugar (or cook 15 oz (400 gm) prunes in syrup made from 4 oz (100 gm) sugar and 1 cup of water and rub through a sieve). Bake pancakes from wheat flour, lay in a deep dish greased with butter and sprinkled with fine-ground dried bread-crumbs, and cover with a layer of the plum paste. Do the same several times. The top layer has to be made of pancakes. Sprinkle it with sugar and butter and brown slightly in an oven. Beat four egg-whites, mix with $1/2$ cup of sugar, cover the pancake-like pie with it and let it gradually brown in the oven.

Decorate with the candied fruit or fruit jelly. Serve cream or milk.

SWEET PANCAKE-LIKE PIE

1/2 cup flour, 1/2 cup egg-yolks, 1 cup butter, 1/2 cup cream, 1 cup sugar, and 1 lemon

Mix well the flour, egg-yolks, cream, melted butter, sugar and lemon peel, add the remaining egg-whites beaten into spume; brown in small frying-pans. Put the pancakes one on another and lay in a dish. Spread the following kind of sauce over each pancake: mix the juice from one lemon with 1/4 cup of fruit juice and 1/4 cup of sugar; spread 4 beaten egg-yolks mixed with 1/4 cup of sugar all over the walls of the mound; stand in an oven for several minutes. Decorate with jam and serve.

ROUND LOAF FROM PANCAKES WITH RICE AND EGG FILLING

Pancakes, dill, parsley, 2 eggs, 5 oz (150 gm) rice, and butter

Bake 1/2 portion of wheat pancakes. Chop the dill and parsley, add 2 chopped hard-boiled eggs. Boil the rice until crumbly, pour 1 table-spoon of warm butter into it, mix with the eggs, dill, and parsley and salt. Grease a dripping-pan with butter, sprinkle with dried bread-crumbs, and cover the bottom and walls with the pancakes. Put a layer of rice, then a layer of chopped eggs, then the pancakes again, etc. Cover the top with the remaining pancakes. Sprinkle with dried bread-crumbs and butter, let it gradually heat and be browned in an oven. Serve butter.

ROUND LOAF FROM PANCAKES WITH BOILED BUCKWHEAT AND EGG FILLING

Boiled buckwheat (crumbly), pancakes, butter, onions, and 2 eggs

Cook crumbly buckwheat. Bake pancakes from wheat flour without sugar, browning them on both sides. Then make a round loaf the way the round loaf from pancakes with rice filling is made. Serve butter.

Pies, Rolls, and Spice-cakes

LEAVENED DOUGH
First Way

Dilute 2 oz (50 gm) yeast and 1—2 teaspoons of sugar in a small amount of warm milk, add some warm liquid, flour, and melted fat. Nead dough (make sure it does not stick to your hands). Grease the dough with the melted fat, cover with a clean napkin, and put in a warm place for it to rise.

Second Way

Mix yeast with sugar, add some warm liquid, pour about half a portion of flour into it and wait until done. It must become at least three times as much in volume. Add some salt, the mixture of yeast and sugar, flour, and melted butter. Nead dough until it is smooth, resilient, shiny, and not sticky. The time needed for the dough to rise depends on the quantity and quality of the yeast and the temperature in your kitchen. The dough's volume must increase twofold. When the dough is ready, nead it 2—3 times.

KULEBYAKA
(PIES WITH MEAT, FISH, OR CABBAGE FILLING)

The dough: 3 cups flour, 1 tbsp. butter, 2/3 oz (20 gm) yeast, 1 tsp. salt, 1.5 sugar, 2 eggs, water

The meat filling: 1.5 lb (600 gm) meat, 3 eggs, 7 oz (200 gm) butter; herbs, pepper, and salt to taste

The fish filling: 1 lb (500 gm) fish, 3 tbsp. rice, 2 onions, 7 oz (200 gm) butter; herbs, pepper, and salt to taste

Make sourdough (2nd way) and roll it into

an oblong layer $1/3$ in (1 cm) thick. Put the filling all along the length of the layer, fold and join its side edges together. Transfer the *kulebyaka* into a fat-greased dripping-pan. Before baking, spread an egg over it, jab in several places to let the steam out, and bake for 40 minutes with the temperature of 210—230°C.

The fish filling
Put the filleted fish through a meat-grinder and salt. Put some boiled rice, the chopped onions, and some herbs in it. Mix thoroughly. The meat filling. Put the meat through a meat-grinder, add some water and stew. Put the preliminarily browned onion and herbs in it. Salt, pepper, and pour in some broth. Mix well.

RYBNIK (FISH PIE)

1.5 lb (600 gm) leavened dough and 1 lb (500 gm) filleted fish

Roll the leavened dough into a sheet, lay a big piece of the filleted fish or a whole scaled and gutted fish with few bones (zander, cod, hake, etc.) on it, salt, pepper, cover with another piece of dough, join the edges of the layers together, let the pie stay for a while and bake.

PIE WITH SIBERIAN FISH FILLING

1.5 lb (600 gm) sourdough, 1 lb (500 gm) filleted fish, 2 onions, and 4 potatoes

Roll the sourdough, put a layer of the finely cut potatoes and large pieces of the filleted fish on it, sprinkle with salt and pepper, put a layer of the minced raw onions on top, cover with another layer of dough, let the pie stay for some time and bake.

PIE FROM LEAVENED DOUGH WITH SAUERKRAUT AND PICKLED MILK-AGARICS

Leavened dough, 1 onion, butter, 1.5 lb (600 gm) shredded sauerkraut, 7 oz (200 gm) pickled milk-agarics, and 1 egg

Make some leavened dough. Chop and brown the onion in some butter. Strain and cook the sauerkraut in some butter in a pot with the lid on. When it is ready, add 7 oz (200 gm) of finely chopped milk-agarics, the browned onion, and 1 table-spoon of butter. Mix well and have it chilled. Roll out the dough and transfer it into a greased dripping-pan sprinkled with flour. Put the filling and fold the dough in the shape of a pie. Spread the egg over it, let it gradually rise and brown in an oven. Serve the butter.

RASSTEGAI PATTIES FROM LEAVENED DOUGH WITH RICE AND ONIONS

Leavened dough, 2 eggs, butter, 0.5 cup rice, eggs

Chop the onions fine and brown in some butter. Boil the rice until it gets crumbly, salt, mix with 1 table-spoon of hot butter and onions. Make leavened dough (see above), roll it out and cut in the shape of flat cakes. Put some filling on each flat cake, fold the edges leaving the centre of each patty open. Put the *rasstegais* in a greased dripping-pan sprinkled with flour, spread the eggs over them, sprinkle with some butter, let the dough rise and brown in an oven.

PATTIES FROM LEAVENED DOUGH WITH CARROTS AND EGGS

Carrots, butter, dill, parsley, leavened dough, and 3 eggs

Chop the carrots and cook in some butter. Mix with 2 chopped hard-boiled eggs, dill, and parsley. Sprinkle with salt. Make

0.5 portion of dough, roll it out, cut out flat cakes, put 1 tea-spoon of filling on each of them, fold up, put in a greased dripping-pan sprinkled with flour. Spread the remaining egg over the patties, let the dough rise and brown in an oven.

MEAT PIE

The dough: *3 cups flour, 9 oz (250 gm) margarine, 1/2 oz (15 gm) yeast, and 0.5 cup milk*

The filling: *1 lb (500 gm) meat, 2—3 onions, 2—3 potatoes, parsley, dill, salt, pepper, 2 eggs, and 0.5 cup meat broth*

Make dough from the margarine, flour, 1 egg, yeast, and salt and put it in the cold. Roll out the dough in a layer 1/3 in (1 cm) thick. Place half of it in a dripping-pan and cover with the meat filling, onions, and herbs. Salt the filling, add some pepper, 1 bay leaf, and finely chopped raw potatoes. Cover with the second layer of dough and spread an egg over it.

Make a hole in the pie and pour some broth through it during the baking. Bake in a hot oven for 30—40 minutes.

RASSTEGAIS

15 oz (400 gm) flour, 2 oz (60 gm) butter, 4 egg-yolks, 1.5 cups milk, 0.5 cup water, 1 tbsp. sugar, 0.9 oz (25 gm) yeast; salt to taste

The filling: *10 oz (300 gm) slightly salted fish, 4 oz (100 gm) viziga, 4 oz (100 gm) rice, 4 oz (100 gm) onion, 3 eggs, 4 oz (100 gm) margarine, 5 tbsp. fish broth, 1 tbsp. finely chopped parsley and dill; salt and pepper to taste*

Make thick sourdough in warm boiled milk: 1 cup of milk for 7 oz (200 gm) flour and 0.9 oz (25 gm) yeast. Pour some flour into a sauce-pan. Separately dilute the yeast in lukewarm water and pour it into the flour without stirring. Add the lukewarm milk and mix well. Knead the dough thoroughly and let it rise. When the dough rises, salt it, add 7 oz (200 gm) of flour, and pour 0.5 cup of warm milk into it. Stir the dough, knead thoroughly and let it rise again. Cut out round flat cakes the size of saucers. Make filling from the rice, viziga, onion, and slightly salted fish. Put some rice, then some cooked onion and viziga in the middle of each flat cake. Top it all with some burbot strewn with the herbs. Fold each flat cake in the shape of a *rasstegai* leaving the middle open. Put a bit of butter in the open middle of each *rasstegai*. Lay the *rasstegais* in a greased dripping-pan sprinkled with flour and stand in a hot oven. Before serving pour some fish broth in the middle of each pie.

The filling

Several hours before cooking soak the viziga in cold water, then pour fresh cold water over it and boil on a high heat with the lid on. When the water starts boiling, lessen the heat and simmer for about two and a half hours until done. When the viziga is cooked, chop it fine and dress with vegetable oil.

Cook the onion, boil the rice until crumbly, and add some vegetable oil. Chop the fish 24 hours before making *rasstegais*, sprinkle with salt and put in a fridge; then wash it and cook until soft the way salted fishes are cooked.

«GURYEVO» PATTIES

10 oz (300 gm) filleted fish, 1 onion, 3 oz (80 gm) vegetable oil, 1.5 oz (40 gm) margarine, 1.5 lb (700 gm) dough

Put the filleted sevruga through a meat-grinder with a coarse grate and brown in the margarine until semi-done. Add the browned onion, salt, and pepper. Make dough the way it is made for regular patties. Put the filling in the dough. Brown the patties in vegetable oil. Serve them hot.

FAST «BABA» PIE

7 oz (200 gm) butter, 2 cups milk, 6 eggs, 1/2 cup sugar, 15 oz (400 gm) flour

Rub the butter through a sieve, gradually adding the warm milk shaken

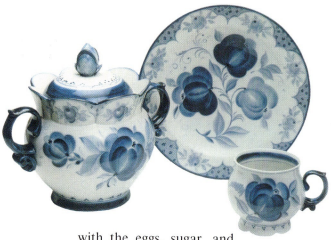

with the eggs, sugar, and flour. Put in a deep container greased with butter and sprinkled with dried breadcrumbs. Let it brown in an oven.

«BABA» WITH CARDAMOM

2 cups milk, yeast, 1.5 cups sugar, 6 eggs, 15 oz (400 gm) flour, and cardamoms

Shake 2 cups of warm milk with the yeast, gradually add, stirring, the sugar, eggs, flour, and pounded cardamoms. Let the dough rise, put in a deep form greased with butter and sprinkled with flour. Have it gradually browned in an oven.

SWEET BUNS STUFFED WITH CANDIED FRUIT

1.25 cups milk, yeast 15 oz (400 gm) flour, 7 oz (200 gm) candied fruit, $3/4$ cup sugar, 4 oz (100 gm) butter, 5—6 eggs, icing and vanilla

Make sourdough from the warm milk, yeast, and 7 oz (200 gm) flour. When the dough begins to bubble and rise, add the warm butter, 4 eggs, 1 tea-spoon of salt, $3/4$ cup of sugar, and 7 oz (200 gm) flour. Nead dough until it begins to come off your hands. Pour the chopped candied fruit into the dough and let it rise again. Roll the dough into a layer $3/4$ in (2 cm) thick, cut out rings, lay them in a dripping-pan greased with butter and sprinkled with flour. Spread the remaing eggs over the dough-rings, sprinkle with butter, let them rise and brown in an oven.

Sprinkle with the icing and vanilla.

MERCHANT'S PATTIES WITH JAM

Make leavened dough. When it rises a second time, put a spoonful of margarine and one table-spoon of sugar and lemon peel in it. Mix well, roll relatively thin, cut out rings, put a spoonful of the jam on each ring, moisten with water, cover with another ring, fold into patties, grease them with butter, and stand in a heated oven. When the patties rise and are browned, take them out, sprinkle with sugar or icing and serve.

ARKHANGELSK BALL-SHAPED LOAVES

4 cups barley flour, 3 eggs, 1 cup sour cream, 2 tbsp. butter, 1 cup sugar, $1/2$ tsp. salt

Nead dough from the components above. Have it chilled, roll into a layer $3/4$ in (2 cm) thick. Cut out rings with a wine glass, put in a dripping-pan, and bake.

DOUGHNUTS WITH POPPY-SEEDS

Make doughnuts from leavened dough. Brown them and grease with poppy-seed oil. To make the poppy-seed oil pound the poppy-seeds with the sugar, add some butter and nead with a pounder. Have the mass chilled and keep in the cold.

PLAITED BUNS (ROLLS)

Roll sourdough into plait and cut into pieces 4 oz (100 gm) each. Roll the pieces in the shape of oval flat cakes. Grease the cakes with butter and fold lengthwise into rolls joining the edges and pressing them tight to each other so that the rolls would not unfold. After that cut the rolls lengthwise, unfold along the cut like a book, and put on greased dripping-pans. Spread an egg over the surface of each roll and bake.

SQUARE-SHAPED RYE BUNS

1 cup milk, yeast, 10 oz (300 gm) rye flour, 2 oz (50 gm) butter, 2 eggs, 1 tsp. salt

To make leavened dough mix 1 cup of milk

with the yeast and 4 oz (100 gm) rye flour. When it begins to bubble, add 2 oz (50 gm) of warm butter, 2 eggs, 1 tea-spoon of salt, 7 oz (200 gm) of rye flour, and let the dough rise. Roll the dough into a finger-thick layer, cut into squares, put in a dripping-pan greased with butter and sprinkled with flour. Pierce the squares with a fork and spread butter over them. Have them gradually browned in an oven.

BREAD MADE FROM WHEAT PASTE

2.5 cups milk, yeast, 2 lb (800 gm) flour, 7 oz (200 gm) butter, 2 tsp. sugar, 4 eggs, 3 tsp. salt

Shake 2.5 cups of warm milk with the yeast and pour in 15 oz (400 gm) of wheat flour. Stand in a warm place. When the dough rises and begins to bubble, add the butter, 15 oz (400 gm) of flour, and salt. Nead dough (until it begins to come off your hands). Let it rise again. Grease a form with some butter, sprinkle with flour, put the dough in it, make small holes in the surface with a fork, grease the top and sides with butter, let the dough rise and have it browned in an oven.

LEAN RYE BREAD

2 lb (800 gm) flour from ground rye, 2 full tsp. salt, 2 cups water, and butter

Grind about 2 lb (800 gm) of rye. Nead dough from the rye flour, add 2 cups of warm water, and salt. Transfer the resulting dough into a small thin-walled basin greased with butter and sprinkled with flour, pierce holes with a fork, moisten with water, sprinkle with flour again, and have it gradually browned in an oven. Each loaf should weigh not more than 2 lb (800 gm) for it to be baked well.

PIES WITH PICKLED MILK-AGARIC FILLING

The dough: 1.5 cups vegetable oil, 1 lb (0.5 kg) sour clotted milk, $^1/_2$ cup granulated sugar, flour (to taste), a pinch of citric acid, and salt to taste

The filling: 2 lb (1 kg) pickled milk-agarics, 4 onions, 4 oz (100 gm) vegetable oil, and pepper to taste

Dissolve the sugar in the sour clotted milk. While stirring, gradually add the vegetable oil, citric acid, and flour to make the dough soft. Nead the dough well. Roll $^3/_4$ of the dough into a sheet, put it in a greased dripping-pan, lay the filling on it (in an even layer), and cover with the remaining sheet of dough. Close up the side edges of both layers, make a hole in the middle of the top layer to let the steam out of the filling during the baking. Spread some egg over the pie and bake in an oven on medium heat.

The filling

Mince the onions and brown in heated vegetable oil in a sauce-pan. The moment the onions begin to grow yellow, add the washed and finely chopped milk-agarics, pepper to taste, and brown together with the onions.

KULEBYAKA WITH FRESH CABBAGE FILLING

The dough: 2 lb (1 kg) pancake flour, 15 oz (400 gm) margarine, 10 oz (300 gm) sour cream, $^1/_2$ cup sugar, and salt to taste

The filling: 2 lb (1 kg) fresh cabbage, 1 oz (30 gm) dried mushrooms, 2 big onions, 3 tbsp. vegetable oil, 2 eggs; salt and pepper to taste

Rub the margarine through a sieve, gradually rub the sour cream, sugar, and salt into it. Nead dough from the pancake flour and keep it at a room temperature for about 2 hours. Then divide the dough in two. Put half the dough on a board sprinkled with flour, roll into a sheet, and transfer into a dripping-pan greased with vegetable oil. Lay the filling (in an even layer) on the dough. Roll the remaining dough into a

Pies, Rolls, and Spice-cakes

sheet and cover the filling with it, at the same time joining the upper layer with the lower one. Spread the beaten eggs over the dough. Put the pie in a well-heated oven. When the dough is browned enough, lower the oven's heat until done.

The filling

Mince the cabbage and boil it in slightly salted water. Strain the liquid through a piece of cotton cloth. Wash the mushrooms well, boil until done, chop fine, put in a sauce-pan, add the margarine and 3 tablespoons of water, and go on cooking with the lid on. Cook the eggs until hard-boiled, chill them in cold water, remove the shells, and pound with a fork. Mince the onions, brown them and mix with the cabbage and mushrooms, with the addition of salt and pepper to taste.

SOCHNI PIES

The dough: *5 cups flour, 1 cup water, 1.5 oz (40 gm) butter*

The filling: *1.5 lb (600 gm) cottage cheese, 3 eggs, 4 tbsp. sour cream, and 6 tbsp. sugar*

Make lean dough from the flour and water. Roll into flat cakes $1/3$ in (1 cm) in diameter and have them dried in a clean frying-pan. Put some cottage-cheese filling on half a flat cake, cover with the other half, close up the edges shaping the sochni into a half-moon, and bake in an oven. Pour the butter over each sochni and serve.

The filling

Put the cottage cheese, eggs, sour cream, and sugar in a basin and mix thoroughly.

RICH PIE WITH BLACK-CURRANT FILLING

3—4 cups flour, 7 oz (200 gm) butter or margarine, 4 oz (100 gm) sugar, 2 tbsp. sour cream, 2 tbsp condensed milk, 2 oz (50 gm) kefir, 3 eggs, 0.5 tsp. soda, 1 cup black-currant jam, and sugar icing

Pound the margarine with the sugar. Beat the mass and gradually add the eggs, sour cream, kefir, and condensed milk. Pour in the sifted flour mixing it preliminarily with the soda. Roll the dough into four round flat cakes 3—4 mm thick, spread the black-currant jam over them, fold into rolls, and bake in an oven at a temperature of 220—240°C. Sprinkle the rolls with the icing. Have the rolls chilled and cut into slices.

CHEEASE CAKES WITH JAM FILLING

15 oz (400 gm) flour, 2 oz (50 gm) butter, 7 oz (200 gm) sour cream, 4 eggs, 4 oz (100 gm) sugar, apple or black-currant jam

Nead dough from 15 oz (400 gm) of flour, 3 eggs, 2 oz (50 gm) of butter, 7 oz (200 gm) of sour cream, and 4 oz (100 gm) of sugar. Roll it out, put in a dripping-pan greased with butter and sprinkled with flour. Fold the edges and spread the egg over them. Have them slightly browned in an oven, cover the middle of the surface of each cheese cake with the apple jam and black-currant jam on the sides. Keep in the oven until done.

APPLE PIE

3.5 cups flour, 5 oz (150 gm) butter, 3 eggs, 0.5 cup sugar, 1 cup sour cream, 2 tbsp. sour clotted milk, $1/2$ tsp. salt, $1/2$ tsp. soda, 2 lb (1 kg) apples, 1 tbsp. cinnamon, and 1 cup raisins

Sift the flour and soda, add the sour cream, sour clotted milk, butter, and salt, and nead dough. Peel the apples, remove the core from each of them, and grate or chop them into slices. Roll half the dough into a flat cake $1/3$ in (1 cm) thick, put it in a dripping-pan greased with butter. Put an even layer of the apples on the dough and sprinkle them with the sugar, ground cinnamon, and raisins. Roll another flat cake from the remaining dough, cut into strips and lay them on the pie in the shape of netting. Spread an egg over the pie and bake in an oven for 25—30 minutes at a temperature of 180—200°C.

SUGAR-COVERED *BARANKAS* (RING-SHAPED ROLLS)

15 oz (400 gm) flour, 4 oz (100 gm) granulated sugar, 1 egg, $1/2$ cup milk, 1.4 cup sunflower oil

Pour the flour onto a board in the shape of a mound, make a hollow and pour some milk and sugar into it. Mix the egg, milk and sunflower oil into it with a knife. Stir well. Chill the paste, roll into a thin cylinder, and cut into slices. Roll the slices into thin cylinders again, join their ends in the shape of *barankas* (roll the paste without adding the flour to it). Put the *barankas* in a dripping-pan greased with sunflower oil, spread some egg over them, sprinkle with the sugar, and bake in an oven.

SHORTCAKES

1 cup sour cream, 2 oz (50 gm) melted butter, 2.5 cup flour

Shake up the sour cream with the melted butter. Pour the flour into a large flat basin. Shape it into a mound, make a crater-like hollow, gradually pour the sour cream and melted butter into it, mixing with the flour (at first with a spoon and then by hand). The dough must be like thick sour cream. Roll it thin and cut out round flat cakes. Put them in a dripping-pan greased with butter and sprinkled with flour, pierce with a fork, have them browned in an oven.

HONEY CAKES

1 lb (500 gm) honey, 1 tsp. potash, 15 oz (400 gm) flour, 4 oz (100 gm) butter, 5 oz (150 gm) almonds, 5 oz (150 gm) candied fruit

Bring the refined honey to a boil, pour 1 tea-spoon of potash dissolved in a little water into it, and stir well. Gradually pour in 7 oz (200 gm) of the flour, constantly pounding the paste and adding 4 oz (100 gm) butter, another 7 oz (200 gm) of the flour, 5 oz (150 gm) of finely chopped almonds, and 5 oz (150 gm) of finely chopped candied fruit. Let it rise for 48 hours. Shape the paste into different kinds of cakes, put them in a dripping-pan (on oil paper), and have them browned in an oven. Serve cream or butter.

CAKES COOKED IN VEGETABLE OIL

10 oz (300 gm) flour, 1 cup sugar, 1 egg, 4 oz (100 gm) vegetable oil, 1 cup kefir, vanilla, lemon peel (1 lemon), $1/2$ tsp. soda dissolved in 2 tsp. 6% vinegar

The icing: *1 tbsp. sugar and 1 tsp. water*

Mix well the soda, kefir, sugar, lemon peel, and vanilla powder with the vegetable oil. Nead paste, put it in a refrigerator for 30 minutes. Roll the chilled paste and cut into rings. Put the flat cakes in a dripping-pan, greased with vegetable oil and sprinkled with flour. Bake in an oven until brown. Take the cakes out of the oven and cover them with the hot icing.

ROUND LOAF

1 long loaf, 4 oz (100 gm) sugar, 2.5 oz (70 gm) butter, 2 eggs, and 1 cup milk

Grate 1 stale loaf of wheat bread on a grater, pour the boiling milk over it, and stir thoroughly until even. Let the mass stay for about 45 minutes and stir again. Add the sugar, salt to taste, 2.5 oz (70 gm) of butter, 2 eggs, and mix well. Grease a tin container with butter, sprinkle with pounded sugar, put the resulting mass into it, and bake for 30—40 minutes.

APPLE CHARLOTTE (PUDDING) SPRINKLED WITH DRIED RYE BREAD-CRUMBS

1 cup finely dried rye bread-crumbs, butter, 12 big apples, sugar, 3 cups milk, 3 egg-yolks, 1 egg

Mix the dried bread-crumbs with half a cup of sugar. Peel the apples and cut them into slices. Grease a special tin container with some butter and sprinkle with the dried bread-crumbs. Put the apple slices in it (layer upon layer) sprinkling each layer with the bread-crumbs and butter. Shake up 3 cups of milk with 3 egg-yolks and pour the mixture over the pudding. Spread the egg over the charlotte, sprinkle with the sugar and butter, and have it browned in an oven. Serve cream or butter.

PASTRY STRAWS

10 oz (300 gm) flour, 1 cup sour cream, 3 egg-yolks, 0.9 oz (25 gm) vodka, 10 oz (300 gm) sunflower oil, 1 tbsp. sugar, 4 oz (100 gm) castor sugar, 2 oz (50 gm) vanilline, $1/2$ tsp. salt

Mix the sour cream with 3 egg-yolks, sugar, salt, and vodka, add the flour and nead thick paste. Roll it into a very thin layer and cut into strips (like noodles). Make lengthwise cuts in the strips and put one end of each strip into the cut, in the manner of a loop. Bring the vegetable oil to a boil in a deep frying-pan. Dip the strips in the sizzling oil, turning them over with a fork.

Take out the browned pastry straws with a skimmer, let the vegetable oil flow away, and sprinkle the straws with the castor sugar mixed with the vanilline.

MERINGUE (LIGHT PIE)

15 oz (400 gm) apples, 2 oz (50 gm) gelatine, 1.5 cups sugar, 6 eggs, citric acid

Bake the apples and rub them through a sieve. Pour cold water over the gelatine and let it swell for 3—4 hours. Bring the gelatine to a boil, add 1.5 cups of sugar, and continue boiling. The moment the syrup is ready (to test its readiness make sure a drop of it keeps its shape in a saucer), put the apple paste in it and bring to a boil again. Beat 6 egg-whites and trickle them, stirring, into the hot mass. You can also add a little citric acid to it. While the mass is still warm, pour it out into small tin containers moistened with water or into a dripping-pan. When it hardens, cut the layer into portions. Instead of apples some other fruit can be used.

DIFFERENT KINDS OF KVASS AND *SBITEN*

Kvass is an old Russin beverage. Especially popular is the kvass made from grains. It is used not only as a drink but as the basic component of the famous Russian *okroshka* (cold kvass soup). In old Russia women made various sorts of kvass. Here we offer you the recipes of some of them.

Sbiten, too, was once very popular. It is an old Russian drink with honey as one of its components.

BREAD KVASS

To make kvass one must use stainless-steel, enameled or wooden (preliminarily steamed) vessels. Cut 4 lb (2 kg) of rye bread into small cubes, dry in an oven or a stove until brown and put in vessels. Bring 20 pints (10 litres) of water to a boil, chill to 90°C, pour over the dried bread cubes, let them stay that way for 10—12 hours, and strain the liquid through cheese-cloth without pressing out the bread mass. Stir 4 oz (100 gm) yeast and 3 table-spoons of wheat flour in a small amount of the remaining bread dregs and stand in a warm place to let the yeast rise.

Pour boiling water over the mint and keep boiling within several minutes. Strain the liquid and add sugar. Pour the risen yeast and strained peppermint tea into the bread liquid, stir well, cover with a napkin, and leave in a warm place until thick scum comes up. Skim the scum to prevent the kvass from overfermenting. Carefully pour out the kvass (through a sieve covered with a piece of cloth or cheese-cloth) trying not to shake up the dregs, and pour it into bottles. Cork up the bottles and lay them horizontally in a basement or a fridge. After 12 hours the kvass is ready for drinking.

KVASS FOR *OKROSHKA*

2 lb (1 kg) rye bread, 15 pints (7 litres) water, $1/2$ cup sugar, $1/3$ stick compressed yeast, 2 cups flour

Cut the rye bread into small slices, dry until brown, put in a sauce-pan, pour boiling water over them, put the lid on, and let them stay that way for 3—4 hours. After that strain the liquid and add the sugar and yeast. Before that dilute the yeast with warm water with the addition of the flour and keep it that way for 1 hour.

Keep the kvass in a warm place for 4—5 hours and then have it chilled. Pour the ready kvass into jars or bottles, stop them up and keep in a cold place.

«PETROVSKY» KVASS

2 pints (1 litre) bread kvass, 1 horse-radish, 1 tbsp. honey, and ice

Dissolve the honey in the slightly heated kvass. Add the finely chopped horse-radish. Stop up the bottles or jars and stand in the cold for 10—12 hours. Strain and serve with ice.

KVASS FROM DRIED RYE BREAD-CRUMBS WITH RAISINS

2 lb (1 kg) dried rye bread-crumbs, 15 pints (8 litres) water, 3 cups sugar or syrup, 1 tbsp. raisins, $1/3$ stick compressed yeast

Pour hot water over the finely ground dried rye bread-crumbs, stir well, and keep them that way for not less than 3—4 hours. Carefully pour the liquid out into some other vessel, add the syrup or sugar, and the yeast. Mix well and let it ferment for 3—4 hours. Pour the kvass into bottles, putting 1 raisin in each of them and keep at a room temperature until bubbles of carbonic acid gas begin to surface. Cork up the bottles and stand in the cold. Lay them horizontally and keep for 24 hours.

KVASS FROM FRESH APPLES OR PEARS

30 apples or 40 pears, 7 oz (200—400 gm) sugar, 0.9 oz (25 gm) yeast, and raisins

Cut 30 unpeeled medium-size apples or 40 juicy medium-size pears into thin slices and put in a clay pot. Pour 30 cups of boiling water over them, stir well, and have them chilled. Add 0.9 oz (25 gm) yeast, mix well, put the lid on and stand in the sun. When the kvass starts fermenting, strain and pour 7 oz (200—400 gm) sugar into it. Stir well. Pour the kvass into bottles, put 2 or 3 raisins into each and cork them up. Lay the bottles horizontally and keep in the cold.

KVASS FROM DRIED APPLES

1.5 lb (700 gm) dried apples, 10 pints (5 litres) water, 1.5 cups sugar, $1/2$ oz (15 gm) yeast

Slightly brown the apples in an oven and put them in an enameled pan. Pour boiling water over them, put the lid on and chill. Pour out the liquid, pour in the sugar, and chill to 25°C. Mix the yeast with a little sugar, add the mixture to the apple liquid, and put in a warm place. When scum appears, pour the kvass into bottles, cork them up, and stand in a cold place. The kvass will be ready in 2 or 3 days. Serve cold.

ROWAN KVASS

3 lb (1.5 kg) rowans, 1.5 lb (600 gm) sugar, 0.9 oz (25 gm) yeast, and raisin

Crush the rowans with a spoon, pour 9 cups of water over them, and bring to a boil three times. Transfer into a clay pot and pour in 30 cups of boiling water. Have it chilled, add 0.9 oz (25 gm) of yeast, mix well, put the lid on, and take outside. When it starts fermenting, strain the kvass, add the sugar, stir well, and bottle putting two or three raisins in each one. Cork up and lay the bottles in a cold place.

RHUBARB KVASS

2 lb (800 gm) rhubarb stalks, 10 pints (5 litres) water, $1/2$ cup sugar, 0.9 oz (25 gm) yeast

Wash, clean, and mince the rhubarb's stalks or cut them into bars $3/4$ in (2—3 cm) long. Put in boiling water and boil for 5—7 minutes. Strain through a piece of cheese-cloth and chill. Add the sugar and yeast, and put in a warm place.

The kvass will be ready in 8—10 hours. Pour it into bottles or jars and keep in the cold.

CRANBERRY KVASS

3 lb (1.5 kg) cranberries, 8 pints (4 litres) water, 1.5 cups sugar, 0.9 oz (25 gm) yeast

Sort out and wash the cranberries. Pour water over them, boil for 10—15 minutes, and crush the berries with a wooden spoon. Strain through two layers of cheese-cloth and press out the berries. Add the sugar, a piece of lemon peel, bring to a boil, chill, add the yeast, and let it ferment for 1—2 days. When the kvass is covered in scum, strain it, pour into bottles, and leave in a cold place. Serve cold.

CARROT KVASS

4 lb (2 kg) carrots, 8 pints (4 litres) water, 2 lb ($1/2$ kg) sugar, 1 oz (30 gm) yeast, 2 oz (50 gm) rye bread, 1 tsp. citric acid, clove and cinnamon

Peel, wash, and grate the carrots. Pour warm boiled water over them. Add the sugar, citric acid, clove, cinnamon, yeast pounded with sugar, and a slice of rye bread. Stir well and put in a warm place for 10—12 hours. Strain the kvass through two layers of cloth-cheese, pour into bottles, cork them up, and leave at a room temperature for 24 hours. Serve cold.

Different Kinds of Kvass and *Sbiten*

BIRD-CHERYY KVASS

3 lb (1.5 kg) bird-cherries, 2 lb (1 kg) sugar, 1 tbsp vanilla sugar, 2 tbsp. lemon juice, and 20 pints (10 litres) water

Sort out, wash thoroughly, and pound the berries. Add the sugar and mix well. Pour in warm boiled water, the lemon juice, and the vanilla sugar. Mix erything well and stand in a warm place for fermentation.
When the foam appears strain through a piece of cheese-cloth and pour into sterilized bottles for further fermentation.
The bird-cherry kvass will be ready in two days.

MINT KVASS

5—6 sprigs (dry) mint, 4 oz (120 gm) dried rye bread-crumbs, 2—3 tbsp. sugar, 3 pints (1.5 litres) water, $1/2$ oz (15 gm) yeast, 3 tbsp. raisins

Pour the water over the bread-crumbs in an enamel sauce-pan, stir well, tie up with a cotton cloth and keep this way for 2 hours, stirring from time to time. Strain the must through a cheese-cloth, pour the yeast diluted with warm water into it, add the sugar and mint, and again leave it in a warm place for 10 hours. Strain the kvass through cheese-cloth again and bottle it adding a few raisins to each one.
Stop up the bottles and keep them this way for another 2—3 hours at a room temperature. Keep the bottled kvass in a refrigerator.

BEET KVASS

3 lb (1.5 kg) beetroots, 0.75 cups sugar, 4 pints (2 litres) water, 1 small piece rye bread, and a little salt

Peel and wash the beetroots in running water. Grate on a grater. Put the grated beetroots in a clean three-litre glass jar. Add the sugar, salt, and bread, and pour cold boiled water over it. Cover the jar with a cheese-cloth and stand in a warm place for 3—4 days.
Strain the kvass through a two-fold cheese-cloth and pour out into sterilized bottles.

YEAST DRINK WITH A LEMON

1 lemon, 4 oz (100 gm) yeast, 4 tbsp. honey, and 5 cups water

Dissolve the yeast in 1 cup of water, add the honey, and leave it for about 45 minutes for the yeast to rise. Put the water with the yeast and honey on a burner and bring to a boil. Add, stirring, some lemon peel. Remove from the burner and chill. Strain the chilled drink through a cheese-cloth, dilute with 4 cups of cold boiled water, and squeeze the juice out from the lemon. Mix well.

HONEY AND LEMON DRINK

3 lemons, 5 tbsp. honey, 0.5 cup water

Squeeze the juice out from three lemons, strain through a cheese-cloth, add the warm boiled water and honey. Stir thoroughly. Serve cold or hot, to this end pouring the drink into an enamel sauce-pan and heat without bringing to a boil.

HONEY AND GUELDER ROSE DRINK

0.05 oz (1.5 gm) guelder rose berries, 0.009 oz (0.25 gm) water, 1 lemon, and 4 tbsp. honey

Sort out and wash the guelder rose berries. Put the berries in a sauce-pan and pour the water over them. Set on a burner and bring to a boil. Remove from the burner, chill a little, and squeeze the juice out through a cheese-cloth. Strain the juice again through the cheese-cloth.
Add the juice from the lemon and honey to the guelder rose juice. Stir everything well. Serve the drink cold.

ORDINARY *SBITEN*

7 oz (200 gm) honey, 2 pints (1 litre) water; spice to taste

Put the honey, cinnamon, clove, hop, and mint in 2 pints (1 litre) of hot water and simmer for 30 minutes.
Drink it hot, like tea.

HOT SBITEN

5 oz (150 gm) sugar, 5 oz (150 gm) honey, spice, and 2 pints (1 litre) water

Dissolve the sugar and honey in 2 pints (1 litre) of water. Add the spice (clove, cinnamon, cardamom, and ginger to taste). Boil for 5—10 minutes removing the scum. After 1 hour, strain it. Heat the resulting *sbiten* and drink it hot.

HOLIDAY SBITEN

1 lb (500 gm) honey, spice, 2 oz (50 gm) yeast, 3 pints (1.5 litres) water

Boil the honey in 3 pints (1.5 litres) of water all the while skimming the scum. Add crushed seeds of cardamom, ginger, cinnamon, and sweet pepper, boil again and chill. Dilute the yeast with water, mix with the honey liquid, pour into bottles, and stand in a warm place for 12 hours, whereupon cork up the bottles and leave them in the cold for 2—3 weeks. You can keep this kind of honey undamaged for quite a long time if the bottles are sealed with wax.

You can add to the sbiten 1 lb (500 gm) of virgin cranberry juice.

HOT-PUNCH SBITEN

8 tbsp. honey, 5 cups water, hot punch from 1 tbsp. sugar, 1 bay leaf, caraway-seeds, and cinnamon

Keep 1 spoon of sugar over low heat until it turns into a dark-brown syrup. Dissolve the honey in 5 cups of water and boil for 20—25 minutes. Add the spice and boil for another 5 minutes. Strain the mixture through a piece of cheese-cloth and add the hot punch for coloration.

Serve hot.

POPULAR SBITEN

1 cup natural honey, $1/5$ oz (6 gm) hop, a little cinnamon, and 2 pints (1 litre) water

Put the honey, hop, and cinnamon in hot boiled water, set on a burner, and boil, stirring, for 2 hours, removing the scum. Remove from the heat and strain. Serve cold.

SPICY HONEY

2 lb (1 kg) honey, 4 oz (100 gm) yeast, 8 pints (4 litres) water, $1/3$ oz (10 gm) spice: pepper, cardamom, and cinnamon

Pour the water over the honey. Set it on a burner and bring ti a boil, skimming the scum. Add the spice and boil for about 10 minutes. Remove from the heat and chill. Add the yeast to the still warm drink and let it ferment in a warm place for 12 hours. Bottle and stop up the drink. Take the bottles out into the cold and keep them there until done. The drink will be ready in 2 weeks.

SAUCES, DRESSINGS, AND GRAVIES

Not being an individual dish, sauces lend food special taste poignancy. From olden times mustard and various dressings with it, as horseradish and sauces, have been widely used in Russian cooking.

WATERY MILK SAUCE

1 cup milk, 1 tsp. wheat flour, 2 tsp. butter, and salt to taste

Slightly fry the wheat flour until light yellow, stir thoroughly in a little milk (boiled), pour the mixture into boiling or diluted (with water) milk, and boil, stirring, for 5—10 minutes. Add the butter and salt, stir well and heat without bringing to a boil.

SOUR-CREAM SAUCE

1 cup sour cream, 1 tbsp. butter, 1 tbsp. flour, and salt to taste

Mix the slightly browned flour with a little sour cream and butter. Pour the mixture, stirring, into the remaining boiling sour cream. Simmer for 10 minutes and strain. To make the sauce tastier, add some vegetable or mushroom liquid to it. This sauce can be made without butter.

CREAM SAUCE

3 tbsp. flour, 2 oz (50 gm) butter, 2 cups cream, 1 cup milk, and 2 egg-yolks

Bring 1 cup of milk to a boil and trickle, stirring, 0.5 cup of cream shaken with the flour. When it boils and thickens, add the butter, 1.5 cups of cream shaken with the egg-yolks, and salt. Heat without bringing to a boil.

SAUCE «WATERY BECHAMEL»

3 tsp. flour, 3 cups cream or milk, 2 oz (50 gm) Swiss cheese, 3 eggs, and 2 oz (50 gm) butter

Mix the butter with 3 tea-spoons of flour, bring to a boil, pour 1.5 cups of hot cream (or milk) into it. Add 2 oz (50 gm) of grated Swiss cheese, 1.5 cups of slightly heated cream (or milk) shaken with 3 eggs. Mix well and pour the mixture over the dish. Sprinkle with finely ground dried breadcrumbs, grated cheese, and butter. Have it gradually browned in an oven.

«THICK BECHAMEL»

3 eggs, 7 oz (200 gm) sour cream, 2 oz (50 gm) Swiss cheese, 6 tsp. flour, and 2 oz (50 gm) butter

Shake up 3 eggs with 7 oz (200 gm) of sour cream. Gradually add, grating all the while, the Swiss cheese, 1 cup of the sour cream (or milk), 2 oz (50 gm) of melted butter, and 6 tea-spoons of flour. Heat, stirring, without bringing to a boil.

DUTCH SAUCE

2 oz (50 gm) butter, 2 egg-yolks, 2 cups vegetable liquid, 1 cup cream, and 4 tsp. flour

Stir 2 oz (50 gm) of melted butter, add the egg-yolks, stirring all the while. Bring 1 cup of vegetable liquid to a boil and have it chilled. Trickle, stirring, 1 cup of the chilled liquid shaken with 4 tea-spoons of flour into it. Bring to a boil. When the sauce has thickened, add the butter, egg-yolks, and 1 cup of cream, salt, heat well without bringing to a boil.

FISH TEA

2 oz (50 gm) melted butter, 2 cups fish tea, 2 pickled cucumbers, 2 boletusses, 10 olives, 2 tbsp. tomato paste, 1 tbsp. flour, parsley and celery

Mix the flour and melted butter. Boil the

Sauces, Dressings, and Gravies

mass, stirring it from time to time. Pour 2 cups of strained fish bouillon boiled with the sprigs of parsley and celery, into the mass. Boil on low heat until thick. Peel the cucumbers and remove the seeds. Cut them into small rectangular pieces. Cook the boletusses and cut them fine. Add the chopped cucumbers, mushrooms, and olives to the thickened liquid. Let the sauce boil for a while and add the tomato paste. Serve the sauce hot with a large boiled fish.

WHITE FISH SAUCE

1 tbsp. flour, 1 tbsp. melted butter, 2 cups fish bouillon, 1 onion, 1 sprig parsley, salt, pepper, 1 tbsp. lemon juice

Brown the flour in the melted butter, trickle, stirring, the hot fish bouillon into it. Boil for 40—50 minutes and strain. Separately heat the chopped onion and parsley in a little butter without letting their colour change. Join the ingredients, salt and pepper the sauce, sprinkle it with the lemon juice, simmer for 5—7 minutes, and serve with boiled fish. You can add chopped eggs and parsley to the sauce.

SOUR-CREAM SAUCE FOR FISH

3 egg-yolks, 1 tsp. flour, 9 oz (250 gm) thick sour cream, 1 dessert-spoon melted butter, salt, and 1 dessert-spoon mustard

Mix the egg-yolks, flour, sour cream, melted butter, and a little salt. Pour the mixture into a sauce-pan and cook on low heat, stirring until a semi-thick mass forms. Add 1 dessert-spoon of mustard and mix well. This sauce can be served with fish or vegetables.

SAUCE FOR COLD FISH

6 egg-yolks, 1 tsp. mustard, 4-5 tbsp. vegetable oil, salt, sugar, pepper, and vinegar

Pound 3 hard-boiled and 3 fresh egg-yolks, mustard, a little salt and sugar, and refined vegetable oil (preferably olive oil), adding it drop by drop, into a spumy mass. Add some pepper (to taste), vinegar or lemon juice. You can serve this sauce with cold fish and other cold dishes.

SAUCE «PROVENCAL»

8 egg-yolks, 4 tsp. sugar, 2 cups olive oil, and 1 lemon

Stir the egg-yolks with 4 tea-spoons of sugar. Gradually add, stirring, the olive oil, at first drop by drop, and then in a trickle. When it thickens, gradually pour, stirring, the juice from 1 lemon, salt, and chill.

EGG SAUCE

7 eggs, 7 egg-yolks, 10 oz (300 gm) sugar, 1 pints (0.5 litre) grape juice, and 1 lemon

Boil the lemon and remove the peel. Stir the eggs and egg-yolks with the sugar, pour in the grape juice, add the lemon peel, and boil on low heat beating the mass with a mixer. Serve when the sauce is three times as much in volume and turns into light spume. Otherwise, ten minutes later the spume will sag and become watery.

«MAYONNAISE» SAUCE

1 cup vegetable oil, 2 egg-yolks, 1 tsp. mustard, 2 tbsp. 3% vinegar or lemon juice, about 1 tsp. sugar

Rub one hard-boiled egg-yolk through a sieve, put in a porcelain or enamel basin, and stir with a small amount of vegetable oil. Add one raw egg-yolk, keep on stirring with the vegetable oil, pouring it in drop by drop until thick. Salt, add the mustard, lemon juice or vinegar, and sugar. This mayonnaise must be used within 24 hours.

SALAD DRESSING

1 cup vegetable oil, 1 cup 3% vinegar, 1 tbsp. sugar; salt and pepper to taste. The proportion of the dressing's individual components, in particular that of vinegar and oil, can be changed depending on one's taste

Mix the vinegar, vegetable oil, salt, pepper, and sugar. It is made immediately before dressing a salad.

138 Sauces, Dressings, and Gravies

HOT HORSE-RADISH SAUCE

3 cups milk (or boiled vegetable liquid), 2 tbsp. butter or sour cream, 6 tbsp. grated horse-radish, 4 tsp. flour

Bring 2.5 cups of milk (or vegetable liquid) and grated horse-radish to a boil. Trickle, stirring, 0.5 cup of cold vegetable liquid or milk (shaken with 4 tea-spoons of flour) into it. Bring to a boil and let it thicken. Add some butter or sour cream, and salt. Heat without boiling.

COLD HORSE-RADISH SAUCE

6 egg-yolks, 3 tsp. sugar, 2 tbsp. olive oil, 1 lemon, 6 tbsp. grated horse-radish, dill, and parsley

Stir the egg-yolks with the sugar, gradually trickle, stirring, 2 table-spoons of olive oil and the juice from 1 lemon into it. Add 6 table-spoons of grated horse-radish, salt, chopped dill, and parsley. Mix well and let it congeal in the cold.

GRATED HORSE-RADISH WITH SOUR CREAM

3 tbsp. grated horse-radish, 1 cup sour cream, and 1 tsp. sugar

Grate 3 table-spoons of horse-radish, add 1 cup of sour cream, salt, and 1 tea-spoon of sugar. Mix well.

RUSSIAN HOME-MADE MUSTARD

5 oz (130 gm) powdered mustard, 0.5 cup water, 0.5 cup 3% vinegar, 3 tbsp. vegetable oil, 2 tbsp. sugar, 1 tsp. salt; bay leaf, cinnamon, and clove to taste

Put the sugar, salt, 1 bay leaf, clove, and cinnamon in hot water. Boil well, strain and pour the liquid into the powdered mustard, stirring thoroughly all the while. Add the vegetable oil and vinegar. Stir well. The mustard paste will be ready in several hours.

MUSHROOM LIQUID

Normally, mushroom sauces are made on the basis of boiled mushrooms' liquid. It can be made from dried or fresh mushrooms. Sort out and wash dried mushrooms several times in warm water. Pour cold water over them and keep for 3—4 hours (1 litre of water for 2 oz (50 gm) of dried mushrooms). Boil in the same water until done. Take the mushrooms out with a skimmer, wash with cold water, chop fine, and use for sauces and soups. Strain the liquid and salt to taste.

MUSHROOM SAUCE

1 oz (30 gm) dried mushrooms, 2—3 tbsp. flour, 1 tbsp. butter, 1 onion, salt, pepper, and sour cream

Wash the mushrooms thoroughly, pour cold water over them, and keep that way for 5—8 hours. Transfer into some other vessel and pour the same liquid (preliminarily strained through a piece of cheese-cloth) over them. Cook on low heat until soft. Wash the cooked mushrooms with hot water and chop fine.

Make a flour dressing from 2 or 3 table-spoons of flour and 1 spoon of butter. Separately heat the finely chopped onion until light yellow.

Slightly chill and dilute the flour dressing with the mushroom liquid. Boil, stirring and skimming the scum. Put the chopped mushrooms and onion in the sauce, salt, pepper, and boil for another 5—10 minutes.

You can add sour cream to the sauce, in which case the mushrooms are cooked in a lesser amount of water.

TOMATO SAUCE WITH MUSHROOMS

10 oz (300 gm) tomato juice, 2 oz (50 gm) mushrooms, 1 small onion, 1 tbsp. vegetable oil, several cloves garlic; salt to taste

Brown the chopped onion in the vegetable

Sauces, Dressings, and Gravies

oil. Cut the boletusses into thin strips. Join the onion and the mushroom strips with the tomato juice and cook for 15 minutes, whereupon add the minced cloves of garlic and salt.

SOUR-CREAM SAUCE BASED ON MUSHROOM BROTH

2.5 cups mushroom broth, 3 tsp. flour, 1 tbsp. butter, and 4 oz (100 gm) sour cream

Bring 2 cups of mushroom broth to a boil, trickle, stirring, 0.5 cup of the remaining cold broth (shaken with 3 tea-spoons of flour) into it. When the liquid boils and thickens, add 1 table-spoon of butter, 1 cup of cream, and salt. Heat without bringing to a boil.

GARLIC SAUCE

1 head of garlic, 4 tbsp. sunflower oil, 1/3 cup water, and 0.5 tsp. salt

Crush the garlic and salt in a mortar and stir, gradually adding the vegetable oil and boiled cold water. Salt to taste.

VEGETABLE BROTH

1 cup water and 9 oz (250 gm) fresh vegetables

Vegetable broth is made from different vegetables and is used for sauces, soups, and other dishes. It lends food the fragrance of a bunch of herbs and besides is very nourishing.

SOUR-CREAM SAUCE BASED ON VEGETABLE BROTH

4 tsp. flour, 2.5 cups vegetable broth or milk, 4 oz (100 gm) sour cream, dill, parsley, and butter

Brown the flour in some butter, pour the broth over it, and bring to a boil. When the liquid thickens, add the sour cream, 1 table-spoon of butter, and salt. Heat without bringing to a boil. Strew with the chopped dill and parsley.

TOMATO SAUCE WITH SOUR CREAM BASED ON VEGETABLE BROTH

1.5 cup vegetable broth, 2 tsp. flour, 4 oz (100 gm) sour cream, 4 oz (100 gm) tomato paste, and butter

Bring a cupful of vegetable broth to a boil. Trickle, stirring, 0.5 cup of the same cold broth shaken with 2 tea-spoons of flour into it. Bring to a boil. When the resulting broth thickens, add 1 table-spoon of butter, sour cream, and tomato paste. Heat without bringing to a boil. Instead of tomato paste you can use fresh tomatoes. Cook them in butter and rub through a sieve.

SAUCE BASED ON VEGETABLE BROTH WITH AN EGG

1 egg, 1 tbsp. butter, 1 tsp. minced herbs, and 0.5 cup vegetable broth

Chop the hard-boiled egg fine, mix with the minced herbs, pour the boiling broth over the mixture, and add 1 table-spoon of butter.

ONION SAUCE

5-6 onions, 4 tbsp. vegetable oil (or 3 tbsp. margarine), 2 cups milk, 4 tbsp. flour, 1 tbsp. butter; pepper, sugar, and salt to taste

Chop the onions fine, brown in the vegetable oil or margarine, add the flour, and, stirring unhurriedly, pour in the milk. Boil for 10—15 minutes. You can add some black pepper, 1 bay leaf, sugar, and salt. Strain the sauce and add the butter. The sauce can be used for baking vegetable dishes.

ONION SAUCE WITH A LEMON

Several onions, 2 oz (50 gm) sugar, 2 cups onion water, 2 tsp. flour, 1 lemon, and 2 oz (50 gm) butter

Boil the onions in slightly salted boiling water and rub them through a sieve. Brown 2 oz (50 gm) sugar. Bring 1 cup of the

Sauces, Dressings, and Gravies

onion water to a boil, trickle, stirring, one more cup of the onion water shaken with the flour into it. When it boils and thickens, add 2 oz (50 gm) of butter, browned sugar, the juice from 1 lemon, and onions. Salt, add some sugar, and heat without bringing to a boil.

APPLE SAUCE

Peel and cut several apples into small bits. Cook in butter until soft. Sprinkle with flour and dilute with citric acid. Add sour cream, salt, and sugar and rub through a sieve.

SUMMER SAUCE

Peel and cut gooseberries into small pieces. Cook in water until soft. Rub through a sieve, cook in butter, flour, and sour cream. You can add 1—2 stirred egg-yolks. Sprinkle with salt and sugar, pour in hot water, add some lemon juice, and boil for 15 minutes.

TOMATO SAUCE

1 lb (500 gm) tomatoes and 4 oz (100 gm) butter

Cut the fresh tomatoes into slices and boil in their own juice (without water). Rub them through a sieve and boil until as thick as cream. Add the butter, salt, and pepper (to taste).

SORREL SAUCE

7 oz (200 gm) sorrel leaves, 3 tbsp. butter, 2 tbsp. flour, and 1 cup sour cream

Remove the ribs from the sorrel leaves. Cut the sorrel leaves fine and put through a meat-grinder. Cook in the hot butter until done. Sprinkle with the flour, brown a little, dilute with water, and boil until thick. Add a big amount of the sour cream and boil again for 3—5 minutes. If the sorrel leaves are still too sour, pour boiling water over them, then mince and cook.

SAUCE WITH DILL AND PARSLEY

2.5 cups vegetable liquid, 3 tsp. flour, 2 oz (50 gm) butter, 0.5 cup cream (or milk), dill, and parsley

Boil 1.5 cup of the vegetable broth, trickle, stirring, 1 cup of the same cold broth shaken with 3 tea-spoons of flour. When it boils and thickens, add 2 oz (50 gm) of butter and 0.5 cup of cream or milk, chopped dill, and parsley. Mix well and heat without bringing to a boil.

DRIED RYE OR WHEAT BREAD

Dried rye or wheat bread

Cut the dried rye or wheat bread into small pieces, brown it gradually and brown slightly in an oven. Crush and sift.

DRIED BREAD-CRUMBS SAUCE

2 tbsp. dried bread-crumbs, 3—4 tbsp. butter, citric acid, and salt to taste

Melt the butter, separate the dregs, add the browned bread-crumbs, citric acid, and salt. Mix well.

BROWNED BUTTER

4 oz (100—150 gm) butter

Bring the butter to a boil in a large saucepan. Stir, heating, until some brown sediment forms.

BUTTER WITH BROWNED DRIED BREAD-CRUMBS

0.5 cup sifted dried bread-crumbs and 4 oz (100 gm) butter

Brown the sifted bread-crumbs with 2 oz (50 gm) of the butter. Add another 2 oz (50 gm) of it, and heat well.

BUTTER WITH BROWNED ONIONS

Several onions and butter

Mince the onions and brown them in sizzling butter. Serve with butter and heat well.

Sauces, Dressings, and Gravies

SAUCE FROM CRANBERRIES AND OTHER KIND OF BERRIES

3 cups juice from different berries, 0.5 tsp. potato flour, and sugar

Make juice from cranberries or different berries. Bring 2.5 cups of this juice to a boil. Trickle, stirring, the remaining cold juice shaken with the potato flour into it. When it boils and thickens slightly, add the sugar, and mix well. Serve hot or cold.

SAUCE FROM BERRY OR FRUIT SYRUP

Berry or fruit syrup and 1.5 tsp. potato flour

Dilute any kind of berry or fruit syrup with the amount of water to have 3 cupfuls. Bring 2 cups of syrup to a boil, trickle, stirring, a third cupful shaken with 1.5 tea-spoons of potato flour. Boil until thick. Serve hot or cold.

SAUCE FROM DRIED FRUIT WATER

3 cups dried fruit water, 1.5 tsp. flour, and sugar

Bring 2.5 cups of dried fruit water to a boil (adding more water if necessary). Trickle, stirring, the remaining cold fruit water shaken with 1.5 tea-spoons of flour into it. Bring to a boil. When it has thickened, add the sugar and mix well. Serve hot or cold.

REQUEST TO READERS

Raduga Publishers would be glad to have your opinion of this book, its translation and design and any suggestions you may have for future publications.

Pleace send all your comments to 4, Aptekarski Lane, building 1, Moscow 105005 Russian Federation